CORRESPONDENCE

OF

WAGNER AND LISZT.

CORRESPONDENCE

OF

WAGNER AND LISZT.

TRANSLATED INTO ENGLISH

WITH A PREFACE,

BY

FRANCIS HUEFFER.

𝔑𝔢𝔴 𝔈𝔡𝔦𝔱𝔦𝔬𝔫 𝔕𝔢𝔳𝔦𝔰𝔢𝔡,

AND FURNISHED WITH AN INDEX, BY

W. ASHTON ELLIS.

VOL. II.

1854—1861.

GREENWOOD PRESS, PUBLISHERS
NEW YORK

Originally published in 1897
by Charles Scribner's Sons

First Greenwood Reprinting 1969

Set SBN 8371-2743-2
Vol. 2 SBN 8371-2745-9

PRINTED IN UNITED STATES OF AMERICA

CORRESPONDENCE OF
WAGNER AND LISZT.

DEAREST RICHARD,

Yesterday (Saturday, January 7th) first performance of *Lohengrin* at Leipzig. The public, very
numerous in spite of double prices, displayed much
sympathy and admiration for this wonderful work.
The first act went tolerably well as far as the artists
were concerned. Rietz conducted in a precise and
decent manner, and the *ensembles* had been carefully
studied. The second and third acts, however, suffered
much from the faults and shortcomings of both chorus
and principals. Further performances will, no doubt,
show an improvement, although the Leipzig theatre does
certainly not possess the proper singers and scenic
artists. The flagging in the second act, which I previously took the liberty of pointing out to you, was felt
very much on this occasion, and the public seemed
painfully and unmistakably tired. The tempi of the
choruses seemed to me considerably too fast, and
there was more than one break-down in this scene.
Altogether, without self-conceit, I may say that the
Leipzig performance is inferior to ours, as you will

I

probably hear from other quarters. On the other hand the Leipzig public is in many respects superior to ours, and I feel convinced that the external success of yesterday's performance will prove very considerable indeed. The grand success of this work can no longer be denied ; of that we should be glad, and the rest will follow sooner or later. The actors, Rietz and Wirsing, were called after the first act, and after the last the representatives of the principal parts had to appear again. T., who had come from Paris for this performance, was very dissatisfied with it. I toned him down, not thinking it advisable to impair the chief thing by detailed criticism. Before all, let it be stated that *Lohengrin* is the grandest work of art which we possess so far, and that the Leipzig theatre by performing it has done credit to itself.

If you have to write to Leipzig show yourself, to please me, friendly and appreciative of their goodwill, and of the success which cannot be denied. The only remark you might make concerns the quick tempo of the choruses in Act II., Scene iii., and of the Lohengrin passage in the third act

Ath - mest Du   nicht die sü - ssen   Düfte

as compared with *your metronomic indication.* This is the more necessary as the chorus practically broke down, and these passages failed to produce their due effect.

On the next birthday of the Grand Duchess (April 8th) *Lohengrin* will be given here, with Götze (at present professor of singing at the Leipzig Conservatoire, late first tenor of this theatre) and Frau Fastlinger, and about the middle of May Tichatschek will sing the part here twice. Zigesar has also asked X. to sing Ortrud, and has offered her as well as Tichatschek very decent terms, but her answer is somewhat vague and undecided : " Unless I have to go to England at that time," etc.

Tichatschek is again behaving splendidly on this occasion, and I thank you for the few friendly lines you have written to him, for he really deserves it by his warm friendship for you and your works. He came to Leipzig together with Krebs, and during the *entr'acte* we met at the buffet, when he told me that you had written to him, which I was very glad to hear. The Härtels have sent you three hundred thalers for the nine pieces from *Lohengrin*.

Farewell, and let me soon hear from you.

　　　　　　　　　　　　　　Your

　　　　　　　　　　　　　　　　FRANZ.

January 8th, 1854.

144.

DEAREST FRIEND,

　　The *Rhinegold* is done, but I also am done for. Latterly I had intentionally dulled my feeling by means of work, and avoided every opportunity of writing to you before its completion. To-day is the first forenoon when no pretext prevents me any longer from letting the long-nourished and pent-up grief break forth. Let it break forth, then. I can restrain it no longer.

In addition to your very kindly notice of the Leipzig *Lohengrin*, I also received that of the *Deutsche Allgemeine*

Zeitung, and discover in it the scornful punishment inflicted upon me for the crime I committed against my being and my inmost conscience when, two years ago, I became unfaithful to my rightful determination and consented to the performance of my operas. Alas! how pure and consistent with myself was I when I thought only of you and Weimar, ignored all other theatres, and entirely relinquished the hope of any further success.

Well, that is over now. I have abandoned my purpose, my pride has vanished, and I am reduced to humbly bending my neck under the yoke of Jews and Philistines.

But the infamous part is that by betraying the noblest thing in my possession I have not even secured the prize which was to be the equivalent. I remain, after all, the beggar I was before.

Dearest Franz, none of my latter years has passed without bringing me at least once to the verge of the resolution to put an end to my life. Everything seems so waste, so lost! Dearest friend, art with me, after all, is a pure *stop-gap*, nothing else, a stop-gap in the literal sense of the word. I have to stop the gap by its means in order to live at all. It is therefore with genuine despair that I always resume art; if I am to do this, if I am to dive into the waves of artistic fancy in order to find contentment in a world of imagination, my fancy should at least be buoyed up, my imagination supported. I cannot live like a dog; I cannot sleep on straw and drink bad whisky. I must be coaxed in one way or another if my mind is to accomplish the terribly difficult task of creating a non-existing world.

Well, when I resumed the plan of the *Nibelungen* and its actual execution, many things had to co-operate in order to produce in me the necessary, luxurious art-mood. I had to adopt a better style of life than before ; the success of *Tannhäuser*, which I had surrendered solely in this hope, was to assist me. I made my domestic arrangements on a new scale ; I wasted (good Lord, wasted!) money on one or the other requirement of luxury. Your visit in the summer, your example, everything, tempted me to a forcibly cheerful deception, or rather desire of deception, as to my circumstances. My income seemed to me an infallible thing. But after my return from Paris my situation again became precarious ; the expected orders for my operas, and especially for *Lohengrin*, did not come in; and as the year approaches its close I realise that I shall want much, very much, money in order to live in my nest a little longer. I begin to feel anxious. I write to you about the sale of my rights to the Härtels ; that comes to nothing. I write to Berlin to my theatrical agent there. He gives me hopes of a good purchaser, whom I refer to the first performance of *Lohengrin* at Leipzig. Well, this has taken place, and now my agent writes that after *such a* success he has found it impossible to induce the purchaser to conclude the bargain, willing as he had previously been.

Confess that this is something like a *situation*. And all this torture, and trouble, and care about a life which I hate, which I curse! And, in addition to this, I appear ridiculous before my visitors, and taste the delightful sensation of having surrendered the *noblest work* of my life so far to the predetermined stupidity of our theatrical mob and to the laughter of the Philistine.

Lord, how must I appear to myself? I wish that at least I had the satisfaction that some one *knew* how I appear to myself.

Listen, my Franz; you must help me! I am **in a** bad, a *very* bad, way. If I am to regain the faculty of *holding out* (this word means *much* to me), something thorough must be done in the direction of prostituting my art which I have once taken, otherwise all is over with me. Have you thought of Berlin again? Something *must* be done there if all is not to come to a stop.

Before all, I must have *money*. The Härtels have been very liberal, but what is the good of hundreds where thousands are needed? If the Berlin purchase had come to something, I might at least have used the *offer* in order to prove to a man of business here that I possessed "capital," and to induce him to lend me the necessary sum for three years, paying back one-third every year. But this hope also has vanished. No one will undertake such an affair unless he has personal confidence in my future (?) successes. Such a *man*, dearest Franz, you *must* find for me. Once more, I want from 3,000 to 4,000 thalers in order to find perfect rest and equipoise. That much my operas may well bring me in in three years IN CASE something real is done for *Lohengrin*, so as to save it. I am willing to lease my rights to the lender; my rights in *Tannhäuser* and *Lohengrin* shall be secured to him in any way he thinks desirable or necessary. If I am not worthy of such a service, then you must own that

I am in a bad way, and all has been a mistake! Help me over this, and I will undertake once more to *hold out*.

Dear friend, do not be angry. I have a claim on you as on my *creator*. You *are* the creator of the person I am now; I live *through you*: it is no exaggeration. Take care of your creation. I call this a duty which you have towards me.

The only thing I want is *money*; that at least one ought to be able to get. *Love* I abandon, and *art*!

Well, the *Rhinegold* is ready, readier than I ever thought it would be. I went to this music with so much faith, so much joy; and with a true fury of despair I continued, and have at last finished it. Alas! the need of gold held me too in its net. Believe me, no one ever has composed in this manner; my music, it seems to me, must be terrible; it is a slough of horrors and sublimities.

I shall soon make a ıclean copy, black on white, and that will probably be the end of it; or shall I give permission to have this also performed at Leipzig for twenty louis d'or? I cannot write more to you to-day. *You are the only person* to whom I could tell such a thing; no one else has an idea of it, least of all the people near me.

Do not think that the news of Leipzig has made me suddenly desperate. I anticipated this, and knew everything beforehand. I can also imagine that the Leipzig failure may still be repaired, that " it is not as bad as we think," and much more to the same effect. It may be, but let me see evidence. I have no faith, and only one hope : sleep, sleep, so profound, so profound, that all sensation of the pain of living ceases. That sleep at least is within my reach; it is not so difficult to get.

Good heavens, I give you bad blood as well! Why did you ever come across me?

The present of the Princess caused me a smile,—a smile over which I could shed tears. I shall write to her when I have lived through a few more days; then I shall also send you my portrait, with a motto, which might make you feel awkward after all. How are you? Burn this letter: it is godless; but I too am godless. Be you God's saint, for in you alone I still have faith. Yea! yea! and once more yea!

Your

R. W.

January 15th, 1854.

Something must be done in London; I will even go to America to satisfy my future creditor; this too I offer, so that I may finish my *Nibelungen.*

145.

MY DEAREST FRANZ,

I write once more to try whether I can ease my heart a little.

Dearest friend, this continual suffering is becoming at last intolerable. Always to submit to things, never, even at the risk of one's own perdition, to give a turn to the wheel of suffering and to determine its direction—that must at last rouse the meekest of men to revolt. I must now act, do something. Again and again the thought comes to me of retiring to some distant corner of the world, although I know full well that this would mean only *flight*, not the conquest of a new life, for I am too *lonely*. But I must at least begin something that will make my life, such as it is, sufficiently tolerable to enable me to devote myself to the execution and completion of my work, which alone can divert my thoughts and give me comfort. While here I chew a beggar's crust, I hear from Boston that " Wagner nights " are given there. Every one persuades me to come over; they are occupying themselves with me with increasing interest ; I might make much money there by concert performances, etc. " Make much *money* !" Heavens ! I don't want to make money if I can go the way shown to me by my longing. But if I really were to undertake something of this kind, I should even then not know how to get with decency out of my new arrangements here in order to go where I could make money. And how should I feel there ?

Alas ! this is so impossible that the impossibility is equalled only by the ridiculous position into which I sink when I commence brooding over the possibility of the plan. My work, my *Nibelungen*, would then of course be out of the question.

This *work* is truly the only thing which still ties me to the desire of life. When I think of sacrifices and demand sacrifices, ·it is for this work ; in it alone I discover an object of my life. For its sake I must hold out, and hold out here, where I have got a foothold, and have settled down to work. If I consider it rightly, all my intended action can only have the object of enabling me to hold out till the completion of my work. But for that very reason I can *do* nothing;

all must be done by *others*. On that account I
latterly again felt the liveliest desire to obtain my
amnesty, and thus to gain free access to Germany.   In
that case I might at least be active in helping on the
performances of my operas.   I might at last produce
Lohengrin myself, while as it is I torture myself for the
sake of it.   The most necessary thing for the moment
seems to me to repair the Leipzig disaster; I was on
the point of venturing there without passport and of
endangering my personal liberty (good God! "liberty!"
What irony!).   In calmer moments I intended to write
to the King of Saxony, till this also appeared quite
useless and even dishonourable to me.   Then again,
as lately as last night, I thought of writing to the
Grand Duke to explain my new situation to him and
to ask him for his energetic intercession at Dresden.
But this morning early I came to think that this
also would be in vain, and probably you agree with
me.   Where can *energy* and real *will* be found?   Everything has to be done by halves, quarters, or even
tenths or twelfths, *à la* X.

So I sit down again, cross my arms, and surrender
myself to pure, unalloyed *suffering*.   I can *do* nothing,
except create my *Nibelungen*; and even that I am
unable to do without great and energetic help.

My dearest, my only friend, listen.   I *can* do
nothing unless others do it for me.   The sale of the
rights of my operas must be brought about, unless I
am to free myself from my situation by violent means.
In the way of pure business this has become impossible
by the Leipzig performance, which, if my wish and my
conditions had been observed, would not have taken

place ; it must be simply a work of friendship.   To
no one but you can I explain myself accurately, because
you are the only one who can understand at its true
estimate, and without a shake of the head, my position,
such as it has been brought about by my moods,
inclinations, whims, and wants.   How can I expect
a Philistine to comprehend the transcendent part of my
nature, which in the conditions of my life impelled me
to satisfy an immense inner desire by such external
means as must to him appear dangerous, and certainly
unsympathetic ?   No one knows the needs of people
like us ; I am myself frequently surprised at considering
so many "useless" things indispensable.   To *you*
alone can I explain how painfully I am placed, and
how necessary immediate help is to me.   This is
the *first* and most indispensable thing to preserve me
for my whole future.   Owing to my extreme sensitiveness in this matter, I shall otherwise be compelled—
because for such a frivolous reason I do not want
to take my own life—to start at once and fly to
America.

I am in a pitiful condition, and I know that to
such a friend as you pity comes from love.   Give
me up if you can ; that will settle all.   With my terrible
care my violent nervous disorder has also returned.
During my work I frequently felt quite well ; the
thunder-clouds seemed to have cleared away.   I often
felt beautifully elevated, gently supported ; generally I
was silent, but it was from inner joy ; even hope
wound itself softly round my heart ; the children of
fable came to the weeping elf, saying, "Weep not ; thou
too mayst still be happy."   But the word resounded from

farther and farther distance, till at last I could hear it no longer. Silence ! now the old night holds me again ; let it devour me altogether !

Pardon me. I *cannot* help it.

Farewell, my Franz ; farewell ; farewell.

Your
R. W.

146.

DEAR FRIEND,

You were going to send me your *Künstler*. Why does it not arrive ?

How about the *Faust* symphony ? I am writing the *Rhinegold* at once in full score. I did not see my way to jotting down clearly the introduction (the depth of the Rhine) as a sketch ; so I hit upon the full score. This is a slower way of proceeding, and my head is still a little confused.

The Princess has done well ; greet her and thank her warmly from me. Who knows how it will turn out ? I do not care to know.

This is a sign of life to which you must respond sympathetically.

Your
R. W.

ZURICH, *February 7th*, 1854.

147.

DEAREST RICHARD,

It is a sad fate that we have to live apart from each other. I can tell you nothing but that I think of you constantly and love you from my heart of hearts.

Latterly my time has been painfully occupied by all manner of business, visits, work, etc. I have written to nobody, as you may well imagine, because you did not receive a letter from me.

Together with this I send you the score of my *Künstler* chorus, and between this and the autumn I intend to publish half-a-dozen orchestral pieces, also in full score. By October the *Faust* symphony will be finished, which also will be published soon afterwards.

Let us leave these trifles alone and speak of your *Rhinegold*. Have you really finished it? That has been wonderfully quick work indeed. You know how delighted I should be if you would let me see the score. Send it to me as soon as you can do without it.

In the meantime I have not neglected your pecuniary affairs, and hope that my intentions will not be frustrated. *Candidly* answer me two questions:—

1. Have you pressing debts, and what sum do you absolutely require to meet them?

2. Can you manage to live this year on your present income?

There is a probability that Berlin may come off next autumn, and in that case I shall let you know the little result of my effort in good time. For the present *do not speak about it*. Dorn was here, and conducted the second performance of his *Nibelungen*. The work is to be given at Berlin in six weeks.

Brendel wrote several things to me about the *Lohengrin* affair in Leipzig. In my opinion, nothing further can be done for the moment, and you have every reason to be calm and *satisfied*. Lohengrin's barque is drawn by a swan; the cackling of geese and the barking of dogs are of no avail.

Berlioz is coming to Hanover at the end of March,

and goes from there to Dresden, where he will conduct a few concerts at the theatre. Fischer wrote to me recently about an intended performance o *Cellini* at Dresden. This is as yet a secret, which I, for my part, should like to see made public very soon. The opera is Berlioz's freshest and roundest work, and its failure in Paris and London must be attributed to low villainy and misapprehension. It would be a fine thing if Dresden were to offer him a brilliant *revanche*, such as he deserves.

Brendel will publish his book within a few days. When you have read it, tell me your candid opinion. Raff also has finished a stout volume on the "Wagner Question" (!). He refuses to show me *anything* of it, although he has read parts to several other persons. Fortunately you are no longer to yourself nor to me a *question*. . . .

Ath - mest Du   nicht die hol - den   Düf - te —

Live in your *Rhinegold*, and think lovingly of

F. L.

Weymar, *February 21st*, 1854.

148.

Dear Franz,

Many thanks for your *Künstler*. You had in me a somewhat adverse judge of this composition —I mean, I was not in the mood for it. I have got so unaccustomed to judging in an objective sense that in everything I go entirely by inclination. I take up only what attracts my sympathy, and enjoy it,

without in the least analysing that enjoyment in a
critical manner.   Imagine then the contradictions which
the very choice of the poem necessarily roused within
me.   It is more or less a didactic poem.   In it speaks
to us a philosopher who has finally returned to art,
and does so with the greatest possible emphasis of
resolution ;—in brief Schiller to the life ! Besides
this, a chorus for a concert ! I have no longer any
feeling for that kind of thing, and could not produce it
at any price.   I should not know where to take my
inspiration.   One other thing : my musical position
towards verse and metre has undergone an enormous
change.   I could not at any price write a melody
to Schiller's verses, which are entirely intended for
reading.   These verses must be treated musically in
a certain arbitrary manner, and that arbitrary manner,
as it does not bring about a real flow of melody,
leads us to harmonic excesses and violent efforts
to produce artificial wavelets in the unmelodic fountain.   I have experienced all this myself, and in my
present state of development have arrived at an entirely
different form of treatment.   Consider, for instance, that
the *entire* instrumental introduction to the *Rhinegold*
is based upon the common chord of E flat.   Imagine
then how sensitive I am in these matters and how
startled I was when, on opening your *Künstler*, I hit
upon the exact contrary of my *present* system.   I do
not deny that I shook my head while going on, and
that stupidly I observed in the first instance only
the things which startled me—I mean details,
always details.   At the same time, there was something in these details which seemed to strike me

in spite of my unsympathetic mood. At the close I reflected and arrived at the reasonable idea of letting the *whole* pass by me in full swing. In fact, I imbibed it in a manner with the most fortunate results. I saw you suddenly at your desk, saw you, heard you, and understood you. In this way I received another proof of the experience that it is our own fault if we cannot receive what is magnanimously offered. This your address to the artists is a grand, beautiful, splendid trait of your own artistic life. I was deeply moved by the force of your intention. You give utterance to it, body and soul, at a time, in circumstances, and before people who would be well advised in trying to understand you. You have done well in drawing Schiller's lines out of their literary existence and in proclaiming them loudly and clearly to the world with trumpet sound. You have, as I say, done well. How to do it was your own affair. *You* knew *how* these lines should be proclaimed to the world, for to none but you had occurred the necessity of that proclamation. I at least know nobody who could do something of this kind with such force. *What* an artist intends to do shows to him *how* he should do it, and by this *how* we recognize the *what.* What you intended to do here you could not have expressed otherwise than by this tremendous display of eloquence, of emotion, of overpowering strength. This is my criticism. I have no other. But who will be able to sing this to your liking? Mercy on me when I think of our tail-coated concert singers! During the performance at Carlsruhe you had, probably from your own inspiration, worked yourself into such a state of excitement, that you thought you heard them sing as they should have sung. I suspect, however, that the public heard correctly what was sung, and therefore could of course not understand the matter at all. Dear friend, you require singers such as I want for my Wotan, etc. Consider this! I have become so abominably practical that the moment of actual representation is always before my eyes, and this is another source of my joyful despair.

Thanks then for your *Künstler*. I feel as if it were meant for a present to myself only, and as if no one else were to know what you have really given to the world.

I am hard at work. Can you tell me of any one who would be able to compile a score from my wild pencil sketches? I worked this time quite differently from what I did before, but this having to make a clean copy kills me. I lose time over it which I might employ to better purpose; and apart from this, the continual writing tires me to such an extent that I feel quite ill and lose the inclination for real work. Without a clever man of this kind I am lost; *with him* the *whole* will be finished in two years. For that time I should require the man. If there were a pause in the scoring, he might copy parts in the meantime. Look out for one. There is no one here. It is true that it may seem absurd that I am going to keep a secretary, who can scarcely keep myself.

If you can help me, you will be doing God's work. Am I not worth a few thousand thalers for half a year to some German enthusiast? I will give him full security on the royalties due to me in the autumn.

On Monday I expect Gustav Schmidt, of Frankfort. I have summoned him in order to go through *Lohengrin* with him, and perhaps he will bring his tenor. I am glad to see him so full of zeal.

As to the rest, I shut my ears against all the world. I do not want to know how low I have sunk.

Shall I hear from you soon? If you think of me at all, think of me always as of one hard at work and profoundly melancholy. Farewell, best and dearest friend. The *Künstler* is splendid. Greet all at home.

From your

R. W.

ZURICH, *March 4th,* 1854.

149.

UNIQUE FRIEND,

I am frequently sad on your account; and on my own account I have not much reason to rejoice. My chief object and task is taking a very serious and painful turn. I had no right to expect much else in that direction, and was prepared, but these long entanglements which I have to submit to have caused me much trouble and have jeopardised my pecuniary position, so that at present I am unable to assist a friend. This I feel very much, and prefer to say nothing further about it. You will understand me and not misinterpret my silence. When the time comes, I shall explain my affairs to you by word of mouth; they are not rose-coloured, and another man might have perished, which other men might not have disliked to see.

To-day I only want to tell you that on the day of the performance of the opera by the Duke of Gotha I met

Herr von Hülsen at dinner. He led the conversation to the performance of your works at Berlin, and told me that he was only waiting till you had sold your rights to Messrs. Bote and Bock in order to produce them. I made bold to say that I had reason to doubt very much whether this would be done, and that even if B. and B. bought the scores of *Tannhäuser* and *Lohengrin* I did not think for a moment that you would abandon your previous demand of my being invited to Berlin in order to secure an adequate rendering of your works. Write to me how this matter stands. I do not want to advise you, but I think that the Berlin performance is an important point for you, and that you would gain nothing by altering your previous position—I mean that the performance should not take place except through my medium and according to my directions.

I was told that the Königsberg troupe intended to perform *Tannhäuser* at Berlin this summer. I tell you this because I think that you will not approve of the plan, and will refuse your consent if asked for it.

I am very weary and tired, but spring will give us new strength.

Write soon to your affectionate and truly devoted

F. Liszt.

Gotha, *April 4th*, 1854.

P.S.—This afternoon I return to Weymar. R. Pohl and his wife are there, and I have asked him to give you an account of the impending performances of *Tannhäuse?* and *Lohengrin*.

150.

MY DEAR FRANZ,
        Heaven knows how anxiously I waited this time
for your letter ! I reply at once in order to explain the
" business " part.
        I knew nothing about Messrs. Bote and Bock, but
have now come to the conclusion that they must be the
purchasers of my operas whom my Berlin agent had in
his eye when necessity compelled me last winter to
apply to him. I declare that at present I should not
sell my operas to Bote and Bock or anybody else, for
reasons which I need scarcely tell you. I find it
difficult to understand how Herr von Hülsen can be
naïve enough to think that I should consent to the performance of *Tannhäuser* at Berlin by the Königsberg
troupe. I shall write to Königsberg about it this very
day, and I ask you also to write to Hülsen at once and
to announce my *veto* to him. You may do this in *my
name*, and mention at the same time that I have *once
for all* placed everything concerning my operas at Berlin
in *your hands*, being firmly resolved to treat with Berlin
only through you and according to your opinion, but
never again personally. You may further say that if
Herr von Hülsen intended to give an opera by me, and
was waiting till he had no longer to treat with me, but
with a third person (Bote and Bock, as he thought),
because he had fallen out with me personally, he would
now have a splendid opportunity of settling everything without coming in personal contact with me,
because he would have to deal with you alone ; that, as
my plenipotentiary, you were compelled to protest

against the performance by the Königsberg troupe, but
that in the same capacity you were prepared to arrange
the matter with him in some other way. I think this
would be a good opportunity of bringing the Berlin
affair to a satisfactory conclusion. There is much need
for it, I can assure you. Heaven only knows how I
am to pull through ; and although I do not wish to
torture you any more, I may tell you that in my present
position you can do me a great and very valuable
service by your intercession in another quarter. Listen!
They have performed *Tannhäuser* at Augsburg, badly
enough, it is true, but it has paved the way for Munich.
Dingelstedt has written me an amiable and encourag-
ing letter, and I have sent him the opera which is to
be given there in the summer.   As regards honorarium,
I have entreated him to procure me the best possible
terms, as these operas are my only capital, and I must
mainly rely upon the great court theatres.   I have,
however, made no definite demand, having full confidence in him. You know Dingelstedt intimately, and
you would oblige me by asking him to get me something substantial, royalties in preference. Before all,
I should wish to have some money *before the end of this
month,* either as an advance on these royalties or, if
that is impossible, as the final purchase money, in
which case I think I might ask a hundred louis d'or.
(Dresden always used to pay me sixty louis d'or ; but
as *Tannhäuser* has everywhere proved a great draw,
I think I might expect the lump sum of a hundred
louis d'or from so great a court theatre as Munich.)
He is probably on his travels now, but if you address
to the care of W. Schmidt, inspector of the Court

Theatre, the letter will, I think, be forwarded to him. Do not be angry with me.

It is only a friend like you whom one can ask to be of active help to others while he himself is in such a painful position as you, poor man, seem to be. Although I have a general idea of your situation, I am very desirous to know precisely how your affairs and those of your dear ones really stand. I feel aggrieved because you touch upon them always in a very cursory manner. From all I can make out, I must fear that the Princess has been cut off from her estate permanently and completely, and I must own that such losses are well adapted to upset one's equanimity. I also understand that you look into the future with a heavy heart, as the fate of a most lovable, youthful being is equally involved. If you had to inform me that you three dear ones were now quite poor and solitary, even then I could not be very sorry—so stupid am I—especially if I saw that you had kept up your courage. My dearest, dearest, unique Franz, give me the heart, the spirit, the mind of a woman in which I could *wholly* sink myself, which could quite comprehend me. How little should I then ask of this world. How indifferent would be to me this empty glitter, which, in my despair, I have latterly again been tempted to gather round me as a diversion of my fancy. If I could live with you in beautiful retirement, or, which would be the same thing, if we could live here wholly for each other instead of frittering our beings away with so many insipid and indifferent people, how happy I should be. And " off and on " we should be sure to undertake something to give vent to our energies in the outer world.

But I am talking wildly. Correct me if I deserve it; I shall never be anything but a fantastic good-for-nothing.

Has Eugène sent you my medallion? It is not bad, only a little sickly.

I shall soon have to write again; I have more materials than I can deal with to-day.

The instrumentation of the *Rhinegold* is going on apace. At present I am with the orchestra down in "Nibelheim." In May the whole will be ready, but not the clean copy, only single sheets with illegible pencil sketches on them. It will be some time before you can see anything of it. In June I have to begin the *Valkyrie.* When are you coming? You say nothing about it, and yet you talk of "verbal communications." Schindelmeisser wrote to me yesterday, asking me to come to Darmstadt on the sly on Easter Monday, because *Lohengrin* would be splendid. That I shall leave alone.

Adieu, dearest, dearest Franz. I have so many things to write to you, that I must close for to-day. Convey my best regards.

Your
R. W.

ZURICH, *April 9th,* 1854.

151.

What do you think, dear friend? Would it be of any use if I sent you a letter to the King of Saxony, which the Grand Duke of Weimar might forward to him through a confidential person (perhaps his ambassador)? I admit that the Prime Minister of Saxony would be more important than the King, but to such a person I cannot possibly apply. Would the Grand Duke do this? Something must be done; I must be able to fly from my ordinary condition at least "off and on," otherwise——

How are you? Do write!

Your

R. W.

152.

For five days, dearest Richard, I have been in bed suffering from catarrh and intermittent fever, and shall probably have to be very careful till next week.

I wrote to Dingelstedt long ago, and asked him to reply to you direct and make the contents of his letter as *weighty* as possible. Dingelstedt is a gentleman, and will no doubt behave in such a manner as will satisfy you.

Lohengrin and *Tannhäuser* were given here last week. On the first occasion the house was illuminated, because the Grand Duchess visited the theatre for the first time since her confinement. Götze (at present professor at the Leipzig Conservatoire, previously for fifteen or twenty years tenor at our theatre) sang Lohengrin, and gave the lyrical portions of the part with much greater effect than had previously been the case. He had studied the part thoroughly at numerous performances, both here and at Leipzig, and therefore sang the music with absolute certainty. *Tannhäuser* drew, as usual, a full house; at the *Lohengrin* performance many strangers who had only arrived in the afternoon had to be refused admission.

Pohl's wife played the harp part very well, and I

asked him to write to you about the performance. Pohl is a zealous and warm adherent of yours.

The newspapers announce that you are going to conduct the impending Musical Festival in Canton Valais. Is there any truth in it? What part will Methfessel take in the direction? Let me know about this, as I have been asked several times.

I had got so far in my letter when yours was brought to me.

That is once more a dark, hopeless complaint! To help or to look on calmly—the one is almost as impossible to me as the other.

After the experiences I have had, and of which I told you only the smaller part, I can scarcely believe that the King of Saxony will perform the act of grace desired by us. However, I will try again. Send me your letter to his Majesty. I hope it will be placed before him soon and in the best possible way. Our Grand Duke is for the moment absent, and I shall not be able to see him before next week. Write to me at once, and concoct your letter for Dresden, which you must send to me *open*.

I have looked out for the copyist you require for your *Nibelungen*. It is difficult to find the proper individual who could undertake such a task. I know several young men who would willingly try, but they are not sufficiently skilful and competent. I have sent a message to one of my former friends at Berlin asking him whether he could place himself at your disposal. With him you would be quite satisfied. In case my inquiry leads to a favourable result, I will let you know.

You ask me how I am. . . .

" When need is highest, God is nighest."

Do not be anxious about my indisposition; it will soon be over, and my legs have to carry me a good way further still.

Your

F. LISZT.

153.

DEAR, DEAR FRANZ,

I can never complain to you again. I go on worrying you with my confidences in a sinful manner, while you keep your own grief to yourself. My troublesome candour knows no bounds; every drop of the fount of my sorrow I pour out before you, and—I must hope that that is the very reason why you are so silent as to your own circumstances. But I begin to feel that the best remedy for our sufferings is sympathy with those of others. My only sorrow to-day is that you hide your grief from my sympathy. Are you really too proud to let me know, or do you refrain from giving me back the painful impression I made on you with my complaints, because you were unable to assist me ? Be it so, dear friend ; if you do not feel the want of making a clean breast of it all, be silent ! But if you do feel such a want, then esteem me worthy of listening to your grief. Do not think me as weak as I may appear to be. My difficulty lies in the abominable meanness of my situation; but of that I can take a larger view if some strong sympathy induces me to break with my habit of thought.

I think I have said enough.   If more were needed, even this would have been too much.

Assume henceforth that all is right with me ; that I have no other care but that which your troubles give me.

The letter to the King of Saxony I shall leave alone ; I should not know how to utter any *truth* in it that he would comprehend, and to tell *lies* I do not care ; it is the only sin I know.   I shall finish my *Nibelungen* ; after that there will be time to take a look round the world.   For *Lohengrin* I am sorry ; it will probably go to the d—— in the meanwhile.   Well, let it go ; I have other things in my bag.   Well then, I have once more needlessly troubled you.

Dingelstedt has not replied to me yet ; he will have difficulties ; it is not the custom to pay decently for dramatic work.   Neither do I know how to oust X. from *Tannhäuser*.   He is said to be a complete ass and a blackguard to boot.   Härtinger, the tenor, is very good and full of his task ; but it was just he who told me that he did not see how X., even with the best intentions, could execute such music.   *You* of course I cannot expect to venture into this wasp's nest of Philistines.

The Königsberg manager has replied to me, saying that he has no idea of producing *Tannhäuser* at Berlin. What nonsense Herr H. has been talking to you !   Do you care to write to him about it ?

Do not misunderstand me if now and then I leave something concerning myself unmentioned to you.   The cause generally is that I attach no importance to it. The truth about the Valais Musical Festival is as follows. The committee asked me some time ago to conduct that festival, which I flatly declined, declaring, however,

my willingness to undertake a symphony by Beethoven
(that in A) if they would appoint for the festival proper
another conductor who would agree to that arrangement. This they readily accepted, and engaged Methfessel, of Berne, who is quite devoted to me. In their
announcements they think it useful to put the matter
in such a way as to make it appear that I have undertaken the direction of " the Musical Festival " conjointly
with M. Perhaps it was this that surprised you. Altogether not much that is "musical" can be expected
from this gathering. People frighten me about the
orchestra they are likely to bring together, but there
are even greater doubts as to the collection of a decent
chorus. As, moreover, they are going to have only *one*
rehearsal, you will easily understand why I did not want
to have much to do with the affair, and especially had
no thought of making propaganda. Latterly, it is true,
they have asked me to produce something of my own,
and I have given up to them the *Tannhäuser* overture,
but with the condition that I must see myself whether
they can manage it ; after the rehearsal I shall be at
liberty to withdraw it. The whole thing attracts me
only because it gives me an opportunity for an Alpine
trip (by the Bernese Oberland to Valais). In the same
sense I have sent out invitations right and left, especially
to Joachim, who had already promised me his visit for
the summer, and whom I have asked to arrange so as
to be here about that time ; he might in that case do a
little in the "festivalling" line in Valais. B. I also
invited, but to *you* I had so many other things to write
at the time that I forgot about this invitation, and the
same might easily have occurred again to-day.

However, how do matters stand ? You are sure to come to me, are you not ? And will you follow me across the Alps ? It is to be at the beginning of July.

If Joachim would like on the same occasion to let me hear something, I could easily get him a regular engagement for the festival.

To Brendel I have been owing a letter some time for his book ; I don't know what to write to him. All that is very well, and those who cannot do anything better should do what these people do, but I have no inclination that way any longer.

By your activity, however, I am delighted. What a lot of things you do ! Do not think I am indifferent because I keep silence ; no, I am really glad ! May you succeed in all you do ! About this another time.

The clean copy of my scores I shall, after all, have to make myself. It would be difficult to compile it to my liking, especially as the sketches are frightfully confused, so that no one but myself could make head or tail of them. It will take more time ; that is all. Many thanks for your trouble in this matter also. We may perhaps talk about it ; and if it tires me too much, I may still make use of your Berlin friend.

God bless you, dear Franz ; you must soon let me hear MUCH, ALL !

Have confidence in your devoted

RICHARD.

ZURICH, *May 2nd*, 1854.

While I am composing and scoring, I think only of *you*, how this and the other will please you ; I am *always* dealing with you.

154.

(FROM HERR VON HÜLSEN.)

MUCH-ESTEEMED DOCTOR,

In reference to our conversation when I had the honour of seeing you at Gotha, I beg to ask,—

If I should wish to produce *Tannhäuser* at the beginning of next winter, what would be the conditions ?

Be kind enough, dear sir, to let me have your answer as soon as possible.

With the greatest esteem,

Your obedient servant,

HÜLSEN.

BERLIN, *May* 17*th*, 1854.

[MY ANSWER.]

DEAR SIR,

I have the honour to return the following answer to your question as to the "conditions" of the performance of Wagner's operas in Berlin :—

It need not be explained at length that the performances of *Tannhäuser* and *Lohengrin* which have so far been given by theatres of the second and third rank, satisfactory and creditable for them though many of them have been, cannot be accepted as a standard for the performances contemplated at Berlin. For the very reason that Wagner attributes special importance to the Berlin stage, he has asked and commissioned me to assist him in this matter as a friend and an artist, and has given me unlimited power to act for him. The conditions are really none other than a dignified and adequate representation, which would guarantee a more

than ordinary success for these works. The latter
result is not doubtful to me provided that the representation is worthy of the Berlin stage, and I venture
to think that you, dear sir, would share this opinion
after the final rehearsals. But in order to arrive at rehearsals at all, I consider it necessary that a conclusive
and brief conversation should without delay take place
between you and me to settle the following points :—

    A. The cast.

    B. The arrangement of the rehearsals, at some
       of which I must be present.

If you desire it, I am prepared to come to Berlin at
the end of the theatrical season here (June 24th), in
order to arrive at an understanding with you about the
whole matter, which cannot be difficult.

As to the honorarium claimed by Wagner, I can
assure you in advance that he will make no unreason-
able demands,* and I shall let you know his decision
after communicating once more with him. As a minor
point, concerning my humble self, I may add that
although my personal participation in the performance
of a work by Wagner would involve a stay in Berlin
of about a month, and the sacrifice of time would
therefore be considerable, I should be so delighted at
the anticipated success of this matter, that I should
not like to mix it up with an estimate of my own
expenses.

One other point I must mention : I have heard lately
that Wagner makes my direction of his operas an
absolute condition for Berlin. Highly flattered as I
must be by Wagner's confidence, I take the liberty, in
accordance with my unlimited power, of considering the

question of my direction as a *question reservée*, which I shall decide later on, *according to circumstances.* I hope some means will be found of preserving my responsibility towards Wagner and his works without leading to an intrusion of myself on the Berlin artists.

Accept, etc., etc.

Your obedient servant,

F. L.

WEYMAR, *May* 20*th*, 1854.

* N.B.—Be good enough to send me your final instructions as to this point, whether you want a lump sum down, or royalties, or both. Write to me at once as to this, and leave it to me to get a *plus* or a *minus*, according to circumstances.

As soon as Hülsen takes another step in the matter, you will hear of it at once, dearest friend. Write to me about the money point, and let me know your other wishes as to the Berlin performance.

In the meantime keep the above two letters *to yourself*, as too much has already been said about the Berlin affair.

The arrangement with Dingelstedt has not as yet been settled, but he is coming to Weymar at the end of June. Probably he intends to wait till the Munich Exhibition is over and to produce *Tannhäuser* in the autumn. He writes that he is sorry not to be able to comply with all your wishes as to the honorarium. If you have made any special demands, let me know.

I am rather unwell and weary. This letter-writing, bargaining, and transacting are intolerable to me ; by way of relaxation, I am writing a longish article about the *Flying Dutchman*; I hope it will amuse you. Brendel will publish it completely before the middle of June; in the meantime it is appearing as a *feuilleton* in the *Weymar Official Gazette.*

Eugène Wittgenstein has sent me your medallion, which has given me great pleasure. It is the most faithful likeness of all your portraits.

In five or six days I shall visit Joachim at Hanover; he was here all last week, and showed me a very remarkable overture. Joachim is making a considerable step in advance as a composer; and if he goes on like this for a few years, he will do something out of the way.

God bless you, dearest friend, in joy and sorrow! Write soon to

Your
F. L.

May 20th, 1854.

155.

DEAR FRIEND,

In a very few days I shall write to you at length, and at the same time explain to you why this letter is so short. For the present only this, because it must not be delayed : *royalties,* nothing else. If these royalties are to be lucrative—*i.e.,* if my operas are to be given *frequently*—the manager must be well and sincerely inclined to the cause. Therefore we will treat him nobly. You have written *most excellently.*

In a few days more from your

W. R.

May 26th, 1854.

156.

HIGHLY ESTEEMED HERR INTENDANT,

By your courteous letter of May 29th, I must perceive that you are not inclined to agree with Wagner's artistic views which cause and account for my interference in the performance of his works at Berlin. I sincerely regret that the deplorable circumstances which prevent Wagner from living in Germany are still in existence, and that many things occur thereby which impede the natural progress of the performances of *Tannhäuser* and *Lohengrin*. You, sir, are too well versed and experienced in matters of art to ignore how much the success of important dramatic works depends upon the manner of their performance. The masterpieces of Gluck, cited in your letter, surely owe, in spite of their great beauties, their permanent effect largely to the particular interest taken in them by Spontini and to his personal influence at Berlin. In the same manner, the exceptional successes of Spontini's and Meyerbeer's own operas were enhanced by the special activity of their composers. It would lead me too far to discuss further facts which have been proved so often, and I confine myself to telling you candidly that if the management intends to do no more than give *Tannhäuser* or *Lohengrin just like any other work*, it would be almost more advisable to give any other work and to leave those of Wagner alone.

With Capellmeister Dorn I had several conversations about the whole matter some months ago, and I am convinced that he will not consider Wagner's condition of my undisguised participation in the performance of his works at Berlin to be an unfair demand.

It is of course natural that you, sir, are " not inclined to accept any obligation which would reflect on the dignity and the capability of the institution as well as on the authority of the intendant." Such an intention is, indeed, very far from my mind. You add, sir, " I expect the confidence of the composer in myself and the Royal Theatre." This point also has been settled, and is wholly beyond question or discussion ; but as Wagner has commissioned me to be his substitute at Berlin and has advised you of his resolution, I must, in the interest of the cause and of my position, decline to be reduced gradually to the part of the fifth whist-player, who, according to the proverb, occupies a very inconvenient position " under the table." In consequence I am obliged to ask you, sir, either to agree to the arrangement contained in my last letter, and, in your capacity of intendant of the Royal Theatre, to approve of my participation in the rehearsals and performance of Wagner's works at Berlin, according to his clearly expressed wish, or else to leave the whole matter in its actual *status quo*.

With the highest esteem, I am, sir,

Your obedient servant,

F. LISZT.

WEYMAR, *June 3rd*, 1854.

P.S.—In his last letter Wagner writes that he leaves the pecuniary conditions with regard to Berlin wholly to my decision, and that *Tannhäuser* will satisfy him.

DEAREST FRIEND,—Return Hülsen's letter to me, as I have not taken a copy, and should not like it to fall into other hands. I hope you will approve of my answer. The enclosed rough draft you may keep.

I was four days at Hanover. What will become of me this summer I cannot determine. As soon as I know, you shall hear.

Have you a copy of the pianoforte score of *Tannhäuser* to spare ? Roger, who is here, would like to study the part, and has written and asked for a copy, but hitherto in vain. I told him that I would let you know, and that I was convinced you would send me a copy for him if possible. It is said that the edition of Meser in Dresden is sold out, or else I might order one from there. You might in your next letter write a few lines which, or a copy of which, I could show to Roger. He is fairly musical, and might make a good effect in the part of Tannhäuser.

When will the Musical Festival in Canton Valais take place, and how long shall you stay there ?

157.

Again only a few lines in reply, dear Franz. You of course will not doubt for a moment that I feel sincerely grateful to you for the energy with which you take care of my interest with Hülsen. Let us " save the soul ; " then the body also will fare best. I return Hülsen's letter to you. But I am grieved to give you all this trouble. Let us expect nothing. My opinion is that you should not answer him any more.

About the pianoforte score of *Tannhäuser* I am writing to Dresden ; they must get one somehow and send it to you for Roger. As you know, I have had Roger in my eye for a long time. If, —as I hope he will through you,—he really learns his task carefully and goes to it with love, I have no doubt that he will be the FIRST Tannhäuser to satisfy my intentions entirely. Greet him very kindly.

Your question about the Musical Festival has given me hopes that you might accompany me there. Really, dear Franz, that would be a joy in this sad year. If you could induce the Princess and the Child to make an expedition to Valais by way of the Oberland and the Gemmi, oh, then, then all would be well. Only from the stupid festival itself you must expect nothing. All my compositions I have withdrawn, and shall only produce the A major symphony; there will be many people, but not much music. If you were there, and perhaps J. and B. as well, we might extemporise something purely for our own diversion. May Heaven grant that you may be sufficiently recovered to do a foolish thing and tempt others to it as well.

The festival will be on July 10th, 11th, and 12th. In the first days of the same month we should have to begin our exodus *viâ* the Oberland. I have been trying for some time to vegetate; the copying of the score of *Rhinegold* will have to wait. I must first of all have a go at the *Valkyrie*.

Farewell, dearest, unique Franz. Give me some hope of seeing you and yours.

Your
R. W.

ZURICH, *June 7th*, 1854.

158.

Herewith, dearest Richard, I send you X.'s babble, together with the sketch of my very simple answer. Probably the cart will stick in the mud for some time, and then the transactions will begin again. Well, I have learned to understand people, although the real kernel of their phrases has not been, and cannot be, clearly expressed. I have seen too much of this to be deceived. The difficulty lies neither with Hülsen nor with other people whose names have been mentioned, but with *those* whom we will not name, although we know them a little.

My symphonic poems I will bring you as soon as I find it possible to get away from here for a fortnight. I am very glad you take an interest in them.

Let us be *patient*, and remain in evil days faithful to eternity.

Your

FRANZISCUS.

June 8th, 1854.

159.

DEAR FRANZ,

Here you have the "babble" back again, the possession of which I do not envy you. Let us put this disgusting nonsense on one side; on hearing the jargon, devoid of honesty or character, which these stupid souls call "prudence," one feels as if a hundred thousand fools were gathered together. Our *fortune* lies at bottom in the fact that we do not yield to such people, and our perseverance in this is sufficient gain. To "get" something by it is of course more than we can expect. Thus in this instance I am quite satisfied to know that we shall not do what X. wants; this is alone sufficient to put me in a good temper; what happens otherwise is a matter of indifference to us.

Berlin to us has been the occasion of celebrating a feast of friendship. What else have we to do with or to care about Berlin ?

A thousand thanks for all you are doing and the way in which you do it.

As regards " success " in X.'s practical sense, I shall probably never have it. It would indeed be a kind of satire on my situation and my being. On the other hand, I should at any moment be prepared to die gladly and with a smile on my face if only a really fine opportunity would offer itself. What more can one desire ? As regards my personal future, I sincerely wish for nothing more than a beautiful death, for life is somehow out of joint. I often feel sorry that things around me do not seem to tend in that direction. Every one seems to care chiefly for a " long life," however narrow, thin, and poor it may be. This is sad.

Of all this we will talk when you come, for that you will come is certain, Lord be thanked. Bring your symphonic poems with you ; that will strengthen my thread of life a little.

Do not look out for a copyist. Madame Wesendonck has given me a gold pen of indestructible power, which has once more turned me into a caligraphic pedant. The scores will be my most perfect masterpiece of caligraphy. One cannot fly from his destiny. Meyer-beer years ago admired nothing so much in my scores as the neat writing. This act of admiration has been my curse ; I *must* write neat scores as long as I live in this world.

You will not be allowed to see the *Rhinegold* till it has been completed in this worthy fashion, and that can only be done in certain idle hours of the long winter evenings. At present I have no time for it. I must begin the composition of the *Valkyrie*, which I feel joyfully in every limb.

Greet the Princess and the Child with the full power of greeting. For to-day I must be satisfied with this request ; I can write no more, not even with my gold pen. I might say a good deal more if I were not taken with a fit of weeping, as once on the railway. I have just been called out ; an eagle was flying over our house. A good omen !

"Long live the eagle ; " he flew splendidly. The swallows were very anxious.

Farewell in the sign of the eagle.

Your

R. W.

160.

Let me tell you that tears prevent me from reading on.

Oh, you are unique of your kind !

It has struck me like a thunderbolt. Heavens, what have you written to me there ?

You alone know it !

161.
July 3rd, 1854.

A thousand thanks, dearest Franz. You have helped me out of a terrible difficulty after I had exhausted all other resources. By the autumn, I think, my affairs will be in better order.

When are you coming ? I am going to Canton Valais in a few days, but intend to be back soon. I have no money for roaming about, and while I am enjoying my work nothing else attracts me.

The *Valkyrie* has been begun, and now I shall go at it in good style.

How curious these contrasts are—I mean, between the first love scene of the *Valkyrie* and that of the *Rhinegold*.

Brendel must have surprised you. (Bosh!) God bless you.

162.

DEAREST FRANZ,

You are just the person whom I wanted to be in Leipzig at this moment, and I look upon your passage through that town as a hint of fate that there may be help for me *after all*. In my great trouble I wrote to Brendel some time ago, asking him whether he could get me amongst my Leipzig " admirers " 1,000 thalers on a bill at four or five months' date. Answer: " No, but perhaps A. might manage it through one person or another." As A. had recently paid me a visit, I wrote to him also. Answer: " No." In the course of the next three months I expect this year's receipts from my operas, and to all appearance they will be good and help me once for all out of this last difficulty. The very least I may expect is this sum of 1,000 thalers. I may therefore, with a good conscience, give a bill payable after three months (end of October) to any one who will lend it to me. Härtel must do it. If he should prefer to advance me 1,000 thalers on account of my receipts, it will suit me equally well. He can control those receipts, and I will give orders that all payments of honorarium are to be made to X. till the money has been returned. Whichever way he likes will suit me, only let me get out of this miserable condition, which makes me feel like a galley-slave.

A. wrote to me about certain possibilities of Germany being opened to me for the special purpose of a short journey. I do not believe it, and at this moment do not care much about it; I certainly will not take the least trouble in the matter. Concerning the Berlin affair, be assured that I am only too glad to leave it entirely in your hands. I should be a nice fool if I withdrew it from them as long as you are not tired of it yourself. X. will take good care not to apply to me. All this is idle gossip.

From the Musical Festival at Sitten I ran away. It appeared to me like a great village fair, and I did not care to take part in the music-making. I simply bolted. No " musical festivals " of any kind for me ! I feel quite jealous because you have gone to Rotterdam. I hope you will find time for Zurich as well. Come if you can in the latter half of August, for then I think the Wesendoncks will be back.

Good Lord, my head is a waste. Yesterday early I left the lake of Geneva. Last night I spent in the stage-coach from Berne to Lucerne. At present I am afloat on the lake of Lucerne, from the shore of which I shall fetch my wife, who is going through a cure of curds and whey. After that I return to Zurich, which I *dare* do only in the hope that your attack on the Härtels has succeeded. No one can help me here ; I exhausted everything to secure my existence from last winter till now. If all goes well, I shall continue the composition of the *Valkyrie* after August 1st. Work, *this* work, is the ONLY thing that makes life bearable. With the copying of the *Rhinegold* I go on in the intervals; in the late autumn you will, I hope, have the score.

Pardon me for this confused stuff in reply to your beautiful, cheerful letter from the Rhine. Perhaps I shall write in a better spirit soon. I am on the point of landing at Brunnen, where you are still remembered as "double Peps." How cheerful you were at that time.

On board the *Stadt Zurich*, on the lake of Lucerne, *en vue de Brunnen*.

Remember JULY 31ST.

163.

DEAR, GREAT MAN,

A thousand thanks for the autograph, which will give much joy. This Fräulein Soest is a good, excellent girl, who was sent by her parents to England, and was there taken with home-sickness for the "Weymar school," "the music of the future," and the "Wagnerian opera." She managed to escape, and is now settled at Erfurt, where she gives pianoforte lessons, and from where she comes to Weymar to hear your poems.

Ten and a hundred thousand thanks for many other things besides. Liszt was delighted to hear that his articles in the Weymar paper had pleased you. It is a fine thing of you to have understood them so well. They are to go on for some time, and the *Flying Dutchman* will conclude this series. It is truly a wreath of mourning which he binds there; your dark, noble hero lives, and will live.   Sleep and solitude are not death; and his vital strength is such, that for a long time to come he will make the round of Europe at certain intervals.   Beethoven's *Fidelio* is only just becoming acclimatised in London.

I am quite happy that the symphonic poems interest you.   When he is *able* to visit you, he will bring the scores with him.   At the present moment they are, I believe, being partly copied out and partly revised for engraving, etc., etc.   But you, dear, great genius, will be the first to read them.   They have been for the greater part performed here.   The music is most beautiful, very noble, very elevated.

Your letters give us the same joy which a poor man used only to kicks and coarse copper coin would feel at receiving an alms of gold.   Give us that alms frequently, because you are none the poorer for it. Allow Liszt to manage Hülsen, and leave Berlin to him wholly and entirely.   It may go slowly, but it will go *well* and, before all, *decently*.   How good, how prudent, how delicate and patient, *he* is—that I know. Another man would during these six years have sunk and been drowned eighteen times in the storms which have our poor little barque for a plaything.   He alone keeps us still on the surface.

Liszt has written to Berlin to find some one who will copy your *Rhinegold*, the beautiful *Rhinegold*, for which our ears are sighing.   He whom he thought would answer your purpose is not free for the present. What is needed to make you begin the *Valkyrie*?   And oh! that wonderful scene between Wotan and Brynhild

—the divine Brynhild, who saves Sieglinde! Write at great length ; it will do good to our three hearts, which are united and inseparable. The whole atmosphere of the Altenburg is gently illumed when a letter from you has arrived.

Heaven grant that we may say, "*Au revoir!* soon," and that we soon may see your *Rhinegold*, were it but a sketch. If you only knew how Liszt sings your poems! We adored *Lohengrin* long before Beck had studied it, and still listen and weep when he sings it. Do finish your *Valkyrie* as soon as possible. What a work!

Write to us soon. You say that H. does not know what the matter is. Who does when the matter is something beautiful and grand ? When a sculptor wants to make a beautiful statue, he takes granite or marble and wearies his strength in cutting it, but granite and marble are less hard than the heart of man. The sculptor, unless he dies, finishes his statue; when a noble thing has to be done, men are less pliable than granite and marble.

Liszt is indefatigable. He is wholly devoted to your courage and hope. I cannot tell you sufficiently how your dear letter has rejoiced me.

C.

164.

X.'s strong box resists a siege even more obstinately than does Silistria ; storming it will do no good, and I have consequently nothing satisfactory to tell you.

Returning here, I find a letter from Hülsen, definitely declining the performance of *Tannhäuser* at Berlin, and winding up with the following flourish : " It is obvious that, after two vain attempts to produce this work at the Royal Theatre, the management will not undertake a third as long as I have the honour of being at the head of it. I am sorry for this."

From another source I hear, however, that the matter is not to remain in this negative stage, and that in the very highest quarters there is a wish to call me to Berlin. The event must show ; for the present I have only written a few lines in reply to Hülsen.

What is all this story about the Musical Festival ? Why did you bolt ? Let me know when you happen to be in the mood.

After the Rotterdam festival I stayed a few days at Brussels to meet my two daughters.

As soon as my large arrears of correspondence are disposed of, I shall settle down to my *Faust*, which is to be ready by the new year. The other things (symphonic poems) will also be in print by that time.

I still feel very much fatigued after my hurried journey, and my personal regret at not being able to serve you makes me curtail these lines still further. Ah ! good heavens ! what can I say to you while

La vergogna dura

and while there is no means of removing that *vergogna* ?

Your

F. L.

July 28th, 1854.

165.

Dearest Franz,

Did you really think for a moment that I had conceived the idea of giving concerts in order to make propaganda for myself, or to make music, or what not? Did you not see at once that this plan was purely the result of despair at my miserable pecuniary situation, and that the only question that required an answer was whether or not I could make money by it, money in return for an unheard-of sacrifice, an act of self-abnegation, which probably I should not have been able to go through with after all? How badly I must have expressed myself! Excuse me for having given rise to such a misunderstanding, and be thanked all the more for the trouble you took nevertheless.

My dear, worthy friend, how proud and happy was I not three years ago, before I had done anything out of keeping with the full consciousness of my antagonistic position towards our artistic publicity. When at that time you, with your friendly anxiety, were intent upon getting "public recognition" for me and a wider field for my works, I used to smile and guard myself against every temptation. But the demon took hold of me; in my terribly bare life, my inclination began to grow again towards some of the amenities of existence; I yielded to temptation, surrendered my scores, was surprised at their success, and—hoped. I now curse this hope. I feel humiliated before myself, because I seek in vain release from this grief of self-reproach.

Hülsen has told X. that the whole thing in connection with me was *done*. Fortunately I was able to comfort X. with the thought that *he* had not done it; but

Hülsen is right: the thing is "done for." What finally could enlighten me better as to the truth and genuineness of my successes than the fact that in the very places where they had been gained, and with every conceivable trouble, the loan of—I must speak plainly —1,000 thalers could not be raised amongst my "admirers"? This very trivial matter speaks volumes to me.

Pray, dearest Franz, do not talk to me of my fame, my honours, my position, or whatever the name may be. I am positively certain that all my "successes" are based on *bad*, very *bad*, performances of my works, that they therefore rest on misunderstandings, and that my public reputation is not worth an empty nutshell. Let us give up all diplomatic contrivances, this dealing with means which we despise for ends which, closely considered, can never be achieved, least of all by those means. Let us leave alone this *côterie*, this connection with idiots who in a body have no notion of what we really aim at. I ask you, What satisfaction, what pleasure, can we derive from the assistance of all these silly people, whatever their names may be? I sometimes cannot understand your ironical enjoyment of life, which gets over your disgust at these people by making fun of them. Away with all this stuff, this "glory," this nonsense! We live at a time when glory can bring neither joy nor honour.

Listen to me: *Tannhäuser* and *Lohengrin* I have thrown to the winds; I do not want to know any more of them. When I gave them over to theatrical jobbery, I cast them out, I condemned them to the task of begging for me, of getting me money, *nothing but*

money. Even for that purpose I should not like to
employ them if I were not compelled to do so. Aftei
the insight which I have gained this summer, I should
willingly submit to the penance of selling all my goods
and chattels, and go, naked as I am, into the wide world,
where—I swear it to you—no illusion should tempt me
any more. But my wife could not bear such a violent
step again ; I know it would kill her. Well then, *for hei
sake* I am resolved to go on. *Tannhäuser* and *Lohengrin* must go to the Jews. But I am unable to wait
and see how much more they might bring me in in certain patiently looked-for contingencies than now, when
I am compelled to get rid of them at any price, and the
sooner the better. Tell me, dearest friend, how do matters stand at Berlin ? Did you merely rely upon making
our condition plausible to Herr von Hülsen, or had you
prepared other means of securing your honourable invitation to Berlin ? I am almost inclined to believe
the latter, and to hope in consequence that you will
soon be able to announce our triumph. The want of
Berlin for my operas involves the delay of the rest of
the business, and I assure you that the spreading of my
operas is entirely a matter of *business* to me. This is
the only real point ; all the rest is, and remains, fictitious.
Let us not attempt to look upon the matter in any
serious light except as regards money. I should
despise myself if I paid any attention to anything
beyond this. For me the song of the " world " was
sung to an end long ago.

And do you know what has confirmed me in this
sentiment, inspiring me with new pride ? It is *your
work about the " Flying Dutchman."* In this series of

articles I have once more clearly recognized myself, and have come to the conclusion that we have nothing in common with this world. *Who did ever understand me?* You, and no one else. Who understands YOU? I, and no one else. Be sure of it. You, for the first and only time, have disclosed to me the joy of being wholly understood. My being has passed into yours; not a fibre, not the gentlest tremor of my heart, remains that you have not felt with me. But I also see that *this alone* means being really understood, while all else is misunderstanding and barren error. What do I want more after having experienced this? What do you want of me after having experienced this with me? Let the tear of a beloved woman mingle with this joy, and what else can we desire? Do not let us desecrate our own selves. Let us look upon the world through the medium of contempt alone. It is worth nothing else; to found any hope on it would be deceiving our own hearts; it is bad, *bad, thoroughly bad*: only the heart of a *friend*, the tears of a woman, can dispel its curse. We do not respect the world. Its honour, its glory, or by whatever name its shams may be called, are nothing to us. It belongs to Alberich, to no one else. Let it perish! I have said enough; you now know my sentiment, which is not a momentary emotion, but as firm and solid as adamant. That sentiment alone gives me strength to drag on the burden of life. But I must henceforth cling to it inexorably. I have a deadly hatred of all *appearance*, of all hope, for it is self-deception. But I will work; you shall have my scores, they will belong to *us*, to no one else. That is enough. You have the *Rhinegold*, have you not? I have got

to the second act of the *Valkyrie* : Wotan and Fricka.
I shall succeed, you will see.

Farewell.

Are you going to write to my wife ?

My cordial remembrances !

(What the other people write I cannot bear to read
any longer.   I only read your *Dutchman* article ;
that is the reward, the pride, of my life.)

Farewell.

Your

R. W.

166.

ZURICH, *September* 16*th*, 1854.

Do you know how I can manage to arrange
some concerts at Brussels and perhaps two Dutch
towns, such as I gave last year at Zurich, and do you
think that by such an undertaking I might make 10,000
francs in cash ?   Can you make arrangements so that
my offer may be readily met, and that my programme
may be translated into French and Dutch ?   If you can
answer these questions satisfactorily, kindly take the
matter in hand as soon as possible.   I must earn money
at once.   No theatre has asked for my operas ; nothing
is stirring ; I seem to be quite forgotten.   If I could bring
back money from Belgium and Holland, I might probably
resume my work.   For the present all music has been
laid aside.

Your medallion is very beautiful.   Many thanks.   I
care for nothing else, and for good reasons.

Always your faithful

RICHARD.

167.

DEAREST FRANZ,

My wife is going to Germany, in the first instance on a visit to her parents. At present she is with Alwine Frommann, Berlin (10, Linden). In a week's time at the latest she will be in Leipzig (at A.'s, Windmühlengasse). From there she will return *viâ* Frankfort. If she could hear one of my operas— *Lohengrin* of course in preference—at Weimar, she would like to stop a day there. If you can manage this, kindly write to her at Berlin or Leipzig, or, in case you can let me know *by return*, write to *me* at Zurich, so that I can advise her in time.

From H. you will have in a few days the score of *Rhinegold*, which I sent to him in separate pieces for the purpose of having a copy made at Dresden. But as I have recently finished a clean copy myself, I cannot bear the thought that the work should not yet be in *your hands*. I did not want to let you have the fragments, for I consider it an important and significant event to place the *whole* in your hands. Keep it for a month, to have a look at it occasionally ; after that I shall ask you to return it for a time, so as to get the complete copy done.

My best love to Daniel, the foolish boy.

I write nothing else, either about myself or about your article. If I once began about these two things, I should not know where to stop. It is a great pity that I did not see you this year. Altogether I feel so boundlessly miserable that I begin to despise myself for bearing this misery. Enough. Farewell.

The worker in plaster-of-Paris has not yet returned

your medallion; the margin was a little damaged. Why do you keep the "Indian fairy tale" to yourself? I have plenty of prosaic things around me, and could find a place for it.

My best remembrances to the Princess.

Your

ZURICH, *September 29th,* 1854.   RICHARD.

168.

DEAR FRANZ,

I begin to find out more and more that you are in reality a great philosopher, while I appear to myself a hare-brained fellow. Apart from slowly progressing with my music, I have of late occupied myself exclusively with a man who has come like a gift from heaven, although only a literary one, into my solitude. This is Arthur Schopenhauer, the greatest philosopher since Kant, whose thoughts, as he himself expresses it, he has thought out to the end. The German professors ignored him very prudently for forty years; but recently, to the disgrace of Germany, he has been discovered by an English critic. All the Hegels, etc., are charlatans by the side of him. His chief idea, the final negation of the desire of life, is terribly serious, but it shows the only salvation possible. To me of course that thought was not new, and it can indeed be conceived by no one in whom it did not pre-exist, but this philosopher was the first to place it clearly before me. If I think of the storm of my heart, the terrible tenacity with which, against my desire, it used to cling to the hope of life, and if even now I feel this hurricane within me, I have at least found a quietus which in wakeful nights helps me to sleep. This is the genuine, ardent longing for death, for absolute unconsciousness, total non-existence; freedom from all dreams is our only final salvation.

In this I have discovered a curious coincidence with your thoughts; and although you express them differently, being religious, I know that you mean exactly the same thing. How profound you are! In your article about the *Dutchman* you have struck me with the force of lightning. While I read Schopenhauer I was with you, only you did not know it. In this manner I ripen more and more. I only play with art to pass the time. In what manner I try to amuse myself you will see from the enclosed sheet.

For the sake of that most beautiful of my life-dreams *Young Siegfried*, I shall have to finish the *Nibelungen* pieces after all; the *Valkyrie* has taken so much out of me that I must indulge in this pleasure; I have got as far as the second half of the last act. The whole will not be finished till 1856; and in 1858, the tenth year of my Hegira, the performance may take place, if at all. As I have never in life felt the real bliss of love, I must erect a monument to the most beautiful of all my dreams, in which, from beginning to end, that love shall be thoroughly satiated. I have in my head *Tristan and Isolde*, the simplest but most full-blooded musical conception; with the "black flag" which floats at the end of it I shall cover myself to die.

When you have had enough of *Rhinegold*, send it to Chorusmaster Fischer at Dresden, instructing him in my name to give it to the copyist Wölfel, so that he may finish the copy which he has begun.

Your cheering words about the *Rhinegold* were splendid, and it has really turned out well. I hope there will be enough counterpoint in it to please Raff. My anxiety as to this troubles me very much. Is M. ill? How can I do anything to help her? She should come in the summer to Seelisberg, on the lake of Lucerne. It is the dearest discovery I have made in Switzerland; up there all is so joyful, so beautiful, that I long to return—to die there.

There we must meet next summer; I mean to write *Young Siegfried* there, and you must assist me. Perhaps I shall assist you too. How full my heart is when I think of it! Many thanks to the Princess; at her desire, I send the enclosed autograph. Nothing about business! What do we care about such miserable things? When shall I see your symphonic poems, your *Faust*?

Farewell, my Franz.

169.

Brynhild sleeps; I am, alas! still awake.

To-day I was asked, on the part of the Philharmonic Society of London, whether I should be inclined to conduct its concerts this year. I asked in return, (1) Have they got a second conductor for the commonplace things? and (2) Will the orchestra have as many rehearsals as I may consider necessary? If they satisfy me as to all this, shall I accept then? If I could make a little money without disgrace, I should be pleased enough. Write to me at once what you think of this.

How are you otherwise?

170

First of all, dearest friend, my best wishes for the new year 1855! May it turn out luckier for us than its predecessors have been.

I have permitted myself a little indiscretion in Brendel's paper, and have written for the specimen number of the journal (which is going to have a new publisher), as well as for the first number of the new year, a few columns about your *Rhinegold*. I hope you will not be angry with me. My intention was good, and it will do no harm to draw a little public attention to the matter. The score I shall one of these days send to Fischer at Dresden, according to your instructions.

The offer of the Philharmonic Society is very acceptable, and your friends will be pleased with it. You do not say whether it is the Old Philharmonic Society or the New Philharmonic Society which has invited you. The latter Berlioz conducted for one or two seasons, in conjunction with Dr. Wylde, a protégé of one of the chief shareholders of that Society, whose name I forget. In both Societies you will find a numerous orchestra and ample materials. You will know how to bring life into them and to do something extraordinary. If I can possibly get away from here, I shall perhaps visit you in London during the season. In the meantime let me know something more about this Philharmonic business, which will probably turn out to your satisfaction. I recommend you, by your leave, some caution, and the tedious but useful method of waiting.

I have heard nothing from Berlin, and shall write to Alwine Frommann before long.

Our theatre will not be able to perform your works
for several months to come. Frau von Milde is in
interesting circumstances, and cannot appear before the
middle of April, and our public would tolerate no other
Elizabeth, Elsa, or Senta. Besides this, our first tenor
has lost his voice, and will be replaced next month by
C., who sang Tannhäuser here in November on
trial.

I expect Berlioz about the middle of February. Do
you know the score of his *Damnation de Faust*?

My *Faust* symphony is finished. There are three
movements : *Faust*, *Gretchen*, and *Mephistopheles*. I
shall bring it to you at Zurich next summer.

Remember me to your wife, and continue to love

Your

F. L.

January 1st, 1855.

The Princess sends her thanks and congratulations.

171.

DEAR FRANZ,

I am able to-day to send you particulars about
London. Mr. Anderson, treasurer of the Philharmonic
Society and conductor of the Queen's band, came
specially to Zurich to arrange the matter with me. I
did not like the idea much, for it is not my vocation
to go to London and conduct Philharmonic concerts,
not even for the purpose of producing some of my
compositions, as is their wish. I have written nothing
for concerts. On the other hand, I felt distinctly that
it was necessary for me to turn my back once for all
upon every hope and every desire of taking an active

part in our own artistic life, and for that reason I
accepted the hand held out to me.

London is the only place in the world where I can
make it possible to produce *Lohengrin* myself while
the kings and princes of Germany have something
else to do than grant me my amnesty. It would please
me very much if I could induce the English people next
year to get up a splendid German opera with my works,
patronised by the court. I admit that my best introduction for that purpose will be my appointment as
conductor of the Philharmonic (THE OLD), and so I
consented at last to the sale of myself, although I
fetched a very low price : £200 for four months. I shall
be in London at the beginning of March to conduct
eight concerts, the first of which takes place March
12th, and the last June 25th. At the beginning of
July I shall be at Seelisberg. It would be splendid
if you could visit me in London ; in any case I must
produce something of yours there. Consider this.

Do not forget Joachim; when I am once in London,
I can easily arrange the matter.

It is splendid that you have finished *Faust*, and you
may imagine that I am most anxious to see it ; on the
other hand, it is a pity that you will not show it me
sooner. At the same time, I shall be glad to go through
it *with you* at the piano, and to make its acquaintance
in that way, seeing that my attendance at a good
performance under your direction is for the present
out of the question. The vivid idea which you know
how to convey cannot even approximately be replaced
by anything else ; and I am more than ever intent upon
getting the right impression from the first, for I greatly

distrust acquaintances made by means of the abstract notes.

It is an absurd coincidence that just at this time I have been taken with a desire to remodel my old *Faust* overture. I have made an entirely new score, have rewritten the instrumentation throughout, have made many changes, and have given more expansion and importance to the middle portion (second motive). I shall give it in a few days at a concert here, under the title of "A *Faust* Overture." The motto will be—

> "Der Gott, der mir im Busen wohnt,
> Kann tief mein Innerstes erregen ;
> Der über allen meinen Kräften thront,
> Er kann nach aussen nichts bewegen;
> Und so ist mir das Dasein eine Last,
> Der Tod erwünscht, das Leben mir verhasst !"

but I shall not publish it in any case.

I was at first startled at your new year's article, but soon perceived that here again I am indebted to your ever-increasing sympathy. If, however, you represent my work as something colossal, you mistake, in my opinion, the standard of measurement ; to me our artistic publicity, the spirit of our means of representation, etc., appear to be very small and miserable, while my work is just in accordance with ordinary human proportions, and appears gigantic only when we try to confine it to those unworthy conditions. When therefore we call our plan chimæric and eccentric, we in reality flatter the actual worthlessness of our artistic publicity, and in a manner mark it as the just and rational measure. We should not give that wrong impression to people.

Every one of your letters is worth to me gold, and more, but *answers* in the proper sense I scarcely ever receive from you, and you treat many of my questions as if they had never been asked. Instead of that you always give me something new ; that is splendid, but an answer also would sometimes be useful.

Well, let me hear something good of you soon, and in London let me *see* you. I shall take my work with me, and hope to finish the instrumentation of the *Valkyrie* there.

Adieu, dearest Franz.

How are you ? Best remembrances from my wife and many greetings from me to you all.

Your

R. W.

Zurich, *January* 19*th*, 1855.

172.

Dearest Richard,

The London Philharmonic comes in very aptly, and I am delighted. As lately as six months ago people used to shake their heads, and some of them even hissed, at the performance of the *Tannhäuser* overture, conducted by Costa. Klindworth and Remeny were almost the only ones who had the courage to applaud and to beard the Philistines who had made their nests of old in the Philharmonic. Well, it will now assume a different tone, and you will revivify old England and the Old Philharmonic. I commend to you Klindworth, a Wagnerian *de la veille*. He is an excellent musician, who formerly acted as conductor at Hanover, and there gave a performance of the *Prophet* at the Tivoli Theatre, of which the newspapers were full some years ago. He is also a splendid pianist, who studied eighteen months with me at Weymar, and you must allow me to send Klindworth a few lines of introduction to you. As far as I know, there is in London no pianist like him ; but, on account of his determined and open sympathy with the so-called " music of the future," he has placed himself in a somewhat awkward position towards the Philistines and handicraftsmen there.

I was present at the first performance of *Tannhäuser* at Gotha. Capellmeister Lampert had taken much trouble, as had also Beer (Tannhäuser), and the performance was, comparatively speaking, very satisfactory. The musical part is better with us, but it is different with the dresses and scenery, which are much more tasteful at Gotha than at Weymar. I have spoken very strongly on that point here ; and as my prayers and admonitions in this respect have so far been of little avail, I am determined not to conduct *Tannhäuser* and *Lohengrin* again until the necessary improvements in the scenery have been made. This negative measure, which I had kept in reserve, will probably be effective. In the meantime our opera remains in a stagnant condition. Since the last performance of *Tannhäuser* (December 10th), I have not been at my desk, neither shall I conduct the festival performance of *Belisario* on February 16th. Nothing can be done till after the confinement of Frau Milde.

Apropos, what do you think of Meffert, the tenor ? Would he be any good to us, and how old is he ? Write to me about this.

You accuse me in your last letter of rarely giving you an answer. This alludes, I presume, to two things :

Berlin and Dresden. Alas! alas! I cannot report from either place what I should wish and, in spite of all, still hope to report. With wranglings and trifles I do not care to trouble you.

Stop; one thing I forgot to write to you : your *Tristan* is a splendid idea ; it may become a glorious work. Do not abandon it.

You were quite right in arranging a new score of your *Faust* overture. If you have succeeded in making the middle part a little more pliable, this work, significant as it was before, must have gained considerably. Be kind enough to have a copy made, and send it me *as soon as possible*. There will probably be some orchestral concerts here, and I should like to give this overture at the end of February.

Härtel is having the scores of Nos. 3 and 4 of my symphonic poems (*Les Préludes* and *Orpheus*) engraved. I am as yet uncertain whether I shall publish the nine pieces together or these two numbers (3 and 4) in advance. In any case I shall send you the proofs of *Les Préludes* and *Orpheus* before your departure to London, so that my scribbling may amuse you too. I am sincerely grateful for your friendly proposal of producing something of mine at the Philharmonic, but I think it will be more advisable to leave it till next season (1856). For the present you will have your hands full enough with your own things, and during the first year you ought to play a waiting game. The chief thing for you is to gain firm ground in London, and first of all to impress your conception of Beethoven, Gluck, etc., on the orchestra and the public. At the same time, the people should learn to listen to and understand the *Tannhäuser* and *Faust* overtures, and finally to rejoice in and be elevated by the prelude to *Lohengrin*. Your plan of conducting next year performances of *Tannhäuser*, *Lohengrin*, and the *Flying Dutchman* with efficient artists is very good. We talked about this at Weymar in the year 1849; and, in my opinion, the enterprise can be made to succeed completely. This year must serve you as a preparation; and when you are once accustomed to London air, it may be expected that you will settle there comfortably. Beware of the theatrical speculators, who will be sure to try and make the best of you, and might be dangerous both to your purse and to your position.

Once more, good luck!

Your
F. L.

Weymar, *January 25th*, 1855.

Best remembrances to your wife. For the first year she will, I suppose, remain at Zurich.

Do not keep me waiting too long for a letter, and send me your *Faust*. The Princess and the Child greet you cordially.

I shall send you in a few days an English translation of your three opera poems in manuscript; it may be of use to you in London.

173.

Pardon me, dearest Franz, for writing a few lines to ask you a favour. I did not communicate with you before because I waited for the copy of my *Faust* overture to be ready. I expect it in a few days, and shall send it you at once, together with a proper letter. For to-day only the following :—

The French ambassador is going to give me his *visé* of my passport through France after repeated applications in Paris, but this is subject to all manner of chicanery, which is disgusting to me, and must be got out of the way, so that in future I may be able to pass without difficulty and at any time through and into France. I shall therefore pay a visit to the Minister of the Interior in Paris, and see whether I can succeed in putting a stop to these vexations. It would, no doubt, be very useful if some one of the court of Weimar (no one better than the Grand Duke himself, perhaps through his minister in Paris) could give me an introduction which would make me favourably known to the people there and teach them a little reason. I am prepared to make every necessary promise in return. Do see what you can achieve.

I start in a fortnight ; therefore no delay, please.

You will hear in a few days from

Your
R. W.

February 9th, 1855.

174.

DEAREST RICHARD,

The Grand Duke has been in bed for several weeks, and I shall probably not be able to see him for a fortnight. Apart from this, it will not be quite so easy to settle offhand the matter you have entrusted to me, but I promise that I shall not fail to take the proper steps, and I hope to send you satisfactory news within twelve days or a fortnight.

Berlioz has been here since Sunday, and is busily engaged conducting rehearsals for the performance of his "Trilogie Sacrée" (*L'Enfance du Christ*) and his "Symphonie Phantastique," including the second part thereof, which he calls a *monodrame lyrique*. I send you programme and libretto.

He tells me that he is not going to London till May, and will conduct only two concerts of the New Philharmonic. As a kind of prelude to the Paris *Exposition Universelle*, he will perform his Te Deum on the 1st of May in the Church of St. Eustache.

During this week of the year we are generally in a state of great confusion. Six years ago, on the 16th of February, *Tannhäuser* was performed for the first time, and on the same date two years ago the *Flying Dutchman*; for to-day *Belisario* is announced, which at any rate I prefer to the silly *Le Maçon*, which has been the delight of Dresden and Weymar during the winter. Even some of our friends were simple enough to call this rotten *musique de portières* charming and a model of its kind.

The Cologne people have done better than this: they have bravely swallowed *Lohengrin* without choking over it. This has delighted me. From Hamburg also I hear that the public are gradually being educated up to it.

How far have you got with the *Valkyrie*?

Difficult as I find it to part with your *Rhinegold*, I promise to send the score to Fischer in a few days. He can send me the pianoforte arrangement later on.

My best remembrances to your wife. I shall soon write again, and also hope to hear from you.

Most thine own,　F. Liszt.

Weymar, *February* 16*th*, 1855.

175.

These lines, most incomparable friend, are intended to introduce to you Carl Klindworth, about whom I have spoken and written to you several times. You will find him an excellent musician and pianist, who is cordially devoted to you, and has not in vain lived several years with me at Weymar. Since last year he has been settled in London, where I cordially commend him to your protection.

Your

F. LISZT.

WEYMAR, *February* 16*th*, 1855.

176.

Herewith, dearest Franz, you receive my remodelled *Faust* overture, which will appear very insignificant to you by the side of your *Faust* symphony. To me the composition is interesting only on account of the time from which it dates; this reconstruction has again endeared it to me : and with regard to the latter, I am childish enough to ask you to compare it very carefully with the first version, because I should like you to take cognisance of the effect of my experience and of the more refined feeling I have gained. In my opinion, new versions of this kind show most distinctly the spirit in which one has learned to work and the coarsenesses which one has cast off. You will be better pleased with the middle part. I was of course unable to introduce a new motive, because that would have involved a remodelling of almost the whole work; all I was able to do was to develop the sentiment a little more broadly, in the form of a kind of enlarged cadence.

Gretchen of course could not be introduced, only
Faust himself :—

> " ein unbegreiflich holder Drang,
> trieb mich durch Wald und Wiesen hin," etc

The copying has unfortunately been done very badly,
and probably there are many mistakes in it.

If some one were to *pay me well* for it, I might still be
inclined to publish it. Will you try the Härtels for
me ? A little money would be very welcome in
London, so that I might the better be able to save
something there. Please see to this. All this, however,
is only the prelude to your *Faust* symphony, to which
I look forward with infinite pleasure. I have nothing
further to tell you, except that I have been fool
enough to take more trouble about a performance of
Tannhäuser at the local theatre than had been my
intention. It will take place to-morrow, and, considering the miserable conditions, will turn out fairly well.
But I shall not conduct.

Cordial thanks for your pieces of advice, which have
my full approval. I intend to appear in London only
as a conductor, and to be very tough about my compositions.

The score of the first act of the *Valkyrie* will soon be
ready; it is wonderfully beautiful. I have done nothing
like it or approaching it before. My complaint that you
seldom *answer* me in the proper sense of the word you
have misunderstood. It did not refer to *external* matters,
like Dresden and Berlin, but exclusively to *internal* ones,
for which I thought I had given you plenty of material.

After having been in Paris together, should we not
try to meet in London also ? How can we manage it ?

And how about the translation? I am looking forward to it with immense pleasure, and shall use it for learning English after all.   Shall I receive it here? I start on the 25th.   If you find it necessary to write to me at once at London, address to Ferdinand Präger, 31, Milton Street, Dorset Square.   I shall stay with him till I have found a convenient lodging.   Could you give me an introduction to the London Erard and ask him to put a nice grand piano in my room?   I shall be glad to see Klindworth.   Farewell for to-day.   Give me another pleasure soon, and remember me at home.

Your
R. W.

177.

DEAREST, DEAREST LISZT,

Pray let me have the *letter to Erard* for which I asked you concerning the piano.

More after the concert.

178.

DEAREST RICHARD,

You have entirely forgotten to let me have your address; and although your fame has reached the point of immortality, it is just possible that the London postmen might have heard nothing of *Tannhäuser* and *Lohengrin*.   Be kind enough therefore to tell me in your next letter the street and the number of the house.

These lines you receive through Klindworth. Enclosed is the letter to the *maison* Erard, which is represented in London by M. Bruzot.   If Erard himself should be there, pay him a visit at once, but I doubt whether he is sufficiently recovered to occupy himself with pianoforte and harp matters.   A few

months ago my children wrote to me from Paris that
Erard was very ill, and, after fruitless trials of baths
and medicines, had been taken to a private hospital.

I have not neglected your passport affair, and have
induced the Grand Duke and another important person
to recommend you specially in Paris. I hope these
transactions will not be without result.

The changes you have made in the *Faust* overture
are excellent, and the work has decidedly gained by
them. I have sent the score to the Härtels. If you
are satisfied with an honorarium of twenty louis d'or,
write to me simply, " Yes," and the full score and parts
will soon be published. To a larger honorarium the
Härtels would not agree, but they will make the edition
better and handsomer than would any one else, and
I should therefore advise you to answer me in the
affirmative.

I shall have to work hard for several months to come.
The Cardinal Primate of Hungary has set me the task
of composing a grand mass for the inauguration of the
cathedral of Gran. The ceremony will take place in
August at the latest. The Emperor will be present,
and I have undertaken to conduct the mass, etc., for
which purpose I have to be in Gran (three hours'
distance from Pesth) a month before.

This task gives me much pleasure, and I hope to
produce an edifying work.

Farewell, dearest Richard, and write soon to

Your

FRANZ.

March 12th, 1855.

The letter to Bruzot is meant for the *firm* of Erard ;

if he should be absent, give it to the representative of that firm.

Your letter to B. has been forwarded.

179.

Good gracious! here comes your and M.'s dear, dear letter! In my terrible mood, it has quite upset me. You will have heard of my letter containing my disgraceful decision regarding *Tannhäuser* in Berlin. In this matter I feel in turns trivial, sublime, and contemptible. The latter mood you have just revived in me, and I am inclined to repent that I have been trivial. But it is almost too late now. By giving up *Tannhäuser*, and at last even *Lohengrin*, to the theatres without reserve, I made such humiliating concessions to the reality of our miserable artistic circumstances that I can scarcely sink much lower. *Once again* I say, How proud and free was I when I reserved these works to *you* for Weimar ; now I am a slave and absolutely powerless. One inconsistency involves another, and I can dull my unpleasant feeling only by being still more proud and contemptuous, in the sense that I look upon *Tannhäuser* and *Lohengrin* as altogether done with and no longer belonging to me, and that I keep my *new creations* all the more sacred for myself and my true friends. This is my only comfort. What I am creating at present shall never see the light except in perfectly congenial surroundings ; on this I will in future concentrate all my strength, my pride, and my *resignation*. If I die before having produced these works, I shall leave them to you ; and if you die without

having been able to produce them in a dignified manner,
you must burn them : let that be *settled*.

Klindworth has probably not yet had time to write
to you about my first appearance, but he is going to do
so.

After the first rehearsal the directors of the Philharmonic were so delighted and full of hope that they
insisted upon my performing some of my compositions
at the very next concert. I had to yield, and chose the
pieces from *Lohengrin*. As for that purpose they granted
me two rehearsals, I also fixed upon the Ninth Symphony,
at which I am pleased, for I should not have given it
with one rehearsal. The orchestra, which has taken a
great liking to me, is very efficient, and possesses great
skill and fairly quick intelligence, but it is quite spoilt
as regards expression ; there is no *piano*, no *nuance*.
It was astonished and delighted at my way of doing
things. With two further rehearsals I hope to put it
tolerably in order. But then this hope and my intercourse with the orchestra are all that attracts me here ;
beyond this all, all is indifferent and disgusting to me.
The public, however, have distinguished me very much,
both in receiving me and even more at the close.
Curious to me was the confession of some Mendels-
sohnians that they had never heard and understood the
overture to the *Hebrides* as well as under my direction.

Enough of this.

Many thanks for your introduction to Bruzot ; I long
for a piano and for my work. To the Grand Duke also
I am much indebted.

Let the Härtels have my *Faust* overture by all means.
If they could turn the twenty louis d'or into twenty pounds,

I should be glad. In any case they ought to send the money here as soon as possible. I do not like to dun the Philharmonic for my fee, and therefore want money. The proofs of the score they must also send to me for correction.

The publication of this overture is, no doubt, a weakness on my part, of which you will soon make me thoroughly ashamed by your *Faust* symphony. When shall I hear something of that? I am afraid my chances of seeing you here have declined, since you write about this Hungarian commission. I can imagine how the invitation has pleased you; and I too am pleased and most curious to see your work. But when shall I see something of all this, you reticent person? Do you not feel how I must long for such cordials amongst the trivial surroundings in which I always live? I must confess, however, that I always prefer becoming acquainted with your creations through yourself. In that manner everything is disclosed to me at once that otherwise I have to disclose to myself painfully. This happened to me in the case of your *Künstler*, while all that you gave me yourself at the piano at once penetrated me by dint of unconditional and perfect artistic enjoyment.

When shall we see each other, you most amiable and nobiest of men?

Most stupidly I was unable at Paris to remember the address of your children, nor could I think of Belloni's address. By taxing my memory I went half mad. Now, stupid fool that I am, it occurs to me that I need only have gone to Erard's. In this manner I deprived myself of the pleasure of seeing them once more, which grieves me very much. Please let me have the address for my return journey.

A thousand thanks to dear M. for her beautiful and kind lines. You all appear to me like a family of saints. Ah, we are all holy martyrs; perhaps I shall one day be a real one, but in that case all will be over for me with art—that beautiful delusion, the last and the most sublime, to hide from us the misery of the world.

Farewell, dear, glorious friend.

Remember me cordially at home, and continue to love me.

22, PORTLAND TERRACE, REGENT'S PARK.

180.

22, PORTLAND TERRACE, REGENT'S PARK, LONDON.

DEAREST FRANZ,

I am in the absurd position of having to demand of you a friendly service of a peculiar kind. I *cannot* delay the Berlin *Tannhäuser* affair any longer; my pecuniary position is so unfortunate that I cannot afford to forego the hope of Berlin receipts. Hülsen has applied to me once more, through Alwine Frommann, and, as he says, for the last time. He promises all manner of things; the opera is to be given in the autumn, and the preparations are to begin as early as the spring. I must adopt the "trivial" view of this matter, the same view which unfortunately I am compelled to take of the entire fate of my operas. In spite of D. conducting, *Tannhäuser* will probably have the same kind of effect in Berlin which it has had everywhere else; to connect higher hopes with it seems vain. Let the matter therefore take the only course which apparently is open to it, but I regret very much that you have wasted so much trouble and submitted to so many stupid things in endeavouring to accomplish the condition made by me. We are, as we now see, powerless.

The fate which we must expect is, after all, the *common lot.* Our best efforts always appear before the world in a truncated and distorted form. I am going to write to Alwine Frommann that she is to accept Hülsen's offer without further conditions and to tell him that this has been your advice. The truth is that in this manner you will avoid a struggle which, in my opinion, would be fruitless.

Klindworth, for whom I am grateful to you, will probably write to you about my doings in London; I can only say that I do not exactly see what I am here for. The only interesting thing to me is the orchestra, which has taken a great liking to me, and believes in me with enthusiasm. By that means I shall at least be able to have a few good performances, to which the people are quite unaccustomed. All other things, especially public, press, etc., are very indifferent to me. The directors insisted upon my performing some pieces from *Lohengrin* and the Ninth Symphony as early as the second concert, and granted me *two* rehearsals for the purpose.

I am still without a piano. I long to resume my work. *Where* and *when* shall I see you again?

Taken all in all, I am *very*, very depressed. I am disgusted with the world.

Adieu. Remember me to all at Altenburg; and if you can, continue to love me.

181.

DEAREST RICHARD,

It would have been difficult to make Härtel consent to the change of louis d'or into pounds, and after considering the matter I simply wrote to him that you had left the *Faust* overture to me, and that in your name I accepted the honorarium of twenty louis d'or, asking him at the same time to send you that little sum to London.

We will not let our hair turn grey over the *Tannhäuser* affair at Berlin. I anticipated this all along, although, for my part, I could not and did not wish to bring it about. I do not grudge your Berlin friends the satisfaction which this issue of the affair will give them, and hope that many other occasions will turn up on which I shall not be superfluous or inconvenient to you.

The day before yesterday I sent the score of the *Rhinegold* (beautifully bound) to W. Fischer at Dresden.

Has B. finished the pianoforte arrangement? In that case I would ask him to let me have it later on, and at my next visit you will sing and represent the whole to me.

I am hard at work at my Mass, of which the Kyrie and Gloria are already finished.

Apart from this, I have to conduct many rehearsals.

Schumann's *Genoveva* will be performed on April 9th, and will give me another opportunity of studying and conducting an opera, which I have not done for the last four months.

Next Sunday (April 1st) the oratorio *Die Verklärung des Herrn*, by Kühnsted, professor at Eisenach and organist of Wartburg *in spe*, will be given at the theatre; and on April 20th Raff is going to give a concert, at which half a dozen of his larger compositions —amongst others, an orchestral suite, the hundred and twenty-first Psalm, a violin concerto, etc.—will make up the entire programme.

This is the musical news of Weymar, which probably will be of less interest to you than to me. Of my life, my hope, my endurance, I have nothing to say that is cheerful. . . .

Whether the great political event, the death of the Emperor, will have a softening influence on my personal fate, remains questionable. In a few weeks I shall have direct news. Whatever it may turn out to be, I cannot waver or hesitate. To you, dearest Richard, remains cordially and invariably attached

Your

F.

I am constantly being asked for introductions to you. Generally I refuse them, but in a few cases I have to yield.

Tell Klindworth he is to write to me about your Philharmonic concerts. His cousin, a very amiable lady, will shortly bring you news of Weymar, where she has been staying several months.

182.

DEAR, GREAT MAN,

For a long time I have been wishing to write to you, but had not the courage to do so. Alas! how can I speak to you from my heart? To-day a sheet of paper with a red border comes under my hand; so many symbols are comprised in that colour ! It is devoted to love, it is the purple of kings, and the image of human blood. It is therefore suited to both of us : to you as the emblem of your sovereign genius, to me as that of an ardent attachment, the flames of which are my happiness and my glory ; to both of us as the sign of the wounds which destiny has inflicted on us without touching our souls. Need I tell you how much I should like to see you again, and how sincerely I desire that your sojourn in London will be agreeable to you in one way or another ? I can do nothing, nothing, except the best thing of all : to love, to bless, to admire.

Your affection is very dear to us ; continue in it ; it is the sun of our starless sky.

May God be with you. Our hearts are always yours.

CAROLYNE.

March 27th, 1855.

183.

DEAR FRANZ,

You have punished me in your amiable manner. I reproached myself very much about this Berlin affair ; in any case I was too rash, and settled the matter too quickly after my fashion. I ought to have asked you, as you were my plenipotentiary, to cede the opera finally to Hülsen ; that would have been better, and you would, no doubt, have undertaken this last transaction to please me. But the whole matter had long ago become so disgusting to me that I lost all energy in connection with it, and felt inclined to finish it as abruptly as possible, so as to hear no more of it. Do not believe that I was brought to this resolution through my

" Berlin friends," but exclusively through my pecuniary position, which is accurately known to you, and which has tied my hands as to this point.   I was *compelled* to think of raising money.   I have therefore asked for an advance of a hundred louis d'or on account of royalties, and as to the rest have ceded the opera without any conditions.   To tell you the truth, everything else in connection with my operas has become a matter of perfect indifference to me.   Looking at it carefully, it seems to me that my wish that you should be called to Berlin for the performance of *Tannhäuser* has by no means been frustrated thereby.   The decision of this matter was never really within the power of the inten- dant of the theatre.   The King alone can suspend the usual order, and *his* decision is quite independent of what the intendant can do on his own authority.   It appears to me therefore that our condition was made to an authority which could not have granted it.   My giving or not giving the opera to the management was a thing apart ; and as regards the invitation to you, this remains a matter which we ought to work with the King direct.   Unfortunately it seems that you have little hope of this.   What could be done to get some- thing out of the King after all ?   Should I have the impudence to write to him and to try in my own way what seems impossible in any other ?   The thought of accomplishing my wish after all is the only thing which suddenly places this Berlin affair once more in an interesting light.   What do you think of it ?

For your news and for the beautiful lines of the dear Princess I am cordially grateful.

Unfortunately I have nothing reasonable to tell you

in return. My whole existence here is a perfect anomaly. I am in a strange element and in a thoroughly false position. If at Zurich I conduct symphonies now and then, it is done for the sake of amusement and to please a few friends ; to make a vocation of it, in the sense that I am to be judged as an artist by a wholly unsympathetic public and press on these grounds, is simply an absurdity. I sincerely regret that I am here, and shall never in my life come again. Pecuniary success is out of the question ; and even if they were to offer me a larger fee for next year, I should probably feel bound to decline it : the misery I have to undergo is too great. This is not my business, and if at my present age, and in the unsettled condition of my health, I cannot at least abide by *my business*, I would rather not abide at all ; I have quite enough to bear without that.

Perfect performances, which in the long run could alone console me, I cannot achieve. The rehearsals are too few, and everything is done in too businesslike a manner. Although the pieces from *Lohengrin* were favourably received, I am sorry that I have given them. My annoyance at being compelled to produce such trifling specimens of my work and to have my whole being judged thereby is too great. I also hate like poison to have to take a single step in order to gain the favour of that wretched pack of journalists. They continue abusing me to their heart's delight, and the only thing that surprises me is that the public have not so far allowed themselves to be misled. In short, I would have nothing to do with these contemptible matters even if I happened to please the people.

Let me finish my *Nibelungen* ; that is all I desire. If

my noble contemporaries will not help me to that, they may go to the devil, with all their honour and glory. Through London I have got into awful arrears with my work; only yesterday was I able to finish the instrumentation of the first act of the *Valkyrie*. Body and soul are weighed down as by a load of lead. My chief wish for this year—to begin *Young Siegfried* at once after my return at Seelisberg—I shall have to give up, for it is very unlikely that I shall get beyond the second act of the *Valkyrie* here. Such as I am, I want a soft, clinging element around me, in order to feel gladly inclined for work. This eternal need of self-condensation for the purpose of self-defence supplies me with obstinacy and contempt, but not with the love of expansion and production.

Klindworth has probably written to you; at least he was startled when I recently conveyed your reminder to him. He was ill, and is not doing well here, but how am I to help him? Blackguardism, obstinacy, and religiously nursed stupidity are here protected with iron walls; only a blackguard and a Jew can succeed here.

Upon the whole, you were right in retiring to Weimar; as much solitude as possible, that alone can save us.

The Härtels sent me the bill of exchange yesterday; many thanks. Cannot B. do the pianoforte arrangement?

He had only just begun the *Rhinegold*, when I took the score away from him to send it to you. As soon as the copy at Dresden has been finished, he is to have it for the completion of the pianoforte arrangement; and after that, if you wish it, it is to be sent to you. Shall we see each other this year, perhaps on your return from Hungary? That would be something like it! Perhaps at that time I should have recovered my voice, which here has disappeared entirely.

Farewell, dearest friend. Patience—that is all that remains to us. Remember me to all at Altenburg. Much luck to your mass!

Farewell, dear, dear Franz.

184.

Klindworth has just played your great sonata to me. We passed the day alone together; he dined with me, and after dinner I made him play. Dearest Franz, you were with me; the sonata is beautiful beyond anything, grand and sweet, deep and noble, sublime as you are yourself. It moved me most deeply, and the London misery was forgotten all at once. More I cannot say, not just after having heard it, but of what I say I am as full as man can be. Once more, you were with me! Ah, could you soon be with me wholly and bodily, then we might support life beautifully.

Klindworth astonished me by his playing; no lesser man could have ventured to play your work to me for the first time. He is worthy of you. Surely, surely, it was beautiful.

Good-night. Many thanks for this pleasure vouchsafed to me at last.

Your
R. W.

London, *April 5th,* 8.30 *evening.*

185.

DEAREST RICHARD,

I had nothing to tell you that was pleasant or

important, and therefore did not write to you for a long time. During these last weeks I have spun myself into my mass, and yesterday at last I got it done. I do not know how it will sound, but may say that I have *prayed* it rather than *composed* it. On my return from Hungary in September, I shall bring you the mass and my symphonic bubbles and troubles, half of which will by that time be in print. If my scores should bore you, that will not prevent me from deriving sweetest enjoyment from your creations, and you must not refuse me the favour of singing the whole *Rhinegold* and *Valkyrie* to me. In the meanwhile all other musical things appear to me "stupid stuff."

How do you feel in London?

Troublesome though it may be, one must try to bear the inevitable and immutable; to take pleasure in it would be a lie.

The English edition of Philistinism is not a whit pleasanter than the German, and the chasm between the public and ourselves is equally wide everywhere.

How, in our wretched conditions, could enthusiasm, love, and art have their true effect?

"Patience and resignation" is our device, and to it we sing

Pardon me for being your hollow echo, and let us endure what cannot be cured.

I am very grateful to you for being so kind to Klindworth. In a few days his cousin will come to London and bring you news of me, as she has spent the whole winter at Weymar. Your letter about the sonata has highly delighted me, and you must excuse me for not having thanked you at once. You are often so near to me that I almost forget writing to you, and I am seldom at the right temperature for correspondence. Well, in September I shall be with you; and (D.V.) we will have some bright, comforting days together.

Your

F. L.

Weymar, *May 2nd*, 1855.

186.

Dear Poet, Dear Friend,

Our hearts are with you, and suffer with you; that you know, and cannot be ignorant of.

Let us hear from you soon, and forgive me if, in the midst of the preoccupations of your heart and of your grief, I ask you for a trifle; but it will cost you so little to grant it me, and you will give such great, such very great, pleasure by it. It is the fate of poets and women sometimes to give what they have not themselves—I mean happiness. Take a piece of paper and write on it the following verses, which, as you know, appear to me written with the purest blood of my veins:—

> " Nicht Gut, nicht Gold,
>   noch göttliche Pracht;
>   nicht Haus, nicht Hof,
>   nicht herrischer Prunk,
>   nicht trüber Verträge
>   trügender Bund,
>   noch heuchelnder Sitte
>   hartes Gesetz:
> selig in Lust und Leid
> lässt—die Liebe nur sein!—"

Sign this with your name, your great name, enclose it in an envelope, address it to me, and put it in the post. Forgive me for asking you this small thing—small in its material aspect, but great as the world in its significance.

I press your two hands with mine, dear, dear, great man.

CAROLYNE.

May 7th, 1855.

187.

Cordial thanks, dearest Franz, for your kind note, which I had been expecting a long time. The hope which you open to me of seeing you in September is my only light in the night of this sad year. I live here like one of the lost souls in hell. I never thought that I could sink again so low. The misery I feel in having to live in these disgusting surroundings is beyond description, and I now realise that it was a sin, a crime, to accept this invitation to London, which in the luckiest case must have led me far away from my real path. I need not expatiate to you upon my actual situation. It is the consistent outgrowth of the greatest inconsistency I ever committed. I am compelled to conduct an English concert programme right down to the end; that says everything. I have got into the middle of a slough of conventionalities and customs, in which I stick up to the ears, without being able to lead into it the least drop of pure water for my recreation. "Sir, we are not accustomed to this"—that is the eternal echo I hear. Neither can the orchestra recompense me. It consists almost exclusively of Englishmen, that is clever machines which cannot be got into the right swing ; handicraft and business kill everything. Then there is the public, which, I am assured, is very favourably inclined towards me, but can never be got out of itself, which accepts the most emotional and the most tedious things without ever showing that it has received a real impression. And, in addition to this, the ridiculous Mendelssohn worship !

And even if all this were better than it is, what business have I with such concerts ? I am not fit for them. It is quite a different thing if I conduct one of Beethoven's symphonies before a few friends, but to be a regular concert conductor, before whom they place the scores of concert pieces, etc., so that he may beat the time to them—that, I feel, is the deepest disgrace. This thoroughly inappropriate character of my position led me to the resolution of sending in my resignation after the fourth concert. But of course I was talked out of it, and especially my regard for my wife, who would have heard of this sudden resignation and of all that would have been written about it with great grief, determined me to hold out till the last concert. The infernal torture this is to me I cannot express. All my pleasure in my work is disappearing more and more. I had made up my mind to finish the score of the *Valkyrie* during the four months here, but that is out of the question. I shall not even finish the second act, in so terribly dispiriting a manner does this false position act upon me. In July I wanted to begin *Young Siegfried* at Seelisberg, on the lake of Lucerne, but now I think of delaying that beginning till next spring. This dislike of work is the worst feature of all. I feel as if with it eternal night were closing around me, for what have I still to do in this world if ₁I cannot do my work ?

Through this hell my study of Dante, to which I could not settle down before, has accompanied me. I have passed through his Inferno, and am now at the gate of Purgatory. Really I am in need of this purgatory ; for if I consider it rightly, I was brought to London by a really sinful degree of thoughtlessness, which now I have to repent with fervour. I must, I must be resigned ; my experience long ago convinced me of the necessity of resignation in the widest sense of the word, and I must now subdue altogether this terrible, wild desire of life, which again and again dims my vision and throws me into a chaos of contradictions. I must hope that I may at some future time rise from purgatory to paradise ; the fresh air of my Seelisberg will perhaps help me to this. I do not deny that I should like to meet Beatrice there.

In all other respects things are going badly and crookedly. Poor Klindworth has been ill all along, and the fact that I could undertake nothing with him has deprived me of a great pleasure. He is better now, but not yet allowed to take a walk with me. Besides him, my intercourse is limited to Sainton, the leader of the orchestra, who caused my ill-fated appointment here, and a certain Lüders, who lives with him. Both are ardently devoted to me, and do all in their power to make my stay here pleasant. Apart from this, Ifrequently go to Präger, a good soul. Quite recently a Mr. Ellerton, a rich amateur, approached me very cordially. He has heard my operas in Germany, and my portrait has been hanging in his room for two years. He is the first Englishman I have seen who does not care particularly for Mendelssohn. A fine, amiable mind. Klindworth has made the pianoforte arrangement of the first act of the *Valkyrie*, which he plays beautifully. Unfortunately I have lost my voice entirely, and can sing very little, so that I am afraid I shall not be able to be of much service to you in that way.

You will have to do all the work next September. You owe me a great debt, you reticent man. If I look forward to anything in the future as pure happiness, it is my becoming acquainted through your means with your new compositions. Do not forget to bring me every one of them. I congratulate you on your mass from the bottom of my heart. Let us hope that you will derive much pleasure from it at Gran.

And how is the Princess? Joyful and sorrowful? Does she still preserve her bright enthusiasm? And Beatrice—I mean the Child? Greet her for me a thousand times.

Farewell, dearest, most unique of friends. Believe me that the thought of you is an ever-new delight to my heart. Be thanked for your love!

Farewell.

Your

R. W.

London, *May* 16*th*, 1855.

188.

22, Portland Terrace, Regent's Park, London,
May 26*th*, 1855.

Once more, dearest Franz, I must make a complaint about the *Faust* overture. The Härtels have sent me an abominable arrangement for four hands, of which I cannot possibly approve. Did not you tell them that B., who, I believe, had already made a beginning, would best be able to make this arrangement ? Klindworth also would be prepared for it. In any case it should be a pianist of that type. The actual arrangement, which I yesterday returned to the Härtels through a music-seller, must not appear.

However, some wrong notes in this arrangement have drawn my attention to the fact that very probably there are many errors in the score as well. You will remember that it was a copy which I sent to you for your own use, asking you to correct such errors as might occur in your mind, or else to have them corrected, because it would be tedious for me to revise the copy. For the same reason I urgently requested the Härtels, if they printed the score, to send me a proof. You are in frequent communication with the Härtels, and the edition of this overture is really your doing. Be not angry therefore if I ask you to set the matter completely right when convenient. For heaven's sake, forgive me for troubling you with this trifle. The day after to-morrow I have my sixth concert, and a month afterwards I start for home.

Shall I hear from you soon ?

A thousand greetings.

Your

R. W.

189.

DEAREST RICHARD,

I returned here yesterday from the Düsseldorf Musical Festival, tired and dull. Hiller, who conducted the whole, had invited me, and it interested me to go through the whole thing for once, to hear *Paradise and the Peri*, and to applaud Jenny Lind. I need not tell *you* anything about it, and I am not much the wiser myself. Although the whole festival may be called a great success, it wanted something which, indeed, could not have been expected from it. In the art world there are very different kinds of laurels and thistles, but you need care very little about such. " The eagle flies to the sun."

Then you are reading Dante ? He is excellent company for you. I, on my part, shall furnish a kind of commentary to his work. For a long time I had in my head a Dante symphony, and in the course of this year it is to be finished. There are to be three movements, *Hell*, *Purgatory*, and *Paradise*, the two first purely instrumental, the last with chorus. When I visit you in autumn, I shall probably be able to bring it with me ; and if you do not dislike it, you must allow me to inscribe it with your name.

With the Härtels little can be done. If the arrangement for four hands of the *Faust* overture has already been made, I do not advise you to propose some one else. The only thing that can be done with the four-hand arrangement is to ask Klindworth to make some corrections in accordance with your instructions, and to have some of the plates newly engraved without mentioning Klindworth's name on the title-page. Another time it would be a practical thing to send in the four-hand arrangement together with the score, and to come to terms with the publisher about it.

The attitude of the Härtels towards us is naturally

always a little reserved. I, for my part, cannot complain of them, and they have always treated me in a decent and gentlemanly manner. But I should not rely upon them for many things, because their intimate friends are decidedly adverse to us; and for the present we shall not be able to arrive at more than a peaceful, expectant footing with them. Although this may sometimes be inconvenient, I think it best to let it continue.

I am surprised that you found so many mistakes in the proofs of the *Faust* score, for, amongst other advantages which they possess as publishers, one is bound in justice to admit that the Härtels have excellent readers (Dörffel, Schellenberg, etc.). Therefore use time and patience in correcting, and where necessary let the plates be engraved over again.

When shall you be back in Zurich? At Düsseldorf they were saying that you had already left London, and jealous Philistia received the news with a joy which I was not sorry to spoil. Whatever may happen, and however it may happen, I implore you to

Hold out and persevere.

In your capacity of *poeta sovrano*, you must, as Dante says of Homer, pass on your way quietly and undisturbedly, *si come sire.* All this dirt does not touch you. Write your *Nibelungen*, and be content to live on as an immortal!

Later on I shall ask Klindworth to let me see the pianoforte arrangement of the first act of the *Valkyrie*. How about that of the *Rhinegold*? Has H. kept it?

Write to me about it, so that I may know how to get at it.

I have advised H. to settle in Berlin, where his position at the music school will be very useful to him. There is not much to be got by travelling about in our days. Later on he may go to Paris and London, but for the next few years Berlin will be a good field for his activity.

I shall stay here during the summer, until I start for Gran at the end of August. The musical task which occupies me is a new and considerably altered score of my choruses to *Prometheus*, which I want to publish next winter. As soon as it is finished I shall return to my Dante symphony, which has partly been sketched.

Farewell, dearest, most unique of friends, and write soon to your serf, body and soul,

F. L.

WEYMAR, *June 2nd*, 1855.

The Princess and the Child send cordial greetings.

190.

Let me express to you, best of men, my astonishment at your *enormous productiveness*. You have a Dante symphony in your head, have you? And it is to be finished in the autumn? Do not be annoyed by my astonishment at this miracle. When I look back upon your activity in these last years, you appear superhuman to me; there is something very strange about this. However, it is very natural that creating is our only joy, and alone makes life bearable to us. We are what we are only while we create; all the other functions of life have no meaning for us, and are at bottom concessions to the vulgarity of ordinary human existence, which can give us no satisfaction. All that I still desire in this world is a favourable mood and disposition for work, and I find it difficult enough to protect these from the attack of vulgarity. It is the same thing with you. But what astonishes me and appears worthy of envy is that you can create so much.

A *Divina Commedia* it is to be? That is a splendid idea, and I enjoy the music in anticipation. But I must have a little talk with you about it. That *Hell* and *Purgatory* will succeed I do not call into question for a moment, but as to *Paradise* I have some doubts, which you confirm by saying that your plan includes choruses. In the Ninth Symphony the last choral movement is decidedly the weakest part, although it is historically important, because it discloses to us in a very naïve manner the difficulties of a real musician who does not know how (after hell and purgatory) he is to represent paradise. About this paradise, dearest Franz, there is in reality a considerable difficulty, and he who confirms this opinion is, curiously enough, Dante himself, the singer of Paradise, which in his *Divine Comedy* also is decidedly the weakest part. I have followed Dante with deepest sympathy through the *Inferno* and the *Purgatorio*; and when I emerged from the infernal slough, I washed myself, as does the poet, with the water of the sea at the foot of the Mountain of Purgatory. I enjoyed the divine morning, the pure air. I rose step by step, deadened one passion after

the other, battled with the wild instinct of life, till
at last, arrived at the fire, I relinquished all desire
of life, and threw myself into the glow in order to sink
my personality in the contemplation of Beatrice. But
from this final liberation I was rudely awakened to be
again, after all, what I had been before, and this was
done in order to confirm the Catholic doctrine of a
God Who, for His own glorification, had created this
hell of my existence, by the most elaborate sophisms
and most childish inventions, quite unworthy of a great
mind. This problematic proof I rejected from the
bottom of my soul, and remained dissatisfied accordingly. In order to be just to Dante I had, as in the
case of Beethoven, to occupy the historic standpoint;
I had to place myself in Dante's time and consider the
real object of his poem, which, no doubt, was intended
to advocate a certain thing with his contemporaries—I
mean the reform of the Church. I had to confess that in
this sense he understood marvellously well his advantage
of expressing himself in an infallible manner through
means of popular and generally accepted ideas. Before
all, I cordially agreed with him in his praise of the saints
who had chosen poverty of their own free-will. I had
further to admire even in those sophisms his high
poetic imagination and power of representation, just as
I admire Beethoven's musical art in the last movement
of his *Ninth Symphony*. I had further to acknowledge,
with deepest and most sublime emotion, the wonderful
inspiration through means of which the beloved of his
youth, Beatrice, takes the form in which he conceives
the Divine doctrine ; and in so far as that doctrine
teaches the purification of personal egoism through

love, I joyfully acknowledge the doctrine of Beatrice. But the fact that Beatrice stands, as it were, on the chariot of the Church, that, instead of pure, simple doctrine, she preaches keen-witted ecclesiastic scholasticism, made her appear to me in a colder light, although the poet assures us that she shines and glows for ever. At last she became indifferent to me ; and although as a mere reader I acknowledge that Dante has acted appropriately, in accordance with his time and his purpose, I should as a sympathetic co-poet have wished to lose my personal consciousness, and indeed all consciousness, in that fire. In that manner I should, no doubt, have fared better than even in the company of the Catholic Deity, although Dante represents it with the same art with which you, no doubt, will endeavour to celebrate it in your choruses. I faithfully record to you the impression which the *Divine Comedy* has made upon me, and which in the *Paradise* becomes to my mind a " divine comedy" in the literal sense of the word, in which I do not care to take part, either as a comedian or as a spectator.

The misleading problem in these questions is always How to introduce into this terrible world, with an empty nothing beyond it, a God Who converts the enormous sufferings of existence into something fictitious, so that the hoped-for salvation remains the only real and consciously enjoyable thing. This will do very well for the Philistine, especially the English Philistine. He makes very good terms with his God, entering into a contract by which, after having carried out certain points agreed upon, he is finally admitted to eternal bliss as a compensation for various failures in this world. But what have we in common with these notions of the mob ?

You once expressed your view of human nature to the effect that man is " une intelligence, servie par des organes." If that were so, it would be a bad thing for the large majority of men, who have only " organs," but as good as no "intelligence," at least in your sense. To me the matter appears in a different light, viz.,—

Man, like every other animal, embodies the " will of life," for which he fashions his organs according to his wants ; and amongst these organs he also develops intellect, *i.e.*, the organ of conceiving external things for the purpose of satisfying the desire of life to the best of his power. A *normal* man is therefore he who possesses this organ, communicating with the external world (whose function is perception, just as that of the stomach is digestion) in a degree exactly sufficient for the satisfaction of the vital instinct by external means. That vital instinct in *normal* man consists in exactly the same as does the vital instinct of the lowest animal, namely, in the desire of nourishment and of propagation. For this "will of life," this metaphysical first cause of all existence, desires nothing but to live— that is, to nourish and eternally reproduce itself—and this tendency can be seen identically in the coarse stone, in the tenderer plant, and so forth up to the human animal. Only the organs are different, of which the will must avail itself in the higher stages of its objective existence, in order to satisfy its more complicated, and therefore more disputed and less easily obtainable, wants. By gaining this insight, which is confirmed by the enormous progress of modern science,

we understand at once the characteristic feature of the
life of the vast majority of men, and are no longer
astonished because they appear to us simply as animals ;
for this is the *normal* essence of man. A very large
portion of mankind remains *below* this *normal* stage,
for in them the complicated organ of perception is not
developed even up to the capability of satisfying normal
wants ; but, on the other hand, although of course
very rarely, there are *abnormal* natures in which the
ordinary measure of the organ of perception—that is,
the brain—is exceeded, just as nature frequently forms
monstrosities in which *one organ* is developed at the
expense of the others. Such a monstrosity, if it
reaches the highest degree, is called *genius*, which at
bottom is caused only by an abnormally rich and
powerful brain. This organ of perception, which
originally and in normal cases looks outward for the
purpose of satisfying the wants of the will of life,
receives in the case of an abnormal development such
vivid and such striking impressions from outside that
for a time it emancipates itself from the service of the
will, which originally had fashioned it for its own
ends. It thus attains to a " will-less "—*i.e.*, æsthetic—
contemplation of the world ; and these external objects,
contemplated *apart from the will*, are exactly the ideal
images which the *artist* in a manner fixes and repro-
duces. The sympathy with the external world which
is inherent in this contemplation is developed in
powerful natures to a permanent forgetfulness of the
original personal will, that is to a *sympathy* with
external things for their own sake, and no longer in
connection with any personal interest.

The question then arises what we see in this abnormal state, and whether our sympathy takes the
form of *common joy* or *common sorrow*.   This question
the true *men of genius* and the true *saints* of all times
have answered in the sense that they have seen nothing
but *sorrow* and felt nothing but *common sorrow*.   For
they recognized the *normal* state of all living things
and the terrible, always self-contradictory, always self-
devouring and blindly egotistic, nature of the " will of
life " which is common to all living things.   The
horrible cruelty of this will, which in sexual love aims
only at its own reproduction, appeared in them for the
first time reflected in the organ of perception, which
in its normal state had felt its subjection to the
Will to which it owed its existence.   In this
manner the organ of perception was placed in an
abnormal sympathetic condition.   It endeavoured to
free itself permanently and finally from its disgraceful
serfdom, and this it at last achieved in the perfect
negation of the " will of life."

This act of the "negation of will" is the true characteristic of the saint, which finds its last completion in
the absolute cessation of personal consciousness ; and all
consciousness must be personal and individual.   But
the saints of Christianity, simple-minded and enveloped in the Jewish dogma as they were, could not see
this, and their limited imagination looked upon that
much-desired stage as the eternal continuation of a life,
freed from nature.   Our judgment of the moral import
of their resignation must not be influenced by this
circumstance, for in reality they also longed for the
cessation of their individual personality, *i.e.*, of their

existence. But this deep longing is expressed more purely and more significantly in the most sacred and oldest religion of the human race, the doctrine of the Brahmins, and especially in its final transfiguration and highest perfection, Buddhism. This also expounds the myth of a creation of the world by God, but it does not celebrate this act as a boon, but calls it a sin of Brahma which he, *after having embodied himself in this world*, must atone for by the infinite sufferings of this very world. He finds his salvation in the saints who, by perfect negation of the " will of life," by the sympathy with all suffering which alone fills their heart, enter the state of Nirwana, *i.e.*, " the land of being no longer." Such a saint was Buddha. According to his doctrine of the migration of souls every man is born again in the form of that creature on which he had inflicted pain, however pure his life might otherwise have been. He himself must now know this pain, and his sorrowful migration does not cease, until during an entire course of his new-born life he has inflicted pain on no creature, but has denied his own will of life in the sympathy with other beings. How sublime, how satisfying is this doctrine compared with the Judæo-Christian doctrine, according to which a man (for, of course, the suffering *animal* exists for the benefit of man alone) has only to be obedient to the Church during this short life to be made comfortable for all eternity, while he who has been disobedient in this short life will be tortured for ever. Let us admit that Christianity is to us this contradictory phenomenon, because we know it only in its mixture with, and distortion by, narrow-hearted Judaism, while modern

research has succeeded in showing that pure and unalloyed Christianity was nothing but a branch of that
venerable Buddhism which, after Alexander's Indian
expedition, spread to the shores of the Mediterranean.
In early Christianity we still see distinct traces of the
perfect negation of the " will of life," of the longing for
the destruction of the world, *i.e.*, the cessation of all
existence.   The pity is that this deeper insight into the
essence of things can be gained alone by the abnormally
organised men previously referred to, and that they
only can fully grasp it.   In order to communicate this
insight to others, the sublime founders of religion have
therefore to speak in images, such as are accessible to the
common normal perception.   In this process much
must be disfigured, although Buddha's doctrine of the
migration of souls expresses the truth with almost perfect precision.   The normal vulgarity of man and the
license of general egoism further distort the image
until it becomes a caricature.   And I pity the poet
who undertakes to restore the original image from this
caricature.   It seems to me that Dante, especially in
the *Paradise*, has not succeeded in this ; and in his
explanation of the Divine natures he appears, to me at
least, frequently like a childish Jesuit.   But perhaps
you, dear friend, will succeed better, and as you are
going to paint a *tone* picture I might almost predict your
success, for music is essentially the artistic, original
image of the world.   For the initiated no error is here
possible.   Only about the *Paradise*, and especially
about the choruses, I feel some friendly anxiety. You will
not expect me to add less important things to this
important matter.

I shall soon write again; on the 26th I leave here, and shall therefore have endured to the end.

Farewell dear, dear Franz.

                                   Your

                                   R. W.

LONDON, *June 7th*, 1855.

191.

                         ZURICH, *July 5th*, 1855.

DEAREST FRANZ,

Your late servant Hermann called on me to-day and told me that I should have a letter from you one of these days, that you and the Princess would come to Switzerland *soon* (?), and a thousand other things.

I am longing for direct news from you. I have been back in Zurich since June 30th, after having conducted my last London concert on the 25th. You have probably heard how charmingly Queen Victoria behaved to me. She attended the seventh concert with Prince Albert, and as they wanted to hear something of mine I had the *Tannhäuser* overture repeated, which helped me to a little external *amende*. I really seem to have pleased the Queen. In a conversation I had with her, by her desire, after the first part of the concert, she was so kind that I was really quite touched. These two were the first people in England who dared to speak in my favour openly and undisguisedly, and if you consider that they had to deal with a political outlaw, charged with high treason and " wanted " by the police, you will think it natural that I am sincerely grateful to both.

At the last concert the public and the orchestra roused themselves to a demonstration against the London critics. I had always been told that my audiences were very much in my favour, and of the orchestra I could see that it was always most willing to follow my intentions, as far as bad habits and want of time would allow. But I soon saw that the public received impressions slowly and with difficulty, and was unable to distinguish the genuine from the spurious, trivial pedantry from sterling worth, while the orchestra—out of regard for its real master and despot Costa, who can dismiss and appoint the musicians according to his will—always limited its applause to the smallest and least compromising measure. This time, at the leavetaking, it broke through all restraint. The musicians rose solemnly, and together with the whole thickly packed hall, began a storm of applause so continuous that I really felt awkward. After that the band crowded round me to shake hands, and even some ladies and gentlemen of the public held out their hands to me, which I had to press warmly. In this manner my absurd London expedition finally took the character of a triumph for me, and I was pleased at least to observe the independence of the public which this time it showed towards the critics. A triumph in *my sense* was, of course, out of the question. In the best possible case I cannot really be known in the concert room, and that best possible case—I mean performances fully realising my intentions—could not be achieved, owing principally to want of time. In consequence, I always retained a bitter feeling of degradation, increased by the fact that I was compelled to conduct whole programmes of monstrous length, and put together in the most tasteless and senseless manner. That I did conduct these concerts to the end was done entirely out of regard for my wife and a few friends, who would have been grieved very much by the consequences of my sudden departure from London. I am glad that the matter has been carried through, at least with favourable appearances ; with the Queen I was really pleased, and to individual friends I have given great pleasure ; that must suffice. The New Philharmonic would like to have me next year ; what more can I desire ?

One real gain I bring back from England—the cordial and genuine friendship which I feel for Berlioz, and which we have mutually concluded. I heard a concert of the New Philharmonic under his direction, and was, it is true, little edified by his performance of Mozart's *G. Minor Symphony,* while the very imperfect execution of his *Romeo and Juliet* symphony made me pity him. A few days afterwards we two were the only guests at Sainton's table ; he was lively, and the progress in French which I have made in London, permitted me to discuss with him for five hours all the problems of art, philosophy, and life in a most fascinating conversation. In that manner I gained a deep sympathy for my new friend ; he appeared to me quite different from what he had done before. We discovered suddenly that we were in reality fellow-sufferers, and I thought, upon the whole, I was happier than Berlioz. After my last concert he and the other few friends I have in London called on me ; his wife also came. We remained together till three o'clock in the morning, and took leave with the warmest embraces. I told him that you were going to visit me in September, and asked him to meet you at my house. The money question seemed to be his chief difficulty, and I am sure he would like to come. Let him know exactly when you will be here.

Klindworth was to play a concerto by Henselt yesterday at the last New Philharmonic concert, conducted by Berlioz. I made the acquaintance of Dr. Wylde, a good man, and was able to be of some use to Klindworth in that small matter. I sincerely pity him. He is much too much of an artist and a high-minded man, not to be and always remain very unhappy in London. He should try something else.

On once more touching the Continent I felt a little better. The air here suits me, and I hope soon to be again at my work, which at last I gave up in London altogether. Of the *Valkyrie* you will find little ready.

But when are you coming ? If I may not expect you before September, I shall go to Seelisberg till then, starting next Monday, but if, as Hermann led me to hope, I receive a letter before then, announcing your immediate arrival, I shall of course be very happy to remain at Zurich.

Therefore let me soon hear from you. You have kept me waiting long, which indeed I might have expected after my last letter from London, for to communications of this kind your reply has always been silence. But now you must relieve me of my uncertainty as to your visit, which may at last be expected shortly once more. I need scarcely tell you that I am looking forward to it with great pleasure, and that our meeting will be to me the only joy after long trouble.

I am expecting a letter from you with great impatience. Cordial greetings in advance from your

RICHARD.

192.

Welcome in Zurich, dearest Richard, where I hope to see you at the end of September or October.

My Hungarian journey is still somewhat uncertain, as, according to the latest news, the cathedral will probably not be quite finished this year. But in any case I shall come to you this autumn, and shall let you know my arrival in Zurich a few weeks in advance. The satisfactory close of your stay in London has pleased me very much, and, as I know London, I think it would be well if you were to go there again next season. About this and some other business I shall tell you more when I see you.

In the meantime I am delighted at your friendly relations with Berlioz. Of all contemporary composers he is the one with whom you can converse in the simplest, openest, and most interesting manner. Take him for all in all, he is an honest, splendid, tremendous fellow ; and, together with your letter, I received one from Berlioz, in which he says amongst other things : " Wagner will, no doubt, tell you all about his stay in London, and what he has had to suffer from predetermined hostility. He is splendid in his ardour and warmth of heart, and I confess that even his violence delights me. It seems there is a fate against my hearing his last compositions. The day when, at the demand of Prince Albert, he conducted his *Tannhäuser* overture at the Hanover Square Rooms, I was compelled at the same hour to attend a horrible choral rehearsal for the New Philharmonic concert which I had to conduct two days afterwards," etc.

And lower down :

" Wagner has something singularly attractive to me, and if we both have asperities, those asperities dovetail into each other : "

(Berlioz's drawing is more brilliant than mine.)

Many thanks for your Dante letter. By way of answer, I hope to show you the first half of my work at Zurich, together with some other things which will illustrate my aims to you more distinctly than anything I could tell you.

During the next few weeks I shall have to work at my *Prometheus* choruses, which I want to publish soon, and for that purpose I must write an entirely new score. For in the year 1850, when I composed this work, I had too little time (scarcely a month), and was too much occupied by the *Lohengrin* rehearsals to give it the necessary finish. I have now kept in view the means of performance more than before, and although the design and the conception remain essentially unchanged, the whole thing will have a better appearance. It is a similar process as in sculpture, when the artist works in marble. Before the performance a symphonic, and still more, a dramatic work exists, so to speak, only in *clay*. I could easily illustrate this comparison by the new score of your *Faust* overture, and by some of the changes you have made in the *Flying Dutchman*.

Wait a little, dearest Richard, and you will see what a lot of stuff, and how much material for conversation I shall bring with me. The end of last week I spent in Dresden, where I called upon our friends, the Ritters.. Sascha Ritter, our Weymar Court musician, has been blessed with a little daughter, whose god-father I shall have the honour to be. His mother-in-law has been staying here for some weeks, and Johanna Wagner is expected in September.

Our theatrical affairs are in a critical condition. The Intendant, Herr von Beaulieu, is going to leave, and the artistic director, Marr, is also said to have sent in his resignation. I do not trouble myself about these matters, and look forward with perfect peace of mind to the solution of these somewhat unimportant questions.

Gutzkow's call to Weymar, which the papers announced several times, is not in itself unlikely, but will probably be delayed a little, as nothing definite has, as yet, been done.

Farewell, and set to work at your *Valkyrie*. Go up your mountains, and bring the very skies down to your music. In September, or at the latest, in October, we shall meet.

Your

F. L.

Your kindness and friendship for Klindworth have obliged me particularly, and I ask you to continue them.

WEYMAR, *July* 10*th*, 1855.

P.S.—I shall remain here all the summer.

193.

DEAREST FRIEND,

I think of nothing now but our meeting and being together. I am glad you did not come sooner, because at present I should be able to show you very little of the *Valkyrie*, and I am pleased therefore to have a good deal of time for the completion of the score. By November I shall have finished, at least, the first two acts, even the clean copy of them.

Consider this, and bear in mind that it will be a *climax of our lives*, for the sake of which all common things must be got over and brought into order. I count upon your magnanimity.

Farewell for to-day. I send you many greetings from a longing heart.

Your

R. W.

194.

DEAR FRANZ,

You are my court business agent, once for all. Be kind enough to forward, through the Weimar minister at Hanover, the enclosed letter to the king as soon as possible. My theatrical agent, Michaelson, has exceeded his legal rights by selling *Lohengrin* to the Hanover theatre without asking me, and for a much smaller sum than they had previously paid me for *Tannhäuser* on my direct application. The Intendant will not hear of my cancelling the sale, and all that remains to me is to apply to the king himself.

You will take care of this, will you not?
Why did you not answer my last question?
One million greetings from

Your

R. W.

195.

In spite of many attempts and inquiries backwards and forwards, I have not found a sure way of obtaining a hearing from his Majesty, the King of Hanover. It appears to me that the best thing you can do in this matter is to write a few lines to Joachim or, in case he should be absent on his travels, to Capellmeister Wehner at Hanover, and to enclose your letter to the king. I, for my part, cannot undertake this commission, as I have no relations with Hanover just now, and should not like to be responsible for a failure. Wehner (I am not quite certain as to the spelling of his name) is on very good terms with the king, and will be glad to be of service to you. It will be necessary, however, that you should write to him a few lines direct, in which please mention me. I herewith return your letter to the king. Kindly excuse this delay; I was absent for several days, and some other measures, which I thought had been taken for the purpose, have come to nothing.

In November you will see me, and I agree to everything that is agreeable to you. By then several of my scores will be in print, which will make it easier for us to read them. During these last months I have been occupied so much by visits, correspondence, and business matters that I could scarcely devote a few hours to my work. I am sometimes angry and wild at the ridiculous troubles I have to go through, and long for our days at the Zeltweg.

Write to me later on when my visit will be most convenient to you, in November or at Christmas ?

The Princess and her daughter stayed several weeks at Berlin, and for the last week they have been in Paris. I do not expect them back here till the middle of September. In the meantime my son Daniel—who at this year's *concours* at the *Lycée Bonaparte*, as well as in the *Concours Général*, again distinguished himself and carried off several prizes—has arrived at the Altenburg.

One of these days you will receive from Bussenius, with whom you were in correspondence before, your biography. It has been written with the best intentions, and will probably be read far and wide. Under the pseudonym of W. Neumann, Bussenius has edited a biographical collection, "Die Componisten der neueren Zeit," for E. Balde of Cassel, and the success has been such that a second edition of some of the volumes will soon be published. I have asked Bussenius to send you the little book.

My friendly greetings to your wife. Do not forget your

F. LISZT.

196.

MY DEAR FRANZ,

Your silence makes me very anxious. Whenever I look around me and into my future, I see nothing that can rouse me, elate me, comfort me, and give me strength and arms for the new troubles of life except.

our meeting, and the few weeks you are going to devote
to me. If as to the exact time of that period of
salvation I expressed a wish to you, it was done
with the care with which one likes to realise beforehand a supreme blessing, well knowing that it must
be bought with long sadness, both before and
after. But perhaps you misunderstood me after all,
and thought that, apart from the happiness of seeing you again, I was looking for something else,
quite independent thereof, and this perhaps may have
made you angry. Let me know, in a few words, how
things are, and when you are coming. I should certainly like to show you as much as possible of my
Valkyrie, and principally for that reason I did not
object to this delay of your much-desired visit. In my
present condition, however, I have little hope of
gaining much work by this gain of time. My mental
disharmony is indescribable; sometimes I stare at my
paper for days together, without remembrance or
thought or liking for my work. Where is that liking
to spring from? All the motive power which, for a
time, I derived from my dreary solitude is gradually
losing its force. When I commenced and quickly
finished the *Rhinegold*, I was still full of the intercourse with you and yours. For the last two years
all around me has grown silent, and my occasional
contact with the outer world is inharmonious and
dispiriting. Believe me, this cannot go on much
longer. If my external fate does not soon take a
different turn, if I find no possibility of seeing you
more frequently, and of hearing or producing some
of my works now and then, my fountain will dry up,

and the end be near. It is impossible for me to go on like this.

You may imagine, then, how I look forward to your coming, and what I must feel when suddenly I see myself forsaken by you. Comfort me soon. After much trouble the first half of the *Valkyrie*, including a clean copy, has got finished. I should like to show you the two acts complete, but am still waiting for the real love of work. For the last week indisposition has prevented me from doing anything, and if this goes on I almost doubt whether I shall be able to finish this work from the sketches.

Your article about the *Harold* symphony was very beautiful, and has warmed my heart. I shall write to Berlioz to-morrow; he must send me his scores. *He* will never know *me* thoroughly; his ignorance of German prevents this; he will always see me in vague and deceptive outline. But I will honestly use my advantage over him, and bring him nearer to me.

How are matters with you? I hear about you now and then, but you are silent.

Adieu! Imagine a very long sigh here.

197.

DEAREST RICHARD,

I enclose a letter from T. Hagen, of New York, where he has been settled for about a year, and does good work as a musician and musical author. The letters in the *Leipzig Signale*, signed " Butterbrod," are his, and some time ago he published a volume about music in its relation to social interests, the exact title of which I cannot remember. He is a friend of Klindworth's, and associates with your admirers and partisans. With Mason Brothers I have some connection through William Mason, one of my pupils, who lived eighteen months in Weymar. As far as I know, the firm is *solid* and respectable.

Although I do not suppose that you will accept the offer of conducting concerts in America during next winter, I ask you to let me have an answer (addressed to me) soon, because I shall wait for your letter concerning this matter, in order to forward it to Hagen. A Beethoven musical festival in connection with the inauguration of the Beethoven statue at Boston would not be amiss, and the pecuniary result might be very favourable.

Johanna Wagner arrived here the day before yesterday, and she and her parents will stay a week in Weymar with her sister, Frau Ritter. I spent several hours with her last night.

Tannhäuser is to be produced at Berlin in December.

How far have you got with the *Valkyrie*? I am looking forward to our meeting in November.

The Princess and the Child are still in Paris. They study carefully the exhibition of pictures, and see a good deal of Scheffer, Delacroix, and other artistic notabilities, which suits them exactly. About the 25th of this month I expect them here, where, in the meantime, I am terribly bored by the load of tedious things which are imposed upon me, and with the relation of which I will not trouble you. On the 16th the theatre will be opened with Nicolai's *Merry Wives*. After that we shall have *The Huguenots, Cellini*, and Verdi's *I Due Foscari*.

Lohengrin will not be given just yet because Ortrud (Frau Knopp) has left us, and the new prima donna, Fräulein Woltendorff, will at least require three or four months to learn the part. But as *Tannhäuser* and the *Flying Dutchman* have proved " draws," they will be sure to be thrashed out thoroughly.

I, for my part, am sick of the whole theatrical business, but I am compelled to stick to it in a half-and-half sort of way, because, without me, things would probably be still worse.

Your
F. L.

Return Hagen's letter to me.

198.

ZURICH, September 13th, 1855.

Your last but one letter, dear Franz, was the best answer to my last, the two having crossed on the way. As to our final meeting I use all the arts of an experienced voluptuary in order to get the most out of it. As it has been delayed so long, I should almost like to finish the whole *Valkyrie* previously. The completion of this work, the most *tragic* which I have ever conceived, will cost me much, and I must think of recovering what I have put into it by the most cheering impressions, and those *you only* can supply. The thought of being able to go with you through this work also is my only hope of reward. I am quite unable to deal with it on the piano to my own satisfaction. You must introduce it to me. For that reason I am thinking of delaying our meeting till I can go through *the whole* with you. Thus my highest need has made an egoist of me. The first two acts I hope to have finished and copied out at the end of October, the whole by Christmas. You said in your last letter it would suit you equally well to come either in November or at Christmas. This induced me to curb my impatience to see you again till then, so as to make it possible, by the most incessant industry, to place the whole, completed and fairly copied, before you, including the last act, which is so important to me. Must I then *ask* you to delay your visit till Christmas ? It sounds absurd enough, but you will understand my pedantry. If you agree, and if no further delay will become necessary on that account, I shall send you the first two acts for inspection at the end of October, and you can bring them back with you.

What shall I say to you of this New York offer ? I was told in London that they intended to invite me. It is a blessing that they do not offer me very much money. The hope of being able to earn a large sum, say ten thousand dollars, in a short time, would, in the great helplessness of my pecuniary position, compel me, as a matter of course, to undertake this American expedition, although even in that case it would perhaps be absurd to sacrifice my best vital powers to so miserable a purpose, and, as it were, in an indirect manner. But as a man like me has no chance of a really lucrative speculation, I am glad that I am not exposed to any serious temptation, and therefore ask you to thank the gentlemen of New York very kindly, in my name, for the unmerited attention they have shown me, and to tell them that, " for the present," I am unable to accept their invitation.

I puzzle my head about the cause of the journey which the Princess and the Child have taken to Paris ; is it for amusement and nothing else ? Greet them both most cordially for me when they return ; could they not come with you to a poor devil in Switzerland just as well as go to Paris ? If you would let me cater for you I could arrange matters very cheaply. At the *Hôtel* (*Pension*) *Baur au lac*, where you stayed before, one can, during the *winter*, have brilliant, large, and comfortable rooms for *very little*. A family of my acquaintance occupied a whole floor there last winter, and lived very well at a fabulously cheap rate. The Wesendoncks are also staying there, and you might set up a splendid, half-common *ménage*, which would be a great joke. Well, the chief thing will be to have a good piano for our two selves, and of that I will take care, although I cannot provide so splendid an instrument as that which Erard sent me in London, and for which I forgot to thank you. I believe if I had such an instrument I should still learn to play the piano.

I am much annoyed about Hanover. I know of no way to address a reclamation to the King. I have no faith in Wehner's intercession. As a subordinate of Count P.'s, he can risk no step which might compromise him with that official. But these are disgusting things to write about. You also complain of troubles. Tell me, why do not we live together ? Must it be Weimar of all places ? Another time more about this. For to-day farewell, and let me thank you for being in existence.

Your

R. W.

199.

DEAREST RICHARD,

Over America I had forgotten Hanover, and must not omit once more to point out Wehner to you as the best advocate of your claims there. If the matter of the honorarium can be arranged according to your wish, he will be the most likely man to do it. From Joachim I have heard nothing since the Düsseldorf festival. Wehner lives at Hanover, and is in particular favour with His Majesty, and he will be most eager to do you a little service if you will ask him in a friendly manner.

At the end of December, about Christmas, I shall be with you. Then we will feed like the gods on your *Rhinegold* and *Valkyrie*, and I, too, shall contribute some *hors d'œuvre*.

F. L.

WEYMAR, *September 23rd*, 1855.

Write to me, at the first opportunity, whether ten thousand or twelve thousand dollars, with proper guarantee, would be a sufficient honorarium if you were to act as conductor in America for six months.

200.

October 3rd, 1855.

To-day, dearest Franz, I send you the two first acts of the *Valkyrie* finished. It is a great satisfaction to me to place them at once in your hands, because I know that no one sympathises with my work as you do. I am anxious for the very weighty second act; it contains two catastrophes, so important and so powerful, that there would be sufficient matter for two acts; but then they are so interdependent, and the one implies the other so immediately, that it was impossible to separate them. If it is represented exactly as I intend, and if my intentions are perfectly understood, the effect must be beyond anything that has hitherto been in existence. Of course, it is written only for people who can stand something (perhaps in reality for nobody). That incapable and weak persons will complain, cannot in any way move me. You must decide whether everything has succeeded according to my own intentions. I cannot do it otherwise. At times, when I was timid and sobered down, I was chiefly anxious about the great scene of Wotan, especially when he discloses the decrees of fate to Brynhild, and in London I was once on the point of rejecting the whole scene. In order to come to a decision, I took up the sketch, and recited the scene with proper expression, when, fortunately, I discovered that my spleen was unjustified, and that, if properly represented, the scene would have a grand effect even in a purely musical sense. The manner of expression I have in places indicated very accurately, but it still remains, and will indeed be my principal task, to introduce a gifted singer and actor to the very core of my intentions by means of personal communication. You, I firmly hope, will find out the right thing at once. For the development of the great tetralogy, this is the most important scene of all, and, as such, it will probably meet with the necessary sympathy and attention.

If you should like nothing at all in my score, you will, at least, be pleased once more with my neat handwriting, and will think the precaution of red lines ingenious. This representation on paper will probably be the only one which my work will achieve, for which reason I linger over the copying with satisfaction.

I hope, more firmly than ever, to finish the last act by Christmas. That you allow yourself to be ordered about by me is too kind of you, and touches me deeply. In return, I promise to behave very reasonably when you come. In the meantime I shall nurse the feeble remnants of my voice in every way, and during the last weeks before your arrival I shall try a few *solfeggi*, in order to restore the overstrained and badly treated instrument to a tolerable condition. Must I assure you once more, that I look forward to our meeting with a sacred awe !

As far as we require society, it will not be unpleasant this time. You probably know that Semper has been appointed here. I take great pleasure in him—an artist through and through, and of his nature more amiable than before, though still fiery. Carl Ritter also will settle here. He pleases me better than ever. His intellect is vast, and I do not know another young man like him. He loves you sincerely, and understands you well.

Berlioz replied lately to a letter of mine, in which I had asked him, amongst other things, to make me a present of all his scores, if he could get them gratis. That he cannot do, because his earlier publishers will give him no more free copies. I confess that it would interest me very much to study his symphonies carefully in full score. Do you possess them, and will you lend them to me, or will you go so far as to give

them to me ?   I should accept them gratefully, but
should like to have them soon.

The Hanover business has been settled satisfactorily,
the Intendant having apparently seen the error of his
ways.   I thank you for your well-intended advice with
regard to Wehner, and regret to have troubled you
with this trumpery business.

America is a terrible nightmare.   If the New York
people should ever make up their minds to offer me a
considerable sum, I should be in the most awful
dilemma.   If I refused I should have to conceal it from
all men, for every one would charge me in my position
with recklessness.   Ten years ago I might have undertaken such a thing, but to have to walk in such by-
ways now in order to live would be too hard,—now,
when I am fit only to do, and to devote myself to, that
which is strictly my business.   I should never finish the
Nibelungen in my life.   Good gracious ! such sums as I
might *earn* in America, people ought to *give* me, without
asking anything in return beyond what I am actually
doing, and which is the best that I can do.   Besides
this, I am much better adapted to spend 60,000
francs in six months than to " earn " it.   The latter
I cannot do at all, for it is not my business to " earn
money," but it is the business of my admirers to give
me as much money as I want, to do my work in a
cheerful mood.   Well, it is a good thing, and I will
take courage from the thought that the Americans will
make me no such offer.   Do not you instigate it either,
for in the " luckiest " case it would be a great trouble to
me.   Of your dear ones I never have any real news ;
I am frequently asked, and do not know what to say.

But you must greet them all the more cordially for me, and, if you can, love me with all your heart. Will you not? Adieu.

Your
R. W

And how about your great compositions? To know them at last is worth a whole life to me. I have never looked forward with such desire to anything. Let me know *at once* that my score has arrived, so that I may not worry myself about it.

201.

One word, dearest Franz, to say that my score has safely arrived! I am anxious.

Your
R.

202.

Your *Valkyrie* has arrived, and I should like to reply to you by your *Lohengrin* chorus, sung by 1,000 voices, and repeated a thousandfold: "A wonder! a wonder!"

Dearest Richard, you are truly a divine being, and it is my joy to feel after you and to follow you.

More by word of mouth about your splendid, tremendous work, which I am reading "in great inner excitement," to the horn rhythm, page 40, in D:

The scores of Berlioz I possess, but have lent them all to friends for the moment, and shall not be able to get them back for some weeks.

About the middle of November I shall send you a parcel of them. You will find in them much to please you.

The day after to-morrow I am going for a few days to Brunswick to conduct, on the 18th instant, one of the Symphony Concerts given by the orchestra there. For the 21st, Sunday week, your *Flying Dutchman* is announced here, and at the beginning of November there will be a performance of *Tannhäuser* in honour of several Berlin people (Hülsen, Dorn, the operatic stage manager Formes, etc.), who have announced their visit here. I shall send you an account of it.

Go on with your *Valkyrie,* and permit me to adapt the proverb,

"*Quand on prend du galon, on n'en saurait trop prendre,*"

to your case in the following manner :

"*Quand on fait du sublime on n'en saurait trop faire, surtout quand ce n'est qu'une question de nature et d'habitude !*"

Your

F.

WEYMAR, *October 12th,* 1855

203.

November 16th, 1855.

DEAREST FRANZ,

Thank the Child a thousand times for her letter, and tell her that I shall not send the album back till you return from here, because I want to write something good in it which will not be finished till then.

I must write many and reasonable things to the Princess, and that I cannot do at present. So I remain in her debt also, but only to satisfy her. She may see from this how much I value her letter.

I have not yet gone out into the air ; but I am getting accustomed to my room, and do not particularly long for our autumn mists. I am doing a little work too. You are coming, are you not ?

I should like to be silent till then and for ever, for whenever I speak or write it is sure to be something stupid.

Au revoir ! ! !

204.

DEAR FRANZ,

I am making a tentative effort to rise from the sick bed on which I have lain again exactly three weeks.

Carl Ritter has informed you of my condition. The thorns of my existence have now been supplemented by blooming "roses." I have suffered from continual attacks of erysipelas in the face. In the luckiest case I shall not be able to go out into the air this year, and during the whole winter I shall live in continual fear of relapses. For the slightest excitement, accompanied by the least cold, may throw me back on my sick bed for two or three weeks at any moment.

I am now reaping the fruit of my stupid postponement of your visit, for I cannot possibly expect you to visit me in the present uncertain state of my health.

Anyhow, I thus relieve you of the burden which a visit in this evil, hard winter would no doubt have been to you. As concerns myself, nothing can make my mood worse than it is. I am getting accustomed to all kinds of trouble, and the disagreeable and the necessary and natural are to me convertible terms.

I long for news of you, of which you are too chary.

As soon as I get better and am accustomed to sitting up I shall write more. For to-day a thousand greetings to the Altenburg.

Your

R. W.

Zurich, *December 12th*, 1855.

205.

Chronos has made another step across all our heads. How can I write to you, dear poet, without telling you of the kind wishes which I and the Child entertain for you, and the desire we both of us have of seeing you again in the course of 1856? I can assure you that if fate were to send me a messenger with the assurance of this, I should consider it the best New Year's gift, although there are many things which I demand of it.

But one must hope—hope is a virtue. Is not this a beautiful identification ?

It gives us great pain to know that you are suffering. I would accept double and treble the rheumatism which I have caught in this climate, where we have eight months of bad weather, and not four of fine, if I could secure you perfect liberty thereby. Liszt is sad because his travelling plans are disarranged, although he hopes to see you more at his ease another time. He must be at Vienna at the beginning of January in order to conduct a Mozart festival given for the centenary of the Master's birthday; and as Berlioz is coming here at the beginning of February, he will have to leave Vienna immediately afterwards.

The papers have no doubt informed you of his stay at Berlin, where he will soon return to attend the first performance of *Tannhäuser*, two rehearsals of which he almost entirely conducted. Stupid people will not be silenced thereby. To poets living in the tropical regions, where passion expands her gigantic blossoms and her sidereal marvels, stupid people appear like little gadflies which sometimes annoy them and draw blood by their stings, but cannot disturb the enchantment of this luxuriant nature. Liszt also has been honoured by a swarm of these insects, which buzz with all the more noise and self-sufficiency because they can make so little honey. He is quite composed, and goes quietly on his way, only uttering occasionally such *bonmots* as "They have cast me down, but I remain standing none the less," or " What does it matter if other people do things badly so long as I do them well ?" etc., etc.; and so life goes on.

Write to me, dear poet, and do not always wait for a *reason*; and if you will give pleasure to my daughter send her for the New Year the autograph for which she has asked you.

Embrace your wife for me, and convey to her my kindest wishes. She ought to be sure of them, as indeed ought you. Have you resumed the *Valkyrie* ?

The duet between Siegmund and Siegliende has made me shed copious tears. It is as beautiful as love, as the Infinite, as earth and the heavens.

Your devoted,

CAROLYNE W.

December 23rd, 1855.

206.

To-day I ought to be with you and prepare your Christmas tree, where the rays and gifts of your genius should shine. And now we are apart, you troubled with erysipelas, and I with all manner of red roses grown in similar gardens. But this abominable *flora* shall not delay the joy of our meeting too long.

You probably know that I have to go to Vienna, in January, to conduct the Centenary Mozart Festival, which takes place on January 27th, and will require at least a few weeks' preparation. At the beginning of February I shall be back here. Berlioz is coming on the 8th of February, and Johanna Wagner on the 20th. Berlioz's *Faust* and *Cellini* will be given before the 16th, and your niece is announced in three *rôles*. As soon as this is over I shall write to tell you when I can come to Zurich, but I am afraid I shall have to wait for the summer.

At Berlin, where I stayed three weeks, I attended a few pianoforte rehearsals of *Tannhäuser*, by invitation of Messrs. von Hülsen and Dorn, and if the first performance is not delayed after January 6th to 8th (for when it is announced), I shall be able to send you a report of it as an eye and ear witness. Johanna will sing and act Elizabeth beautifully, and Formes is studying his part most conscientiously. Dorn has already had a number of pianoforte and string rehearsals, and makes it a point of honour to produce the work as correctly and brilliantly as possible.

No doubt *Tannhäuser* will become a "draw" at Berlin, which is the chief thing, even for the composer, and I hope that the *critical* treatment which I received at the hands of the critics will redound to the credit of *Tannhäuser*, and that the infallible impression of your work on the public will not be impaired by carping notices. I shall write to you about this at great length.

The day after to-morrow, Boxing-day, we shall have *Tannhäuser* here, which retains its position as a "draw," a distinction which it shares at Weymar, with *Lohengrin* and *The Flying Dutchman.*

Next spring *Lohengrin* is to be mounted again here. Up to the present we still want an Ortrud, and, unfortunately, cannot get a good one from elsewhere. The Leipzig one would, for example, be quite useless, and the voice of Frau Knopp is still much impaired by her late illness.

I am looking forward to *Lohengrin*, that wonderful work, which, to me, is the highest and most perfect thing in art—until your *Nibelungen* is finished.

At Berlin, at Count Redern's, I heard a few pieces from *Lohengrin* splendidly executed by several regimental bands, and was reminded of our pompous entry into the "Drei Könige" of Basle :

Our new Weymar Union has adopted the entry of the trumpets

as its " Hoch," and I wish we could sing it to you in chorus soon.

Of my concert affairs, etc., I have nothing to tell you. When I come to you I shall bring some of my scores with me. The rest will not interest us much. With similar compositions, the only question is, what is *in* them ? The publication I shall delay a few months (although six numbers are already engraved), for the reason that some of my *excellent* friends (an expression which Kaulbach is fond of using for people who do not like him) had the *excellent* intention of producing these things at once by way of a *warning example*. That amiable intention I want to forestall by a few performances under my own direction during the winter.

Try to get better again soon, and remember kindly

Your faithful

F. LISZT.

December 24th, 1855.

Best remembrances to Ritter.

207.

DEAR FRANZ,

I am again, or rather still, unwell and incapable of anything. I was just going to write something in the album, so that the Child might have it for the new year. But it will not do ; my head is too confused and heavy.

I write to you only to tell you so; a real letter I could not accomplish. Apart from this I have nothing to tell you; I mean that I have no materials.

I should like to ask you, however, to return the two acts of the *Valkyrie* to me at once before you start. I have at last found a good copyist to whom I have promised work, and I am anxious to have the copy finished soon,—perhaps for the same reason which induces insects to place their eggs in safety before they die.

If I ever finish the last act I will send you the whole, although you are so great a man of the world. Till then be of good cheer, and remember that if you are abused you have willed it so. I also rejoice in the *fiasco* of my *Faust* overture, because in it I see a purifying and wholesome punishment for having published the work in despite of my better judgment; the same religious feeling I had in London when I was bespattered with mud on all sides. This was the most wholesome mud that had ever been thrown at me.

I wish you joy for the Vienna mud.

Adieu, and do your work well. Of your Christianity I do not think much; the Saviour of the world should not desire to be the conqueror of the world. There is a hopeless contradiction in this in which you are deeply involved.

My compliments and thanks to the Princess, and tell the Child that I was unable to manage it to-day. *When* shall I? Heaven knows! It is largely your own fault.

Adieu. I cannot say more, and have, moreover, talked nonsense enough. Farewell, and enjoy yourself

208.

Telegram.

To R. WAGNER, Zeltweg, Zurich.

Yesterday *Tannhäuser.* Excellent performance.
Marvellous *mise-en-scène.* Much applause. Good
luck.

F. LISZT.

BERLIN, *January 8th,* 1856.

209.

DEAREST RICHARD,

From Berlin I brought home so dreadful a cold
that I had to go to bed for a few days, and to delay my
journey till this evening. I have to supplement my
Berlin telegram by the following notes :—

Johanna was beautiful to see and touching to hear
as Elizabeth. In the duet with Tannhäuser she had
some splendid moments of representation, and her great
scene in the *finale* she sang and realised in an incomparable manner. Formes's intonation was firm, pure,
and correct, and there was no sign of fatigue in the
narration, where his sonorous, powerful voice told
admirably. Altogether Formes is not only adequate
but highly satisfactory, in spite of his small stature,
which, especially by the side of Johanna, somewhat
interferes with the illusion. Herr Radwaner as
Wolfram, although not equal to our Milde, deserves
much praise for the neatness, elegance, and agreeable
style of singing with which he executed his part; and
Madame Tuczek proved herself to be an excellent
musician and a well-trained actress, who may be confidently intrusted with the most difficult part. Dorn

and the band took every pains to carry out your intentions, and the orchestral performance was throughout successful, with the exception of two wrong tempi, in the first chorus

where you have forgotten to mark the tempo as *più moderato*, that is almost twice as slow as before, and in the G major passage (before the *ensemble* in B major), which, in my opinion, was also taken too fast, the rhythmical climax of the second part of the *finale* being considerably impaired thereby.

The chorus had studied its part well, but it is much too weak for Berlin, and in proportion to the vastness of the opera house, scarcely more efficient than ours, which always gives me great dissatisfaction. The stringed instruments, also, are not sufficiently numerous, and should, like the chorus, be increased by a good third. For a large place like this eight to ten double basses, and fifteen to twenty first violins, etc., would certainly not be too many at important performances. On the other hand, the scenery and mounting of *Tannhäuser* left nothing to be desired, and I can assure you that never and nowhere have I seen anything so splendid and admirable. Gropius and Herr von Hülsen have really done something extraordinary and most tasteful. You have heard, no doubt, that his Majesty the King had ordered the decorations of the second act to be faithfully reproduced after the designs for the restoration of the Wartburg, and that he had sent

Gropius to Eisenach for the purpose. The aspect of
the hall with all the historic banners, and the costumes
taken from old pictures, as well as the court ceremonial
during the reception of the guests by the Landgrave,
gave me incredible pleasure, as did also the arrangement of the huntsmen with their horns on the hill, the
gradual filling up of the valley by the gathering of the
hunt (four horses and a falcon bringing up the rear) in
the *finale* of the first act; and, finally, the fifteen trumpets
in the march of the second act

which blew their flourish from the gallery of the hall in
a bold and defiant manner.

I only hope, dearest Richard, that you will hear and
see all this before very long, and when I pay you a visit
in the course of the summer, we shall have some more
talk about it.

Your last letter was very sad and bitter. Your illness must have put you out still more, and, unfortunately,
your friends can do little to relieve you. If the consciousness of the most sincere and cordial comprehension of,
and sympathy with, your sufferings can be of any comfort to you, you may rely upon me in fullest measure,
for I do not believe that there are many people in this
universe who have inspired another being with such
real and continual sympathy as you have me.

As soon as you are well again go to work and finish
your *Valkyrie*. The first two acts I returned to you.
You must sing them to me at Zurich.

I have to ask you yet another favour to-day.

Schlesinger, of Berlin, is bringing out a new edition of the scores of Gluck's overtures, which is dedicated to me, and he wishes to print your close of the overture of *Iphigenia in Aulis* in addition to that by Mozart. For that purpose he wants your special permission, and has asked me to get it from you. If you have no objection to this close—which has already been published in Brendel's paper—appearing in this edition, be kind enough to give me your consent in a few lines, and address your letter, " Hotel Zur Kaiserin von Oestreich," Vienna, for which I start to-night.

I shall conduct the two concerts for the Mozart centenary celebration on the 27th and 28th instant, and shall be back in Weymar on February 4th.

Your speedy recovery and patience is the wish with all his heart, dearest Richard, of

Your faithful
F. LISZT.

WEYMAR, *January* 14*th*, 1856.

210.

ZURICH, *January* 18*th*, 1856.

My letter, dear Franz, you will have received at Vienna through Glöggl. I once more put the question contained therein, and ask you : Can you *give* me the thousand francs, which would be still better, and can you settle the same sum on me annually for two years more ? If you *can*, I know that you will willingly join with those who keep me alive by their pecuniary assistance. My own income is insufficient for the very expensive style of living here, and every new year I am troubled by a deficit, so that I am really no better off now than I was before. If it were not for my wife you

would see something curious, and I should be proud to
go about the world as a beggar; but the continual uncertainty, and the miserly condition in which we live,
affects my poor wife more and more, and I can keep
her mind at rest only by a certain economical security.
More of this when I see you. That I ask you this
question at the present moment when I am sick of life,
and would see the end of it to-day rather than to-
morrow, you will probably understand, when you
realise that from the deepest mental grief I am inces-
santly aroused to nothing but the mean troubles of
existence, this being my only change. I have no doubt
of your *will*, and believe even that it would give you
pleasure to belong to those from whom I receive a
regular pension. It remains to be asked only : Can
you ? I know that some time ago you were not able,
although even at that time you occasionally made real
sacrifices to assist me. Perhaps a change has taken
place since then, and on the chance of this " perhaps "
I venture to trouble you with my question.

One other matter I have to place before you. You
remember that I wrote to you some time ago that I had
at last discovered here an excellent and intelligent
copyist for my musical manuscripts. To him I gave, in
the first instance, Klindworth's pianoforte score of the
Valkyrie, and he brought me the first act beautifully
written; but his charge for the time employed, moderate
enough though I found it, appeared to me so high, that
I could not possibly afford the expense from my yearly
income. I considered what might be done, and found
that, if I really went on with my composition, I should
have exactly three years' occupation for a copyist

This would include the copying of the full scores, the pianoforte scores, and all the vocal and orchestral parts. If the enterprise of the performance should in any way be accomplished, three years' salary for a copyist might well be added to the estimate of the costs, and the question would be whether one could find, at this moment, a small number of shareholders who would advance the necessary funds. I should have to engage my amanuensis for exactly three years, and pay him an annual salary of eight hundred francs. The only awkward part would be that I should have to bind myself to furnish the compositions in this given time. I might, however, as soon as I found myself unable to continue, give notice to both shareholders and copyist. For one year I have more than sufficient work for the copyist, and whatever he had written might, in such a case, be handed over to the shareholders as a security. I think that would be fair enough. Kindly see, dearest Franz, whether you can manage this for me. In the meantime I let him go on with the pianoforte arrangement, but as soon as you are bound to give me a negative answer I shall stop him, for, as I said before, I cannot bear this expense from my housekeeping money.

It was an evil, evil fate that we did not see each other last year. You must come soon, if POSSIBLE this SPRING. I feel that on our meeting this time everything, everything depends. I am continually at war with my health, and fear a relapse at every moment. But let us leave this for to-day. We shall soon meet.

Many thanks for your letter from Berlin, received to-day. Alwine Frommann writes to me every day, always in a great state of anxiety about the positive and permanent success of *Tannhäuser*. It appears that in over-witty and wholly unproductive Berlin everything has to be born anew. "Kladderadatsch" was quite right in taunting me with the fact that I had surrendered *Tannhäuser* to Berlin, solely for the sake of the royalties. That is so. It is my fault, and I have to suffer for it as vulgarly as possible. Very well, I suffer, but unfortunately I do not even get anything by it.

Could I only bring back the state of things of four years ago! Enough. It is my own fault, and it serves me right.

Try to be as little annoyed as possible at Vienna. I am anxious to learn whether you will be at all satisfied.

Your letter has once more done me a great deal of good. Yes, dear Franz, I trust in you, and I know that there is some higher meaning in our friendship. If I could live together with you I might do many fine things yet. Farewell, and be cordially thanked for your glorious friendship.

Your

R. W.

I have no objection to my close of Gluck's *Iphigenia* overture being used, seeing that I have already published it. It would be advisable, however, that the overture should appear with the correct tempi and some necessary marks of expression. Apart from this, Herr Schlesinger, in his musical paper, might adopt a pleasanter tone towards me in case Herr M. will permit him to do so.

R. W.

211.

DEAR FRANZ,

My letters to Vienna seem to have put you in a very awkward position. Forgive me, and do not punish me any longer by your silence!

Before anything else in the world I ask you to pay me as soon as possible the visit, which was so unfortunately postponed. My desire to consult with you definitely about my future life has reached a painful pitch, and my longing for you is unspeakable. I am very unhappy.

Your

R. W.

March 21st, 1856

212.

DEAREST RICHARD,

At last I am able to tell you that you will receive one thousand francs at the *beginning* of May. When you wrote to me at Vienna about this matter it was impossible for me to tell you anything definite, and even now I am unable to undertake an *annual* obligation.

I am always sincerely sorry to have to tell you anything disagreeable, and for that reason I waited for the moment when I should be able to state that the aforesaid sum would be sent to you. I have more than once explained to you my difficult pecuniary situation, which simply amounts to this, that my mother and my three children are decently provided for by my former savings, and that I have to manage on my salary as Capellmeister of one thousand thalers, and three hundred thalers more by way of a present for the court concerts.

For many years, since I became firmly resolved to live up to my artistic vocation, I have not been able to count upon any additional money from the music publishers. My Symphonic Poems, of which I shall send you a few in full score in a fortnight's time, do not bring me in a shilling, but, on the contrary, cost me a considerable sum, which I have to spend on the purchase of copies for distribution amongst my friends. My Mass and my *Faust* symphony, etc., are also entirely *useless* works, and for several years to come I have no chance of earning money. Fortunately I can just manage, but I must pinch a good deal and have to be careful not to get into any trouble, which might affect my position very unpleasantly. Do not be angry, therefore, dearest Richard, if I do not enter upon your proposal, because for the present I can really not undertake any regular obligations. If, which is not quite impossible, my circumstances should improve later on, it will be a pleasure to me to relieve your position.

About my journey to Zurich I can tell you nothing until I know when the consecration of the Gran cathedral is to take place. Some papers state that this solemnity will come off in the course of September. In that case I shall come to you before, at the beginning of August. As soon as I have official news I shall write to you. In the meantime I must stay here. On April 8th, the birthday of the Grand Duchess, I have to conduct *I due Foscari* by Verdi, and at the end of April the performances of your niece Johanna.

Unfortunately I missed Carl Ritter when he called; I had gone to Gotha for that day to hear the Duke's opera *Tony*. Carl Formes sang the title part. I hope

I shall see Carl at Zurich. Remember me kindly to him. Through his sister Emilie you have probably had news of our last *Lohengrin* performance, which went off very well. Caspari sang Lohengrin much better than it had been heard here before. The Princess of Prussia had asked for the performance, and for want of a local Ortrud (Frau Knopp, who used to sing the part here, has given up her engagement and gone to Königsberg) we had to write for Madame Marx, of Darmstadt, in all haste. An overcrowded house and a most attentive public were foregone conclusions. Berlioz was present.

Do you correspond with Counsellor Müller? He is sincerely devoted to you, and well intentioned.

Dingelstedt, who was here lately, intends to give *Lohengrin* next winter, and *not before*. Of the very *decided* success of the performance at Prague you have probably heard. Fräulein Stöger, daughter of the manager there, sang Ortrud, and wrote me a letter full of enthusiasm about the enthusiasm of the public and the musicians. She was engaged at Weymar until last season.

Farewell, and be patient, dearest friend, and write soon to

Your

F. L.

March 25th, 1856.

213.

DEAREST FRANZ,

Your letter has grieved me very much. Do you really think it necessary to explain to me by an exact description of your situation why you cannot comply with my request for new pecuniary assistance? If you only knew how ashamed and humiliated I feel!

It is true that I applied elsewhere first, and then came back to you, because the feeling of having to accept benefits from less intimate friends frequently becomes absolutely unbearable to me.

This induced me to apply for assistance to you, who never allow me to feel the deepest obligations in a painful sense. I thought, of course, more of your protection and intercession than of a sacrifice of your personal income, because I know sufficiently well how limited your resources are. That I spoke in so determined a manner was owing to the eccentric nature of my whole situation, which makes everything concerning my most intimate feeling take a violent form.

About this also I feel the absolute necessity of personal communication with you. Everything here is so delicate, so finely threaded, that it cannot be explained by letter. I want so much patience to preserve courage and love of work in my precarious position, that in my daily efforts to keep up that courage in spite of my miserable circumstances, I can only gain a few moments in which I am happy in my work, and forget all around me. The reason is that delusive possibilities of escape continually haunt my troubled imagination. But about this we must have some definite conversation.

Your offer of help in the circumstances in which you make it to me has placed me in a painful position, and so much is certain, that I cannot accept the sum which you promise to me for May in order to make my life more pleasant. I must put my income on a different basis, that is understood, and you will understand me if I say so. If, on the other hand, you contrive to dispose of that sum in my favour under conditions less troublesome to yourself, I accept it for the purpose of meeting the expenses of the copying of my scores and pianoforte arrangements, which is very expensive here. I have already spent some money on it, and the hole this has made in my income I must fill up somehow. I certainly cannot go on paying for the copying with my own money. I therefore undertake, for the sum already named, to have all the scores and pianoforte arrangements of my *Nibelung* dramas copied, and to place the copies at your disposal as your property, assuming at the same time that you will kindly lend them to me, as soon and as often as I want them. Are you satisfied with this?

The copy of the *Rhinegold* is quite ready, and I expect it back from London, together with Klindworth's arrangement. This therefore, would be at your disposal at once. Of the pianoforte arrangement of the *Valkyrie*, the first two acts will be finished very soon; the third act I recently sent to Klindworth. Hoping that you will accept my proposal, I shall now have the copy of the full score of the *Valkyrie* taken in hand, and this also you can have as soon as it is finished, because Klindworth works from my sketches of the parts. If at this moment you have leisure, and wish to look at it, I will with pleasure let you have the original score of the finished work for some time, and shall occupy the copyist with the pianoforte arrangement of the *Rhinegold* which I expect very soon. I am very anxious to know how the last act will please you, for, besides you, there is really no one to whom I could show it with any satisfaction. I have succeeded, and it is probably the best thing I have written. It contains a terrible storm of the elements and the hearts, which is gradually calmed down to the miraculous sleep of Brynhild. What a pity you will be far from me for so long! Could you not pay me a short flying visit soon?

And am I at last to see some of your new compositions? Their arrival and entry into my home shall be blessed. I have desired to see them ever so long.

Had you nothing more to tell me about Berlioz? I was expecting to hear a great deal of him. And cannot you send me any of his scores? I am, as you may imagine, making a pause in my work now. I am waiting to see what my health will do; my doctor wants to send me to some watering place, but to this I will not, and cannot agree. If I knew how to manage it I should go with Semper to Rome in the autumn. We frequently talk about it, always in the silent hope that you might be one of the party. Here you have my latest whim. A thousand greetings to the Princess and her daughter. She has written me a very cheerful and friendly letter, for which I am deeply obliged to her. I ask you fervently, dearest friend, not again to keep me waiting for a letter so long. Write to me soon and at some length, as we are not going to meet just yet.

Farewell, and continue to love me.

Your
R. W.

214.

MY DEAR FRANZ,

Before taking any steps with regard to my amnesty, I must, once more, take counsel with you, and as this is impossible by word of mouth, as I should have wished, it must be done by letter as briefly as possible.

From Prague the Director of Police there, Baron von Peimann, sent me the advice that I should become a Swiss citizen. In that case the Austrian minister would give his *visé* to my passport for all the Imperial states, and I might then reside there without being disturbed, for if Saxony should claim me, the reply would be that no Saxon subject of the name of R. W. was known. This would give me some air at least in one direction, and although not much would be gained by it, I might make use of it if there were an intention of performing *Tannhäuser* at Vienna, which opera I should let them have there only on condition of my conducting it personally. It is of course more important to me to be allowed to return to Germany proper, not in order to reside there permanently, for I can thrive only in the retirement which I can best secure in a little quiet place in Switzerland, but in order to be present now and then at an important performance, especially of *Lohengrin*, and to gain the necessary excitement, without which I must perish at last. I am *firmly resolved* not to allow *Lohengrin* to be given at either Berlin or Munich *without me*. A performance of my *Nibelungen* can of course not be thought of, unless I have the permission to travel through Germany so as to gain a knowledge of the acting and singing materials at the theatres. Finally I feel the absolute necessity of living, at least part of every year, near *you*, and you may be assured that I should make a more frequent and more constant use of the possibility of visiting

you than you do. To gain all this has now become a
matter of the greatest importance to me, and I cannot go
on living without at last and quickly taking a decisive
step in that direction. I am therefore determined to
apply to the King of Saxony for my amnesty in a letter in
which I shall candidly own my rashness, and at the same
time explicitly state that my promise, never and in no
manner to meddle with politics, comes from my very
heart. The drawback to this is that, if the other side
were ill-inclined, my letter might easily be published
in such a manner that I should be compelled to protest publicly against a false and humiliating explanation
of my step, and this would lead to a permanent breach,
which would make reconciliation impossible. Taking
all this into account, I must think it the best thing
if my request were laid before the King by word
of mouth, through a third person. To satisfy me
completely, and give me a chance of success, this
could only be done by you, dear Franz. Therefore I
ask you plainly, Will you undertake to demand an
audience of the King of Saxony on the strength of
a letter from the Grand Duke of Weimar? What
you should say to the King at such an audience I
need not indicate, but we surely agree that in asking
for my amnesty stress should be laid upon my *artistic
nature*. On account of that nature and of my individual
character as an artist, my startling political excess can
alone be explained and excused, and the reasons for my
amnesty should be considered in the same light. With
regard to that excess and to its consequences, which have
continued for several years, I am ready to admit that I
appear to myself as one who was in error and led away

by passion, although I am not conscious that I have committed a real crime, which would come under a judicial sentence, and I should therefore find it difficult to plead guilty to such a crime. Concerning my conduct in the future, I should be prepared to make any binding promise that could be desired of me. I should only have to announce the modified and clearer view which makes me look upon the affairs of this world in a light in which I did not see them previously, and which induces me to confine myself to my art, without any reference to political speculation. You might also point out that my reappearance in Germany could in no circumstances give rise to a demonstration which, although it might be meant for the artist only, could be explained and applied in a political sense by evil-disposed persons. Fortunately I have, as *an artist*, reached such a stage that I need consider only my works of art and their success, but no longer the applause of the multitude. I would therefore promise, with the greatest determination and quite in accordance with my own wishes, to avoid every public demonstration of sympathy which might be offered to me, even as an artist, such as complimentary dinners and the like. These I should most positively decline, and indeed make them, as far as would be in my power, impossible by the mode of my sojourn in various places. I should not even insist upon conducting the performance of any of my operas in person. All I should care for would be to secure a correct rendering on the part of the artists and the conductor by my presence at the rehearsals. If, for the purpose of avoiding any possible demonstration, it should be thought necessary, I should be prepared to leave the town after the completion of the rehearsals and before the performance, which would show clearly enough what is alone of importance to me. In addition to this, I will undertake to avoid in my writings, even of a purely artistic nature, such combative expressions open to misapprehension as may have escaped me formerly in my irritability. Considering all these declarations, the future need be dealt with no longer, only the past. And over that it would be well, in the case of an artist, to throw the veil of forgetfulness, not to make it a cause for revenge. All this you might in conversation explain in a much more comprehensive and conciliatory manner than I could do by letter, especially in a petition for amnesty.

I therefore ask you most fervently, perform this great service of friendship for me. Sacrifice to me the two days which a visit to Dresden would cost you, and explain the matter with that emphasis which alone can avail. From no other measure can I expect a definite and positive result. You alone can speak for me in the manner which is required. If, for special reasons, you should refuse my demand, it would only remain to me to write to the King myself, and in that case we should have to consider by whom my letter could be forwarded to the King, perhaps through the Weimar ambassador. In case the King should refuse my request I might fall back upon the intercession of one of the Prussian ministers, which has been offered to me for that purpose. But I rely little on that, while I expect everything from you and your personal pleading.

Be good enough then to let me know soon what I had better do.

Farewell, and accept the cordial greetings of your

RICHARD W.

ZURICH, *April 13th*, 1856.

Perhaps you might on the same occasion hand a copy of my *Nibelungen* poem to the King.

215.

DEAREST RICHARD,

I have not neglected the steps for your return to Germany. Unfortunately my late efforts and endeavours have not as yet led to a favourable result, which proves by no means that such may not be the case in the future. Your hint about the roundabout way, viz., Prague, I believe to be an illusion which you ought not to cherish, because it might lead to the most dangerous consequences.

The only thing that I can advise, and which I most urgently request you to do, is to send at once your petition to His Majesty the King of Saxony.

The stage into which this affair has got makes such a step absolutely necessary, and you may be sure that I should not urge you to it if I were not firmly convinced that your return to Germany cannot be brought about in any other way. As you have already told me that you would write to the King, I feel sure that you will do so without delay. Send me a copy of your letter to the King. You should, in the first instance, ask for an amnesty to the extent only *that you might be permitted to hear your works at Weymar*, because this would be necessary for your intellectual development, and because you felt sure that the Grand Duke of Weymar would receive you in a kindly spirit. It breaks my heart to have to prescribe such tedious methods, but believe me, in that direction lies your only way to Germany. When you have once been here for a few weeks the rest will be easily arranged, and I shall give you the necessary information in due course.

In the meantime we must have patience and again patience.

Take heart of grace in the hope which I have by no means abandoned, that we shall see you here.

Your faithful
F. LISZT.

Johanna has been here this last week, and has sung Orpheus and Romeo with the *most enormous* applause.

I shall have to tell you many things about her when we meet.

By this post you receive the three first numbers of my Symphonic Poems, which have just been published.

216.

DEAREST FRANZ,

Your last letter found me again on a sick bed. To-day I am scarcely recovered, and fear another relapse; that is how I am.

To-day I received the second instalment of your Symphonic Poems, and I feel all of a sudden so rich that I can scarcely believe it. Unfortunately it is only with great difficulty that I can gain a clear conception of them. This would be done with lightning rapidity if you could play them to me. I am looking forward with the eagerness of a child to studying them. If I could only be well again !

(Do you want the third act of the *Valkyrie*? My copyist works so slowly that there will be plenty of time for you to let me know your wishes. The copy of the full score of the *Rhinegold* I expect back from Klindworth before long, and shall send it to you.)

I am going to take a purgative in order to avoid the return of my illness. I wish I could, instead, start for Purgatory at once.

Adieu. A thousand thanks for your friendship.

R. W

217.

MORNEX, near GENEVA, *July 12th*, 1856.

MY DEAR FRANZ,

I have flown, as you see, to this place in order to seek final recovery. I could not help laughing when the excellent Princess, with much sorrow and sympathy, announced the impending arrival of the M. family at Zurich. From evils of that kind I am safe. No outsider can know approximately what troubles and tortures people of our stamp suffer when we sacrifice ourselves in the intercourse with heterogeneous strangers. These tortures are all the greater because no one else can understand them, and because the most unsympathetic people believe that we are in reality like themselves; for they understand only just that part of us which we really have in common with them, and do not perceive how little, how almost nothing that is. To repeat it, the tortures of this kind of intercourse are positively the most painful of all to

me, and I am only intent upon keeping to myself.
I force myself to solitude, and to achieve this is my
greatest care. When I was on the point of taking
flight, at the end of May, Tichatschek suddenly called
on me. This good man, with his splendid, childlike
heart, and his amiable little head, was very agreeable
to me, and his enthusiastic attachment to me did me
good. I was specially pleased with his voice, and tried
to persuade myself that I still had confidence in it.

I wanted to take him to Brunnen, but bad weather
delayed our purpose; still we risked it after all, when
the carriage drive brought me another attack of
erysipelas in the face—the *twelfth* this winter. I had
foreseen all this, and therefore during Tichatschek's
stay of twelve days, was in a state of continual, painful
anxiety. This abominable illness has brought me
very low. In the month of May alone I had three
relapses, and even now not an hour passes without my
living in fear of a new attack. In consequence, I am
unfit for anything, and it is obvious that I must think
of my thorough recovery. For that purpose a painfully
strict *regime* with regard to diet and general mode of
life is required; the slightest disorder of my stomach
immediately affects my complaint. What I want is
absolute rest, avoidance of all excitement and annoyance, etc.; also Carlsbad water, certain warm baths,
later on cold ones, and the like. In order to get away
from home as far as possible, and to avoid all temptation to social intercourse, I have retired here, where
I have found a very convenient refuge. I live at two
hours' distance from Geneva, on the other side of
Mont Salève, halfway from the top, in splendid air.

At a *Pension* I discovered a little summer-house, apart from the chief building, where I live quite alone. From the balcony I have the most divine view of the whole Mont Blanc range, and from the door I step into a pretty little garden. Absolute seclusion was my first condition. I am served separately, and see no one but the waiter. A dear little dog, the successor of Peps, Fips by name, is my only company. *One* thing I had to concede in return for the favour of possessing this garden *salon*; every Sunday morning from nine till twelve I have to turn out. At that hour a clergyman comes from Geneva and performs divine service for the Protestants of this place, in the same locality which I, a godless being, occupy for the rest of the time. But I willingly make this sacrifice, were it only for the sake of religion. I fancy I shall meet with my reward. But the thing is frightfully dear, and without your subsidy I could not have undertaken this expedition. I have had to make an inroad into the money which I had destined for the copying of the scores; I could not help it. The money from Vienna arrived exactly on my birthday; accept my cordial thanks for this sacrifice. I know it is infamous that you have to give me money; why do you do it? On the same occasion I was gratified by a few very friendly lines from your relative, of whose existence I was not aware; they somewhat sweetened the bitterness of having to take money from you. Remember me to him, and thank him cordially in my name.

A piano, although not of the first order, stands in my *salon*. I hope I shall soon have the courage to begin my *Siegfried* at last, but first of all I must take your

scores thoroughly in hand.   How many things you
have sent me ! I had been longing to have, at last,
some of your new works ; but now this wealth almost
embarrasses me, and I shall require time to take in
everything properly.   For that purpose it would, of
course, be necessary for me to hear your poems, or for
you to play them to me.   It is very well to read something of that kind, but the real salt, that which decides
and solves all doubts, can only be enjoyed by actual
hearing. In that terrible month of May I was able
only to look at your scores with a tired eye, and as
through dark clouds ; but even then I received the
electric shock, which none but great things produce on
us, and so much I know that you are a wonderful man,
by whose side I can place no other phenomenon in the
domains of art and of life.   So much was I struck by
your conception, and by the design of your execution
in its larger outlines, that I at once longed for something new—the three remaining pieces, and *Faust* and
Dante.   There you see what I am.   Without having
made myself acquainted with the finer details of the
artistic execution proper I wanted to go on, probably
because I had to despair of recognizing these without
hearing them.   For nothing is more misleading and
useless than to attempt this by a laborious, halting and
blundering performance on the piano, while an excellent
and expressive execution in the right tempo at once
produces the right picture in its varied colours.   That
is why you are so fortunate in being able to do
this with supreme excellence.   If I look upon your
artistic career, different as it is from any other, I clearly
perceive the instinct which led you into the path now

trodden by you. You are by nature the genuine, happy artist who not only produces, but also represents. Whatever formerly, as a pianist, you might play, it was always the personal communication of your beautiful individuality which revealed entirely new and unknown things to us, and he only was able and competent to judge you to whom you had played in a happy mood. This new and indescribably individual element was still dependent on your personality, and without your actual presence it did, properly speaking, not exist. On hearing you one felt sad, because these marvels were to be irretrievably lost with your person, for it is absurd to think that you could perpetuate your art through your pupils, as some one at Berlin boasted lately. But nature, by some infallible means, always takes care of the permanent existence of that which she produces so seldom and only under abnormal conditions; and she showed you the right way. You were led to perpetuate the miracle of your personal communication in a manner which made it independent of your individual existence. That which you played on the piano would not have been sufficient for this purpose, for it became only through means of your personal interpretation what it appeared to us to be; for which reason, let me repeat it, it was frequently indifferent what and whose works you played. You, therefore, without any effort, hit upon the idea of replacing your personal art by the orchestra, that is, by compositions which, through the inexhaustible means of expression existing in the orchestra, were able to reflect your individuality without the aid of your individual presence. Your orchestral

works represent to me, so to speak, your personal art
in a monumental form ; and in that respect they are so
new, so incomparable to anything else, that criticism
will take a long time to find out what to make of them.
Ah me ! all this seems very awkward and open to misunderstanding in a letter ; but when we meet I think I
shall be able to tell you many new things which you
have made clear to me.   I hope I shall have the necessary
leisure and sufficient lucidity of expression.   For that
purpose I want good health ; for, failing this, I always
lapse into that fatal irritability which frustrates everything, and always leaves the best things unsaid.   For
the same reason, and because our meeting is to me,
as it were, the goal for which I strive as the one
desirable end, my only care now is the perfect recovery
of my health.   Let us hope that my efforts and
many sacrifices will lead me to it.   I shall take care to
send you accounts at frequent intervals.   My amnesty
is of importance to me for this reason *only*, that in
the case of success my way to you would always lie
open ; if it is granted to me you will have to put up
with me for some time next winter.

Franz Müller has congratulated me on my birthday
in a very touching manner.   I cannot write to him
to-day, but I ask you to give him the news I send you,
and to assure him that his friendship is a great boon to
me.   In case he cannot accompany you when you visit
me, I hope to become thoroughly acquainted with him
at your house in the autumn, if only the Saxon Minister
of Justice will listen to reason.   Even his intention of
visiting me has made me very happy.

A thousand cordial thanks for the letter of the dear

Princess, who soon will have to take the title of private secretary. My best greetings to ALL.

The splendid air and the quiet sympathetic surroundings which I have been enjoying for two days have already cheered me up a little, and I begin to have hopes of perfect health.

Farewell, my dearest, my only friend. For heaven's sake, do not be so chary of your communications.

When we compare letters some day, I shall appear a veritable babbler by the side of you; while you, on the other hand, will make a noble show as a man of deeds. But, dearest Franz, a little confidential talk is not to be despised. Take note of this, you aristocratic benefactor!

Farewell, and write to me soon. I shall once more have a good go at your scores, and hope to get well into them. My address is still *Poste restante, Genève.*

Your

R. W.

Your *Mazeppa* is terribly beautiful; I was quite out of breath when I read it for the first time. I pity the poor horse; nature and the world are horrible. I would really rather write poetry than music just now; it requires no end of obstinacy to stick to one thing. I have again two splendid subjects which I must execute. *Tristan and Isolde,* you know, and after that the *Victory,* the most sacred, the most perfect salvation. But that I cannot yet tell you. For the final *Victory* I have another interpretation than that supplied by Victor Hugo, and your music has given it to me, all but the close; for greatness, glory, and the dominion of nations I do not care at all.

218.

My Hungarian journey has, during the last three weeks, become unexpectedly a doubtful matter, and I did not like, dearest Richard, to write to you before I could tell you something more definite; for the time of my visit must be arranged according to that journey taking or not taking place. The consecration of Gran cathedral is fixed for August 31st, and in case I go there to conduct my Mass, I should be with you in Zurich about September 15th or 20th; but if I am relieved of that duty I shall be at Zurich about the end of August. I hope to know by the end of next week what has been settled, and shall then ask the Princess to let you know particulars. In the meantime, albeit used to waiting, I did not care to wait any longer before I told you that I am an hungered and athirst for being together with you, and going through our programme of *nonsense*; the *hors d'œuvre* (which, as you know, have the quality of exciting both hunger and thirst) of your feast of *Rhinegold* and *Valkyrie* will be my symphony to Dante's *Divina Commedia*, which will belong to you and was finished yesterday. It takes a little less than an hour in performance, and may amuse you.

After that you will speak to me about your *Victory*, the most sacred, the most perfect salvation. . . . What will it be? The few hints in your last letter have made me very curious to know the whole idea.

Your amnesty business will, for the present, remain

in statu quo, but I hope you will come to me next winter, and am preparing your rooms at Altenburg. *Speak to no one about it.* I shall tell you what I have heard when I see you. Before all, take care of your health, and do all you can so that more rosy aspects may open before you than the roses which erysipelas has painted on your face. Unfortunately, with regard to external matters, I cannot present you with many rosy things, although, as far as appearances go, I am counted amongst the happy. It is true I am happy, as happy as a child of this earth can be. I may confess this to *you*, because you know the infinite self-sacrifice and invincible love which have supported my whole existence for the last eight years. Why need I be disturbed by other troubles? All else is only the peace-offering for my exalted happiness.

Do not reproach me any longer for not telling you anything about myself, for in these words I confide to you the secret of my usual silence.

Forgive me for not having written to you so long; the Hungarian troubles, caused by my Mass, were at fault. Let me know soon whether you are back at Zurich, and whether my coming to you about the end of August or the middle of September will suit you. You will receive more definite news before long. You have probably seen in the newspapers that Herr and Frau Milde sang the duet from the *Dutchman* at the Magdeburg Musical Festival excellently, and with splendid success. At the rehearsal I made the horns repeat

several times, till at last they succeeded in pulsating tenderly and passionately.   The critic of the *Magdeburg Gazette* says:—

"Although we were at first not sorry that Wagner's name did not appear in the programme, it was very interesting to hear this scene sung by the two Mildes, who have studied these compositions under the direction of Herr Liszt, the chief representative of the Wagner movement. Both sang beautifully, and in many passages, especially in the second half, with overpowering beauty.   We close our notice with the words of the duet, 'We were conquered by a mighty charm.'"

Criticisms in the newspapers remind me of A., whom, during my stay at Berlin, I found in the most touching state of anxiety about the notices of the performance of *Tannhäuser* that might be published by the Berlin press.   Highly estimating, as I do, her friendship for you, which also keeps up a kind of amiable feeling between us two, I could not avoid offending her a little by my indifference.   Again, during her last stay here, about three weeks ago, she excited me to a few bad jokes by the *enthusiastic* interest with which she attended a performance of Auber's *Le Maçon* at the theatre here.   She was indeed near being seriously offended by my bad jokes at the *many-sidedness* of taste, or rather, the want of taste, shown by her veneration for this *musique de grisettes*.   When an occasion offers I will try to make it up with her.

I have only too many opportunities of experiencing what you so justly say of the troubles and inconveniences which arise to us from intercourse with heterogeneous persons, although I may boast of possessing a thicker and more impenetrable skin, and a much larger portion of patience, than you.

For to-day I must not tax your patience any more by gossip of this kind. In a few weeks we shall communicate without the aid of ink and paper, which is the real and wholesome thing for us.

Perhaps the Princess will accompany me to Zurich this time.

Your

F. L.

219.

MORNEX, NEAR GENEVA, *July 20th*, 1856.

You may easily imagine, dearest Franz, how delighted I was by your letter. Sometimes I grow anxious about you when I do not see you or have proper news from you for such a long time ; I always think then that you care for me no longer. I shall not *write* to you anything rational now, for your letter can be answered only by word of mouth. God knows, I castigate my flesh by this cure chiefly in order to be quite well when we meet at last. As regards my health, I could not have done better than place myself under the immediate guidance and supervision of an excellent French physician, Dr. Vaillant, who conducts a hydropathic establishment here. I conquered my first aversion to the course when I recognized the valour of this Parisian Vaillant. I go thoroughly to work in using this new and careful treatment, and feel sure of being completely cured of my ailment, which, after all, was caused by nervousness. But it is more than possible that I shall be detained by it till the end of August, and I should therefore prefer, after all, if you could

come about the middle of September. This also seems
to me more likely, because I cannot believe that you
will give up Gran altogether. I expect then to see you
crowned with glory on your return from the land of
your fathers.

Your Symphonic Poems are now quite familiar to
me; they are the only music which occupies me at
present, for during my cure I must not think of doing
any work. I read one or other of the scores every
day, just as I might read a poem, fluently and without
stopping. I feel every time as if I had dived into a
deep crystal flood, to be there quite by myself, leaving
all the world behind me, and living for an hour my real
life. Refreshed and strengthened, I rise again to long for
your presence. Yes, friend, *you can do it, you can do it*!

Well, not much can be said about it; the noblest
expressions might easily seem a little trivial in such
a connection. Enough, you will soon be here, and
bring me *my Dante*. This is a beautiful, glorious look-
out; I thank you.

I sent you yesterday a parcel containing the original
scores of *Rhinegold* and the *Valkyrie*. Their fate will
probably be a peculiar one. Let me explain briefly :—

I shall perish, and shall be quite incapable of further
work, unless I find a habitation such as I require, viz.,
a small house to myself and a garden, both removed
from all noise, and especially from the damnable pianoforte noise, which I am doomed not to escape wherever
I turn, not even here, and which has made me so
nervous that even the very thought of it prevents me
from thinking of work. Four years I tried in vain to
realise this wish, which I can accomplish only by buy-

ing a piece of ground and building a house on it. Over this possibility I brooded like a madman, when it occurred to me not long ago to offer my *Nibelungen* to the Härtels, and to get the necessary money from them. They have expressed to me their willingness of doing something out of the way in order to gain possession of my work, and I have in consequence made the following demand: They are to purchase the two pieces which have already been finished, and are to expect *Siegfried* in the course of next year, and *Siegfried's Death* at the end of 1858, paying in each instance the honorarium on the delivery of the manuscript. They also bind themselves to publish the whole in 1859, the year of the performance. I have been led to this by sheer despair; the Härtels are to supply me with means for the purchase of a piece of ground according to my fancy. If we agree, which must be decided soon, I shall have to send them, in the first instance, my two scores, so as to place them in possession of the material for their future publication. But they will only keep them long enough to take a copy, and then return the originals to you. In any case, if I want the money, I must enable them to take actual possession. They must of course lend me the scores, in case they have not yet been copied, during your visit to me; that is understood. As you do not yet know the last act of the *Valkyrie*, I send you the score before taking further steps, so that you, and no one else, may be the first to whom I communicate it. If you have time, read the act quickly, and then keep the whole in readiness for sending it to the Härtels as soon as I ask you.

About this whole matter, however, we must come to a better understanding when we meet.

During my cure here I have become terribly indifferent towards my work.   Lord knows, if I am not much encouraged to finish it, I shall leave it alone.   Why should a poor devil like me worry and plague himself with these terrible burdens if my contemporaries will not even grant me a place for doing my work ?   I have told the Härtels as much ; if they will not help me to a house, detached and situated on an eminence, such as I want it, I shall leave the whole rubbish alone.

Well, if you only will come, I shall not trouble Saxony and the rest of Germany for some time.   Bring the Princess with you, do you hear ?   And the Child, too, must come.   If you put me in a good temper I shall perhaps lay my *Victors* before you, although this will be very difficult.   For although I have carried the idea about with me for a long time, the material for its embodiment has only just been shown to me as in a flash of lightning.   To me it is most clear and definite, but not as yet fit for communication.   Moreover, you must first have digested my *Tristan*, especially the third act, with the black flag and the white.   After that you will understand the *Victors* better.

But I am saying vague things.

Come and bring me the divine comedy, and we shall see then how we can come to an understanding about the divine tragedy.

Thine for ever and aye,
R. W.

I pray you most ardently to let me know AT ONCE *by a line the receipt, or possibly the non-receipt, of my scores.*

I always feel nervous when I know they are on the road.
They left Geneva yesterday.

My address is :—

à *Mornex, Poste restante, No.* 111, *à Genève.*

220.

I say, Franz, a divine idea strikes me.
You must get me an Erard grand!
Write to the widow and tell her that you visit me
three times every year, and that you must absolutely
have a better grand piano than the old and lame one in
my possession. Tell her a hundred thousand fibs, and
make her believe that it is for her a point of honour that
an Erard should stand in my house.

In brief, do not think, but act with the impudence of
genius. *I must have an Erard.* If they will not give
me one let them lend me one on a yard-long lease.

Adieu.

221.

I am leaving Mornex.
I shall be better than ever on September 20th.
Write to Madame Erard that she must send me a
grand piano at once. I will pay her in instalments of
five hundred francs a year without a doubt.
It must be here when you come.
Happiness and joy to you.

222.

I thank you, dearest, most unique of men, for
having sent me your scores of *Rhinegold* and the
Valkyrie. The work has for me the fabulous attractive
power of the magnet mountain, which fetters irresistibly

the ship and the sailor.   H. has been with me for a few days, and I was unable to withhold from him the joy of viewing Valhall. So he tinkles and hammers the orchestra on the piano, while I howl, and groan, and roar the vocal parts; this by way of prelude to *our* great performance at your Zurich palace, to which I am looking forward with longing.

In a week's time I start for Hungary, and my Mass will be performed on August 31st, on the occasion of the Gran ceremony, for which it has been written. For several minor reasons I must, after that, stay at Pesth and Vienna for a few weeks, and shall therefore not be at Zurich till about September 20th. Probably the Princess will come, too, together with her daughter.

Franz Müller will pay you a visit at Mornex about the middle of this month, and will show you his work on the *Nibelungen*.

The two scores I shall leave here in the keeping of the Princess until you write to *her* that they are to be sent to the Härtels.

Your idea of becoming a houseowner at Zurich is quite peculiar, and I congratulate you cordially on the building delights which await you.

Dawison told me recently that his starring engagement had enabled him to buy a villa near Dresden. At the same rate, you ought to be able to purchase with your scores at least the whole of Zurich, together with the Sieben Churfürsten and the lake.

Whether Madame Erard will be inclined to dispose of a grand piano on the advantageous terms you mention is a questionable question, which I shall put to her when I have the chance.

Try, first of all, to get quite well ; the other *arrangements* will come in due course.

May God protect you.

F. L.

August 1st, 1856.

We are just going together with H. (who wishes to be remembered to you), to have another try at the last act of the *Valkyrie.*

223.

DEAREST FRIEND,

In order to give you a little more diversion I herewith introduce to you Herr Zeugherr, an architect, and an acquaintance of Ernst's ; he is in search of a little villa for me to compose in, but has as yet found nothing. Perhaps you will inspire him.

Farewell, and receive best greetings from your

R. WAGNER.

ZURICH.

224.

Friday Evening.

DEAREST FRIEND,

That I ran away from you was a perfect inspiration, which should bring noble fruit both to you and to me.

I shall go to bed at nine ; do you likewise, and sleep by the book, so that we may present to each other tomorrow morning a couple of fresh faces, ready to face the world.

I shall study *Mephistopheles* a little to-day.

If you like we will do some Valkyring to-morrow.

May a thousand gods protect you.

R. W.

225.

DEAR FRANZ,

Believe me, by all that is sacred to you and me, that I am ill, and require the most perfect rest and care to-day, in order, let us hope, to enjoy you again to-morrow. A very considerable, though welcome and wholesome, catarrh weighs down my limbs like lead. It developed during last night, together with an inflamed throat and other addenda. The slightest excitement would impede my recovery.

Au revoir in a rational matter to-morrow.

Yours,

W. R.

226.

MY DEAREST FRANZ,

I must think it really fortunate that you this time cultivate a few other acquaintances, and that I may therefore disappear for a short time without attracting too much attention.

My catarrh has developed so thoroughly and nobly, that I may hope it will rid me of my usual winter illness, if I take proper care of it; even now I perceive the beneficial effect of nature's self-relief, although I feel as if leaden fetters were on me. I am sure that I shall be better in a few days, and am looking forward to offering you the fruits of my recovery in the shape of an excellent temper.

For to-day I am a strict patient, and must not think of a visit to Herwegh. If you will give me the pleasure of seeing you to-day, I inform you that I shall have to perspire from noon to 4 p.m.; before or afterwards my aspect would be less horrible.

The hardest thing was that I had to miss the organ concert yesterday.   But resignation helps me over everything.

I will try to finish the letter to the Grand Duke to-day.

A hundred thousand most cordial remembrances to the whole Rectory.   How are you, indefatigable man ?

227.

Sunday, early.

Here I sit again gazing after you.   My best thanks to your dear Princess for the first news.   My mind was set at rest not a little on hearing that you had been able to continue your journey to Munich without mishap.   There you will be able to rest a little more comfortably than at the Hecht of St. Gallen. Rest ? Ye indefatigable ones !

A thousand ardent blessings follow you everywhere. What you have become to me your hearts will tell you. You are so rich a possession to me that I scarcely know how to realise it.   But on the other hand, you are to me a continual sermon of repentance ; I cannot think of you without being heartily ashamed of myself.

How can you bear with me, who appear so unbearable to myself?

But I am not without good resolutions of amendment. Although I shall palm off great part of the care on my doctor, who is to put me completely on my legs again next spring, I am too well aware that an enormous labour—less watercure than purgatory—lies before me. Yes, I will shut myself up in that *Purgatorio*, and hope, dearest Franz, that I shall do so well that I may greet

you with a *magnificat* soon.   It is true that I shall
never be able to equal you, but then you are the only
genuine virtuoso.

My æsthetic efforts will, I hope, cure my moral pro-
stration to some extent.   I must try to-morrow to break
the news of the death of his mother to Siegfried.   On
Thursday evening I arrived at the Zeltweg, freezing
and empty, with a violent cold and in terrible weather;
since then I have not set foot out of doors.   All
I did was to find a good place for the Madonna
and Francesca, which was a difficult job.   I hammered
like Mime.   Now all is safe and sound.   The Madonna
hangs over my writing table and Francesca over the
sofa, under the looking-glass, where she looks beautiful.
When I begin *Tristan* Francesca will have to go over
the writing table, and the turn of the Madonna will not
come again until I take the *Victors* in hand.   For the
present I will try to inspire myself a little with the
victrix, and to imagine that I could do the same thing.

My studs are much finer than yours, dear Child ;
that any one can see.   Yours have the sole advantage
of moving one to resignation, while mine excite my
vanity terribly—a kind of surreptitious vanity, not
before the eyes of people, but all to myself; merely
for the sake of the studs, not for effect.   It is just the
same with my *Nibelungen.*   You always think of the
effect of the performance, I of the shirt studs that may
be hidden in it.

Well, my blessings on you.   If only the dear " lady
friend " would soon recover her health, so that the great
professors of Munich might delight in the " Rectory
family "!   Dear, good Princess, and dear, dear Franz,

mon bon grand! Good and great you are. My blessings on you! Farewell, and forget all bad and unpleasant things about me. Remember only the kindness of which you thought me worthy. Adieu. I am always yours.

My wife has not scolded me once, although yesterday I had the spleen badly enough. She greets you with all her power, and is thankful for your friendship.

228.

ZURICH, *December 6th*, 1856.

I have not forgotten to convey your greetings and inquiries. Wesendonck has written to me in reply, and enclosed a letter of his wife's to the Princess, which I herewith ask you to hand to her.

I long for news from you. How are you, dear Franz, and does the Princess keep her health ? From her daughter I soon expect a letter, as we have promised to correspond with each other.

I feel so-so. I shall finish the first scene one of these days. Curiously enough, it is only during composition that the real essence of my poem is revealed to me. Everywhere I discover secrets which had been previously hidden from me, and everything in consequence grows more passionate, more impulsive. Altogether it will require a good deal of obstinacy to get all this done, and you have not really put me in the right mind for it.

However, I must think that I am doing all this for myself, in order to pass the days. Be it so.

You may believe me or not, I have no other desire than that of coming to you soon. Do not fail to let me know always what chances there are. I want music, too, and, Heaven knows, you are the only one who can supply me with it. As a musician, I feel perfectly mean, while I think I have discovered that you are the greatest musician of all times. This will be something new to you.

Adieu. Tell M. that I have overhauled the old red letter case, and have got my biography up to December 1st, 1856, into shape.

A hundred thousand remembrances to mother and child.

Farewell, and take care to let me have some of your new scores soon.

Your

R. W.

229.

MUNICH, December 12th, 1856.

DEAREST RICHARD,

I have come to a close of my stay at Munich, and want to send you a few short notes of it before returning to Weymar, which will happen to-morrow evening. First of all about the performance of *Tannhäuser*, which took place last Sunday (apart from the subscription nights) for the benefit of the Munich poor. The Princess had taken two boxes, which we occupied together with Kaulbach, E. Förster, Liebig, Carrière, and others. The scenery and dresses are brilliant, but probably you would not like them particularly, and I, for my part, think them mannered and pretentious. In the orchestra the wind (especially flutes, clarinets, and bassoon) is excellent. The violins and double basses

(six in number) are a little hazy, and lack the necessary
energy, both in bowing, which is short and easy-going,
and in rhythm. The *pianos* and *crescendos* are insufficient, and for the same reason there is no fulness in the
fortes. Lachner has, no doubt, studied the score with
the greatest accuracy and care, for which thanks and
praise are due to him. But in the drama, as you know
and say best, " we must become *wise* by means of *feeling*." " Reason tells us *so it is*, only after feeling has
told us *so it must be*;" and as far as I can tell, Lachner's
feeling says little about *Tannhäuser*, although he was
called several times before the curtain at the first performances. The part of Tannhäuser was sung by Herr
Jung, the husband of Lucile Gran. He succeeded, in
my opinion, better than the public here seemed to think,
which is, as a rule, somewhat lukewarm and stolid.
Frau Dietz, whose figure and personality do not particularly fit her for Elizabeth, sang the beginning of the
second act with intelligence and feeling, but in the last
act she was no longer up to the mark, and the prayer in
the third act was applauded as if it had been " The Last
Rose of Summer." Kindermann's voice is splendid, but
there is no trace of Wolfram about him. Still less was
Fräulein X. able to identify herself with Venus, whom
she seemed to conceive as an ideal Munich barmaid.
Lindemann, the Landgrave, you know, from Hamburg ;
his voice is as powerful as ever, and he might, later on,
serve you as Fafner or Fasolt.

Apropos, your X. is a perfect madman, and I should
certainly not advise you to have anything to do with a
man like him. He asked me to attend a vocal practice of
his pupils, when the poor people had to shout nothing but

four or five notes dö, de, da! X. has entirely surrendered himself to his monomania of method, which to
him has become a kind of dram-drinking. His circumstances are in a very bad way, and I am told that he
keeps himself alive chiefly by acting as clerk in a tailor's
business here. This, of course, is by no means to his
discredit, and I think, on the contrary, that he would
do much better to give up his method, and take to
tailoring *ex professo*.

Our concert at St. Gallen has not been without an
echo at Munich, and Lachner, with whom I lived
on friendly terms, proposed to me soon after my
arrival to write for the parts of the two Symphonic
Poems to St. Gallen, so as to have them played during my stay at the subscription concerts. I thanked
him politely for the distinction intended for me, and
reserved to myself the permission of making use of it
another time. At the theatre I heard *Clemenza di Tito*
(the festival opera on the King's birthday), *Jessonda*,
The Prophet, and *Tannhäuser*; at the subscription concert the D minor symphony by Lachner, his fourth, if I
am not mistaken. *Lohengrin* is promised—that is, they
are talking about it; but amongst the present artists one
would have to search for Ortrud with a lantern. The
Munich public is more or less neutral, more observing
and listening than sympathetic. The Court does not
take the slightest interest in music, but H.M. the King
spoke to me about *Tannhäuser* as something that had
pleased him. Dingelstedt complains of the impossibility
of giving importance to the drama, and gives two or three
operas every week for the sake of the receipts.

Kaulbach and I have become sincere friends. He is

the right sort of fellow who will please you too, for the very reason that many people call him intolerable. As lately as yesterday I roared to him :

He - da!   He - da! He - do!

His designs for Shakespeare's *Tempest* (Ariel as Capellmeister in the air) are splendid. He must paint your portrait for me later on.

Farewell, dearest Richard. I must take care that we meet soon.

Your
F. L.

230.

ZURICH, *December* 16*th*, 1856.

Several times, dearest friend, I made an attempt to write to you on serious, and to me important, matters, but I had many things to settle in my own mind first. At last I feel sufficiently mature, and will tell you in plain words what is in my heart. Your last visit, much disturbed as was our intercourse, has left a decisive impression on me, which is this : your friendship is the most important and most significant event of my life. If I can enjoy your conversation frequently and quietly, and in my own way, I shall have all that I desire, and the rest will be of subordinate value. You cannot have a similar feeling, because your life is just the opposite of mine. You love diversion, and live in it, and your desire of self-concentration is therefore temporary. I, on the contrary, live in the most absolute solitude, and therefore want occasional diversion, which, however, in my

meaning, is nothing but artistic stimulus.   That stimulus
the musical world cannot give me ; you alone can.   All
that I lack, especially as a musician, owing to nature
and insufficient education, my intercourse with you and
no one else can alone give me.   Without this stimulus
my limited musical capacity loses its fertility ; I become
discontented, laborious, heavy, and producing becomes
torture to me.   I never had this feeling more vividly
than since our last meeting.

I have therefore but one desire, that of being able
to visit you when I wish, and of living with you
periodically.

Well, seriously speaking, how does this matter
stand ?   This letter will find you at Weimar.   What
news have you to give me from the Grand Duke ?   I
ask you urgently, let me have conclusive and definite
information soon.   *Much* depends upon it.   Let me
explain about Weimar.   I want to come to the Altenburg, not to Weimar ; and if it were possible I should
be quite willing to live there *incognito*.   As this will
be impossible, my existence might be noticed by the
Court.   If the Court wants anything of me, I am
prepared to appear there in person, either reading my
poems, or performing fragments of my music, such as
the first act of the *Valkyrie*, in conjunction with you,
and after *our* fashion.   I do not want to go before the
public at all.   Can this be arranged, and can the
possibility of my visit to Weimar be accelerated ?

Concerning my income and my recent hopes of a
pension from the Weimar Court separately, or in conjunction with others, you have given me some
important hints, which I have not left unnoticed or

unconsidered. I should prefer to remain without sub-vention from that quarter which would make any subsequent relation to the Weimar Court much easier to me, because it is my nature to give rather than receive.

I do not deny it would be very desirable if you could soon make an arrangement with the Härtels about the *Nibelungen*, for which object, in accordance with your kind offer, I gave you discretionary power. If you should succeed in this, it would certainly be advisable to interest the Weimar Court in my work, to the extent that it might for some time grant me certain advantages on account of the honorarium which I should receive for the publication.

If you could not ask this without loss of dignity, my only way would be to give up the *Nibelungen*, and begin a simple work such as *Tristan* instead, which would have the advantage that I could presumably dispose of it to the theatres at once, and receive royalties in return, although, as you know, the music trade would give me nothing for it.

Let me express my sincere regret at giving you again care and anxiety. If you decline to meddle with what I ask you, I shall think it quite natural on your part; but more depends upon your decision, and especially upon your success, than you may perhaps imagine. I cannot drag on like this.

Since my return from St. Gallen I have not seen a soul except Herwegh. Solitary walks, a little work and reading, constitute my whole existence, in addition to which there were some unpleasant attacks on the little rest I have, which did not allow me to breathe

freely, and impaired my health to an unbearable extent.   The correspondence between Goethe and Schiller
alone pleased me much ; it reminded me of our
relation, and showed me the precious fruits which, in
favourable circumstances, might spring from our working together.

Your Munich news showed you to me in your ever
serene artistic element, which I cordially enjoyed with
you.   Your encounter with X. I regret.   All I told you
of the man was, that at one time I was pleased with
his voice and manner, but could form no judgment
whatever of his method.   As you were no longer able
to hear him sing, and as none of his pupils was
sufficiently advanced to let you hear some real thing,
I can well understand that the poor man must have
bored you terribly with his theory ; but I thank you for
the trouble you have taken, and shall make use of your
hint.   I thought you would have been able to let me
know something about Dingelstedt, and his conduct
towards *Tannhäuser*, etc.   Probably there was nothing
pleasant to tell, and you remained silent in consequence.
A thousand thanks to the most excellent Princess for
the most astonishing cushion, and especially for the
famous German letter.   I sent her a short answer to
Munich, but it probably did not reach you.

To the good Child I shall write shortly ; continue to
love me all three of you.   I need it.   Best remembrances
from my wife.   Farewell, and let me soon hear something comforting.

Yours longingly,

R. W.

231.

DEAREST FRANZ,

I must think of protecting myself against any conceivable unpleasantness in connection with the impending warlike troubles in Switzerland.

Could not the Grand Duke get me from the Prince of Prussia, as chief of the army, a safe conduct against any possible ill-treatment or imprisonment on the part of the Prussian authorities? If this is impossible, I should have to fly to France in case of a Prussian occupation, which would be unpleasant to me. I am sure you will be good enough to do all in your power to set my mind at rest.

Of course the best thing would be if I could soon come to Weimar; but it appears that none of the difficulties of my position will be spared me.

Shall I hear from you soon?

A thousand loving and longing greetings.

232.

January 1st, 1857.

DEAREST RICHARD,

I am in bed once more, covered with the whole *flora* of my Zurich ills. Unfortunately I am no longer near you, and must be content to celebrate the New Year with you by letter. You could not meet with better luck than I wish you from the bottom of my heart. The hope of serving you and, perhaps, of living together with you soon for some time, keeps me active and cheerful, although the external aspects are not of the most favourable kind. At Carlsruhe, where I stayed a day three weeks ago, the Grand Duke and Grand Duchess spoke with the warmest interest of your works. (*Lohengrin* was being studied for production at Christmas.) Our Grand Duke here did the same at my arrival, adding, however, his apprehension, that for the present nothing could be done for you, and that I must have patience. How sick I am of this patience you may easily imagine.

I wrote to the Prince of Prussia the day before yesterday explaining your business at some length to him. I shall probably have a reply, which I will communicate to you in due course. The warlike dangers in Switzerland do not appear to me of a very urgent kind, but I thought this a good opportunity for calling the attention of the Prince to your miserable fate, which is in such glaring contrast to your fame and artistic activity. The Prince is an honourable character, and it may be expected that his intercession will be of service to you later on. In the meantime, you ought, I think, to take no further step, nor waste a single word, because this would lead only to useless humiliation for you.

As soon as the favourable moment arrives which I expect, I shall write to you. On the occasion of the performance of *Lohengrin* for the wedding of the son of the Prince of Prussia, I advise you again to write to the young Prince in the sense previously discussed by us. Probably your affair will have entered a different stage by then.

Tannhäuser was given here on Boxing-day with great success, and *Lohengrin* will follow soon. For the latter we shall have to get Frau Stäger from Prague, because amongst our local artists there is none who could undertake Ortrud. Otherwise everything here is very much in the old groove, and there is little to please me.

I long very much for my work. As soon as I am quite recovered I shall shut myself up in it, and you will be always present to my mind, until we may at last live together in the body.

Your

F. L.

233.

January 6th, 1857.

Is not this a miserable thing, dearest Franz ? I had been looking forward to your letter as to a Christmas present, and now it brings me nothing but sad and comfortless news. That you are once more confined to your bed is the crown of my sorrow.

Ah, heavens! why do we not give in altogether ?

It seems to me that you have not received my long letter, which I sent you at Weimar on the supposition that you would go there straight from Munich, and the same has, I fear, been the case with my letter to M., or else she would have surely sent me a few lines in reply. Concerning my letter *to you*, it touches upon a point to which I must urgently return once more, because I want your definite reply as soon as possible. Since you left me an important change has taken place in my situation ; I have absolutely given up the annual allowance which the R.'s made me. In such circumstances, my only hope is the speedy success of the Härtel affair in connection with the *Nibelungen,* which had been broken off. In accordance with your kind offer, I gave you unlimited power with regard to it. But now you are again tied to your bed, and cannot, in any case for the present, pay the visit to Leipzig which would be necessary for the settlement of such an affair. Consider, therefore, whether you are quite confident that the bargain will be completed after all, provided that I declare myself willing, as I do herewith, to accept any offer, knowing well that, however small the result may be, I could not get more in any other way. If you are quite sure of a final success, the further question would be, how it would be possible to raise some money on account at once. In any case, I ask you, and authorise you, and request you, as soon as possible, to come to a distinct understanding with the Grand Duke as to whether he would be inclined to confirm his favourable opinion of me by granting me a pension, or, at least, a sufficient annual subsidy for the three years which it will take me to complete my *Nibelungen*. In the eventuality of a pension for life I should, of course, accept the obligation of staying every year some time at Weimar, and give him my services according to his wish, as soon as the return to Germany is opened to me. You no doubt remember our discussion of this point, and of the possible concurrence of other princes well inclined towards me. But what I particularly care for is *speedy and absolute certainty*. At this moment, when I am most in need of help, I want to know *definitely* how matters stand. This uncertainty places me in a wavering position of hoping, expecting, wishing, and desiring, which involves my circumstances more and more, apart from demoralising me. In short, I want to know *where* to look for my friends. Therefore, much-tried friend, look upon this as your last attempt at intercession between me and a world, my position towards which I must know exactly. Patience of any kind is no longer in question. My amnesty will be granted no sooner than at the moment when Saxony herself considers that the time has come ; those gentlemen like to appear independent.

Farewell for to-day. I shall very soon write to you about other matters, which, I hope, will be pleasanter to both of us.

Your

R. W.

234.

January 27th, 1857.

DEAREST FRANZ,

Wretched and helpless as I am, I must once more trouble you with something which this time will not be altogether without interest to you. I enclose the letter of the person concerned, so that you may be *au fait* at once. (The enthusiasm displayed for me will, I hope, not excite you.) B. A., according to the testimony of my wife, is a young, very handsome, slender fellow, as, indeed, you may have guessed by the liking of X. for him.

Arrange, therefore, that he may make his *début* as Tannhäuser and Lohengrin at Weimar under your direction. In that manner I shall know that he will be under the surest guidance, and that I shall have the best information as to the value of the young man. Perhaps you will be kind enough to send for him previously.

I have not yet got back to the mood for writing to the kind Princess and the good Child. I am annoyed at being always in a state of lamentation, and must therefore wait for a favourable hour, for I do not like absolutely to deceive you. You yourself are used to my laments, and expect nothing else. My health, too, is once more so bad, that for ten days, after I had finished the sketch for the first act of *Siegfried*, I was literally not able to write a single bar without being driven away from my work by a most alarming headache. Every morning I sit down, stare at the paper, and am glad enough when I get as far as reading Walter Scott. The fact is, I have once more over-taxed myself, and how am I to recover my strength? With *Rhinegold* I got on well enough, considering my circumstances, but the *Valkyrie* caused me much pain. At present my nervous system resembles a pianoforte very much out of tune, and on that instrument I am expected to produce *Siegfried*. Well, I fancy the strings will break at last, and then there will be an end. *We* cannot alter it; this is a life fit for a dog.

I hope you are out of bed again. I wish I were a little more like you. Can you not let me have the *Mountain Symphony*? Do not forget to send it to me.

Adieu, my good, dear Franz. You are my only comfort.

A thousand greetings to all at Altenburg.

235.

February 8th, 1857.

Your sympathy with me makes me hope that you are at present employed in giving the necessary helpful turn to my affairs, and I therefore think it advisable to

describe to you, in a few words, my situation as it has
lately shaped itself, so that you may know accurately
upon what I reckon, and may take steps accordingly.

W. has bought the little country house after all, and
offers me a perpetual lease of it.

As I have given up the allowance of the R.'s, it is
important for me to settle my income on an *independent* basis. It would be foolish if I tried to arrange
my future definitely at this moment, which will probably bring my provisional position to a close. I am
certain that my amnesty will be granted in the course
of 1858 at the latest, and I hope that this will suddenly
change my situation, to the extent, at least, that it
will depend upon myself to find a solid basis for my
social existence. All I can rationally care for, considering that I have no chance of success in any other
direction, must be to secure for myself a free, unen-
cumbered, and not too limited income for the next few
years, until my great work is completed and produced.
Nothing appears more adapted to the achievement of
this purpose than the sale of my *Nibelungen* to Härtel,
whom I have asked to settle with me according to his
own judgment. It is most important to me that this
should come to pass, and I hope, in any case, that if
Härtel accepts the offer I shall receive all that is required. I think they ought to pay me 1,000 thalers for
each score, in each case on delivery of the manuscript
—that is, for the *Rhinegold*, and perhaps for the
Valkyrie also, now at once. *Siegfried* will be in their
hands by the end of this year. However, as I re-
marked before, I must be satisfied even if they give me
a little less. In any case, it will be enough to keep me

going for several years ; and if I once know what I have, I shall make arrangements accordingly, being resolved, in any case, to leave the management of my income in future to my wife.

I need not tell you that if you come to terms with the Härtels other things ought to be *left alone altogether*, for I have made up my mind henceforth to preserve my independence as much as possible.

You now have the complete synopsis of my situation ; let me commend it to your well-tried sympathy.

I hear with great delight that you are well again. I have finished the composition of my first act, and, as soon as I have recovered a little strength, hope to score it before leaving my present house. Of resuming composition proper I cannot think here ; I have suffered too much of late by the musical and unmusical noisiness of my lodging.

Tell the dear Child that she will soon receive one of those letters from me which she likes, but not about "Indian poetry" (droll idea!), but about that of which my heart is full, and which I can call by no other name, than "Orpheus." But I must wait for a favourable mood. You may tell the Child, however, that the "white rose" is now red and in full bloom, and that the "slender stem of the lily" looks right robust, and inspires confidence. The Princess is angry with me— I feel it—but I know that I shall conciliate her. A thousand greetings to her.

Farewell, dearest, dear Orpheus !

Your

R. W.

236.

You could not possibly be forgotten, dearest friend, and the next few days will give me an opportunity of looking after your affairs most carefully. On the 22nd I go to Leipzig to stay there for a whole week. On Thursday, the 26th, *Les Préludes* and *Mazeppa* will be given at the Gewandhaus for the benefit of the pension fund of the orchestra, and on the 28th I am to conduct a performance of *Tannhäuser* in Leipzig for the benefit of Herr Behr (the Landgrave), the Mildes singing Elizabeth and Wolfram respectively. In the interval I hope I shall succeed in getting a little *Rhine copper* for the *Rhinegold* from the Härtels, and shall write to you at once.

Frau X. is announced to sing Ortrud on the 8th of March. She is to sing the part twice, and then appear as Antonina in *Belisario*. If she pleases her engagement is very probable.

I shall write very soon to Herr A., who sent me your letter by way of introduction, and I have in the meantime asked Herr von Beaulieu to let him make his *début* as Lohengrin or Tannhäuser.

To-day, 16th February (the anniversary of the first performance of *Tannhäuser*, in the year 1849), we shall have a gala performance of Gluck's *Armida*, with Frau Köster of Berlin. A new opera, never yet performed, by a Belgian composer, M. Lassen, *Landgraf Ludwig's Brautfahrt*, will be put in rehearsal soon. As far as I am concerned, while

He - da!   He - do!

is hammering in my head I can enjoy nothin else,

either old or new, and dream only of the *Ring of the Nibelung*, which God's grace may soon vouchsafe to me.

Your

F. L.

WEYMAR, *February* 16*th*, 1857.

The three last numbers of my Symphonic Poems will appear by the end of this month, and I shall send them to you at once. A similar thing, *Die Hunnenschlacht*, I completed last week. The Princess of Prussia has commanded *Tannhäuser* for next Sunday.

237.

Please forward the enclosed proof to Brendel, so that the good man may get a notion of his bad editorship.

(To BRENDEL.)

ZURICH, *April* 15*th*, 1857.

DEAR FRIEND,

The somewhat tardy publication of my letter about Liszt I recently read in your paper, and saw, to my regret, that it was very incorrect, and even showed several omissions, disfiguring the sense, owing to the inattention of the printer. At first I thought of forwarding you a list of *errata*, but considered, on reflection, that such corrections are never read in context with the article, and therefore made up my mind to send a revised version to Zellner at Vienna, asking him to print it at once in his paper. My intention is by no means to punish you for the neglect shown to me, but to induce those interested in the matter to read the corrected letter once again. In case you intentionally made such changes as "*purer* form

of art" into "*newer*," etc., you have certainly misunderstood me very much, and in that case you must
look upon my correction as a demonstration against
yourself, although only in private. But I presume
that most of the mistakes were caused by the fact
that instead of my manuscript you received a copy,
which you should not have accepted.

Shall I soon see you ? I live in the greatest retirement,
and do as much work as my health will let me.

Best remembrances from

Your

Richard Wagner.

238.

You have given me a delightful Easter Sunday,
dearest, most unique of friends, by your letter. By
the loving *Azymen* which you offer me with so much
kindness and friendship, you have given me strength,
health, and total oblivion of all other leaven. Receive
my most cordial thanks, and let it be a joy to you to
have given me so much and such heartfelt joy. That joy
shall not be disturbed by a few misprints and omissions. The essential thing is that you love me, and
consider my honest efforts as a musician worthy of
your sympathy. This you have said in a manner in
which no one else could say it. I confess candidly
that when I brought my things to you at Zurich, I
did not know how you would receive and like them.
I have had to hear and read so much about them,
that I have really no opinion on the subject, and
continue to work only from persistent inner conviction, and without any claim to recognition or

approval. Several of my intimate friends—for example, Joachim, and formerly Schumann and others—have shown themselves strange, doubtful, and unfavourable towards my musical creations. I owe them no grudge on that account, and cannot retaliate, because I continue to take a sincere and comprehensive interest in their works.

Imagine then, dearest Richard, the unspeakable joy which the hours at Zurich and St. Gallen gave me when your beaming glance penetrated my soul and lovingly encompassed it, bringing life and peace.

In a few days I shall write to you at greater length about the Härtel affair, which unfortunately remains in a very unsatisfactory stage. At Altenburg things are looking very sad. The Child has been somewhat seriously ill for the last three weeks, and cannot leave her bed. The Princess also had to doctor herself, and is not yet allowed to leave her room ; and I, after having been in bed for quite six weeks, am only just able to hobble about the theatre and the castle. In spite of this, I have better and best hopes for my dear ones and for you, who live in a high place of my heart, and to whom I feel and confess that I wholly belong.

F. LISZT.

April 19th, 1857.

At the beginning of next season Dingelstedt will take the place of Herr von Beaulieu as our theatrical manager. He has been here for the last fortnight, and his position, although not yet officially announced, has been secured by the necessary signatures.

By your recommendation Frau X. will sing Ortrud next Sunday.

Herr A., whom you introduced to me, has also been staying at Weymar for the last month, but I doubt whether I shall be able to serve him in any particular way. His vocal talent is said to be very small as yet. Otherwise he impresses me favourably, and I shall hear him before long.

Once more, my best, best thanks for to-day, when I did not want to write to you about anything else.

239.

Your *Lohengrin* has once more pervaded my whole soul, and in spite of my absurd indisposition, which compelled me to go to bed immediately after the performance, I am brimful of the sublime and tender charm of the incomparable work. I wish I could sing in F and E major " A wonder !" just as you wrote it.

The performance was the best which we have had so far, and the artists were most enthusiastic. Next Saturday there will be a repetition, for which I shall get up again. With Frau Milde you would be pleased ; her singing and acting are full of magnetism. Caspari also gave some passages beautifully, and Milde is always noble and artistically efficient, although he does not quite possess the great volume of voice required for Telramund. Frau X. did not come up to the mark, and Frau Knopp, our former Ortrud, was much more equal to the part. Frau X. had studied it conscientiously, but neither her voice nor her enunciation are particularly adapted to the style. The middle register decidedly lacks strength and ful-ness, and the declamation moves in prosaic theatrical grooves, without individual and deeper pathos. This is between ourselves, for I do not want to injure a good woman and conscientious artist; but I cannot advise her engagement at the theatre here, and prefer to keep the place open which she would have to fill. I believe I told you already that Dingelstedt will assume his office of general intendant at Weymar on October 1st. Perhaps we shall find, in the course of next season, an Ortrud whom I should like a little younger than Frau X.

From Hanover I have been asked to get the original score of the *Flying Dutchman* for Capellmeister Fischer there, who is recommended to me on good authority as a sincere and energetic admirer of your works. Fischer has the scores of *Tannhäuser* and *Lohengrin* in *his* library, and is very desirous not to be without the *Flying Dutchman* any longer. I have been informed by my correspondent that he is in the habit of conducting from *his own* scores, and has taken much trouble to get that of the *Flying Dutchman*, but so far without success. He would of course prefer the original to a copy, which he could take at any time. Perhaps you will be able to find an original copy for him, for which he would have to send you the price agreed upon. Although I do not like to meddle with similar matters, I thought that one might show special attention to Fischer, who has prepared your three operas at Hanover with every care. Write to me soon what I am to tell him. I do not know him personally.

After many verbal and written discussions of the *Nibelungen* question with Härtel (in which I throughout stuck to the chief point of Härtel's *first offer*, without allowing him to swerve from it on the vague chance of some other and lower proposal), the matter has about reached this point, that I may assume that he will not give a negative answer to a letter from you, in which, making reference to his conversation with me, you should simply and a little politely ask him to carry out his former proposal. On this first proposal, I think, the resumption of the transaction must necessarily be based, and I must tell you candidly that Härtel did not appear very ready to act upon it now, because the turn given by you to the matter in your second letter has almost offended him.

Consider, therefore, whether you will write him to this effect, which I should advise you to do, for it cannot easily be anticipated that a better proposal will be made to you from another quarter, and yet it appears important to me that your work should be published.

Concerning the performance itself, I am still in hopes that the Grand Duke will supply the means to me, or rather to *you*, for in that case I should only act as your assistant.

Go on with your gigantic work bravely and cheerfully. The rest will be arranged, and I shall be in it.

F. L.

Weymar, *April 28th*, 1857.

240.

Zurich, *May 8th.* 1857.

At last I sit down to write to you, dearest Franz. I have had a bad time, which now, it is true, appears to give place to a very pleasant state of things.

Ten days ago we took possession of the little country house next to W.'s villa, which I owe to the great sympathy of that friendly family. At first I had to go through various troubles, for the furnishing of the little house, which has turned out very neat, and, according to my taste, took much time, and we had to move out before there was any possibility of moving in. In addition to this my wife was taken ill, and I had to keep her from all exertion, so that the whole trouble of moving fell upon me alone. For ten days we lived at the hotel, and at last we moved in here in very cold and terrible weather. Only the thought that the change would be definnite was able to keep me in a good temper. At last we have got through it all; everything is permanently housed and arranged according to wish and want; everything is in the place where it is to remain. My study has been arranged with the pedantry and elegant comfort known to you. My writing-table stands at the large window, with a splendid view of the lake and the Alps; rest and quiet surround me. A pretty and well-stocked garden offers little walks and resting-places to me, and will enable my wife to occupy herself pleasantly, and to keep herself free from troubling thoughts about me; in particular a large kitchen garden claims her tenderest care. You will see that a very pretty place for my retirement has been gained, and if I consider how long I have been wishing for this, and how difficult it was even to bring it into view, I feel compelled to look upon the excellent W. as one of my greatest benefactors. At the beginning of July the W.'s hope to move into their villa, and their neighbour-hood promises many friendly and pleasant things to me. Well, so much has been achieved.

Very soon I hope to resume my long-interrupted work, and I shall certainly not leave my charming refuge even for the shortest trip before Siegfried has settled everything with Brynhild. So far I have only finished the first act, but then it is quite ready, and has turned out stronger and more beautiful than anything. I am astonished myself at having achieved this, for at our last meeting I again appeared to myself a terribly blundering musician. Gradually, however, I gained self-confidence. With a local *prima-donna*, whom you heard in *La Juive*, I studied the great final scene of the *Valkyrie*. Kirchner accompanied; I hit the notes famously, and this scene, which gave you so much trouble, realised all my expectations. We performed it three times at my house, and now I am quite satisfied. The fact is, that everything in this scene is so subtle, so deep, so subdued, that the most intellectual, the most tender, the most perfect execution in every direction is necessary to make it understood; if this, however, is achieved, the impression is beyond a doubt. But of course a thing of this kind is always on the verge of being quite misunderstood, unless all concerned approach it in the most perfect, most elevated, most intelligent mood; merely to play it through as we tried, in a hurried way, is impossible. I, at least, lose on such occasions instinctively all power and intelligence; I become perfectly stupid. But now I am quite satisfied, and if you hear the melting and hammering songs of *Siegfried* you will have a new experience of me. The abominable part of it is that I cannot have a thing of this kind played for my own benefit. Even to our next

meeting I attach no real hope ; I always feel as if we
were in a hurry, and that is most detrimental to me.   I
can be what I am only in a state of perfect concentra-
tion ; all disturbance is my death.

I am deeply touched to hear that my letter has given
you so much pleasure ; I am sure you have taken the
good will for the deed, for what I wrote cannot mean
much to the many, just because it was so difficult to
write *much* that might have been more useful and
important to the multitude.   A description of your
single poems I had to refrain from altogether, for
the reason which I candidly state in the letter itself.
I cannot and will not attempt such insufficient things
again.   I had, therefore, to confine myself to showing to
INTELLIGENT persons the road which I had discovered for
myself.   Those who cannot follow in this road and afterwards help themselves further along, I cannot help along
either ; that is my sincere opinion.   Concerning the
misprints, I shall send you one of these days a corrected
copy, just for the sake of the joke.   You will then
understand that I might well be annoyed, but the fault
seems to lie less with Brendel than with the copyist of
my manuscript, who has performed his task in a very
perfunctory manner.   I do not speak of the intentional
omissions, which were your doing, and to which you
were fully entitled, but of simple abominations.   However,
that has been set right now, and will not happen again.

Many thanks also for *Lohengrin*.   It must remain a
shadow to me, I really have forgotten it ; I do not know
it.   You do all this amongst yourselves, and seem
scarcely to think that I too might wish to be present.
But I honour the mysterious silence which is so con-

scientiously preserved on the awkward question of my
return by my high and highest patrons.   Joking apart,
the Emperor of Brazil has invited me to come to him at
Rio Janeiro, where I am to have plenty of everything.
Therefore if not at Weymar, then at Rio.

Why do·I hear so much about Frau X.?   I did not
specially recommend her for Ortrud.   In my introduction I only spoke of an experienced singer of second
parts, who, for want of a better, and, if she were taken
in hand properly, might perhaps do for Ortrud.   In
saying this I specially had regard to her agreeable,
although perhaps slightly enfeebled, voice, and her
well-known industry.   But that this unfortunate person
should have been engaged specially for the part of
Ortrud, which she had never studied, and that she
should have been considered as my chosen representative of that part, was a little hard on her and on
me.   Please do not turn me into the "father" of this
débutante, whose interest I should have considered
better if I had arranged her first appearance in some
piece by Verdi or Donizetti, or indeed anything but
Lohengrin.   But enough of such stuff, although I am
grieved to see Herr A., the tenor of the future (if well
prepared), dwindle into thin air also.   May heaven
grant that Caspari will keep on, or that a decent tenor
may come to you from some other place.

Apropos, I must ask you to inform the Royal Capellmeister Fischer in Hanover, that he must make a copy
of the *Dutchman* score do for the present.   The few
autographed copies which were made at the time, not
by myself, but by a copyist, have been reduced to so few
that I cannot possibly spare another.   The first twenty-

five copies I scattered about recklessly, before any cock crowed for this opera, and the very few remaining ones are naturally of value to me. Excuse me, therefore, and refer him to the time when the sale of my works will have become so lucrative that the full scores can be engraved. I am, however, very grateful to him for his sympathy. Hanover has become a perfect repository of my scores.

Many thanks also for your hints regarding the Härtel affair. Candidly speaking, the settlement of it is so important to me, that I immediately followed your advice, and wrote to the Härtels in such a manner that they will probably accept my offer, provided that they have been properly informed of the object by you. This, of course, I assume, and thank you cordially for it. Well, we shall see.

I am being continually and painfully interrupted in these sufficiently frivolous lines by the invasions of workmen, especially of a Saxon locksmith. So I had better come to a close, although to my sorrow, for I regret our ill-sustained correspondence, in which at bottom we never express ourselves thoroughly, but, barring a few violent lucubrations, touch each other in a very superficial manner. I do not say anything to-day on the important point of your failing health. I wrote very seriously about it to the Princess some time ago, and am longing for a conclusive answer. I now hear through you that our magnanimous friend has herself been ill for a long time, and my fears are thus sadly confirmed. So I must ask you, after all, to let me know at least what steps you are going to take for the thorough recovery of your health. Have you really settled to persevere in the musical festival of Aix-la-Chapelle, or have you found a doctor with sufficient courage to prohibit your incessant efforts and sacrifices absolutely, and to withdraw you for a time from the world which spoils you more and more, in order to secure your perfect recovery ? Really, dearest Franz, you will cause me the deepest anxiety unless you satisfy me on this point, and every rational person will see that this can be done only by a long and careful cure, together with absolute rest and abstention from every effort and excitement. To speak plainly, you dear people cannot long go on as you do now. Others would be ruined very soon by this kind of thing, which, at last, must become detrimental to you also. Listen, my Franz, come to me. No one shall know of your presence ; we will live quite by ourselves, and you must submit to our taking the necessary care of your "cure." You will think this very stupid, and will perhaps scarcely believe that it is absolute despair which inspires this advice ; but *something* must be done, and if things appear black to me, the reality of the news which you send me surely does not justify a rosier view. For Heaven's sake, calm my fear, and believe me that no triumphs, not even those gained by yourself for yourself, will give me the least pleasure as long as I know how dearly you pay for them. Well, I must wait for your reply, but please let it not be a superficial, futile one.

Heaven only knows what I have written here ; it must be nice stuff.

Finally, I want to thank you for the last three scores received by me ; they came to me like old friends. I shall take them in hand thoroughly ; they are to conse-

crate me a musician once more, and fit me for the beginning of my second act, which I shall precede by my
study of them.

As I said before, I do not thank you for the sacrifice
you have made for me by your last beautiful performance
of *Lohengrin*. If you had written to me instead, "I
have put *Lohengrin*, you, myself, and everything else
on the shelf, in order to get thoroughly well again," I
should have thanked you with heartfelt tears. Let me
soon know something of the kind, or else I shall never
write to you again, and burn *Young Siegfried* with all
his songs of the smithy.

Adieu, you good, wicked Franz. Greet your dear
women from the bottom of my soul; they are to love
me, and to get well, the dear, wicked women.

Adieu, my good dear Franz.   R. W.

241.

May 19th, 1857.

DEAREST FRIEND,

I received to-day the enclosed letter from the
Härtels. In it they refer to a letter addressed to you,
and in case this latter contains any indications as to how
the business might be settled, I should like you to send
it to me. Otherwise it would be of no use to me.

It is a sad thing that, in order to have a *certain*
income for the next few years, I am compelled to offer
my work for sale in this manner, and in different circumstances I should calmly bide my time in the firm
hope that people would come to me. As it is, I am
compelled to try everything, so as to tempt the Härtels
to this purchase. Above all, I perceive that your time
and occupations will not allow you to acquaint those

gentlemen thoroughly with my music. I have, therefore, invited them to come here this summer, and to
meet Klindworth, who has announced his visit to me.
With his aid I shall give them a piece of my *Nibelungen*,
which will give them some notion of it.

Be good enough, therefore, to return to me for some
time the pianoforte score of *Rhinegold*, which we shall
want for that purpose.

Delight me soon with satisfactory news of you ; you
know what I mean by this.

Farewell, and be greeted a thousand times.

Your   R. W.

(I want Härtels' letter back again.)

You wicked friend! Let me know, at least, by some sign, how you are, and whether you forgive me for my anxiety about you.

May 30th, early in the morning, after a good night.

R. W.

243.

WEYMAR, *June 9th*, 1857.

DEAREST RICHARD,

I returned from Aix-la-Chapelle yesterday, and (barring a little pain in both my feet, which requires some care) I feel so well that I can cheerfully go to my work and various occupations. You must forgive me for not having satisfied your friendly anxiety about my health before this; the fact is, I must endure what is destined to me for your sake and my sake. God be thanked, I do not lack either strength or a certain tough equanimity.

H. wrote to you about the Aix Musical Festival, which, upon the whole, was satisfactory, both in arrangement and execution, although *our friend* Hiller may demonstrate in the *Cologne Gazette* that I have no talent either as a conductor or a composer. The *Tannhäuser* overture went splendidly, and your autogragh " ich lieg und besitze,—lasst mich schlafen " has given me a happy moment.

Owing to the severe illness of the Princess, my frame of mind has been sad and anxious for more than nine weeks. At my return I found her on the way to recovery, but several months may still pass before she is quite well again. At present she can scarcely sit up for half an hour every day.

Forgive me for not having written to you sooner, but

I had nothing but sad news to tell you, and the poor Princess caused me so much anxiety that I scarcely knew how to bear it.

At last you have found a comfortable habitation which has been prepared for you by tender friendship, and must be all the more pleasant and beneficial to you on that account. I cordially participate in this essential improvement of your life at Zurich, and am glad that you can give yourself up to your genius, and complete the gigantic mental mountain range of your *Nibelungen*, without disturbance from neighbouring smiths and pianists. Have the W.'s moved into their villa yet? Convey my humble compliments to the amiable lady, and greet W. most cordially. I hope I shall be able to visit you in the autumn, after the Jubilee of Grand Duke Carl August. It will be celebrated here on September 3rd, 4th, and 5th, on which occasion I shall perform my *Faust* symphony and a new symphonic poem *The Ideals*.

In reference to the Härtel affair I enclose his two letters of March 4th and 16th. At the end of February I had a long conversation about the matter at Leipzig with Dr. Härtel, and tried to persuade him to renew his first proposal to you, because that seemed to me the most advantageous thing for you. After a few days' consideration he sent me the letter, dated March 4th, and I replied in the sense of my conversation with him. I tried to show him as clearly as possible that this matter ought to be looked upon as a grand *enterprise* rather than as a common *commercial speculation*, and that the firm of Breitkopf and Härtel, which already possessed *Lohengrin* and the three operatic poems, would, in my opinion, be the most eligible for that purpose.

I have not kept a copy of my letter, but can assure you that you need not disavow a single word of it. Härtel's letter of March 16th is identical with that addressed to you. As matters stand, I am very doubtful whether the Härtels will make you a new offer of honorarium unless, of course, the immediate impression of your rendering of the work on them should be so powerful as to overcome their commercial timidity. On your part I should not think it advisable to make them a new offer, and you have, no doubt, hit upon the best idea in inviting them to Zurich, so that you may be able to give them at least some previous idea of your work. This, I think, will be your most favourable chance in the circumstances. The intention of the Härtels for the present is, of course, to offer you nothing but an eventual honorarium *after* the publication of the work, and after the expenses of that publication have been covered. You seem to think that I have not had sufficient time and opportunity for determining the Härtels to a different and better proposal, *but there you are very much mistaken*; and you may be quite certain that I should willingly have remained at Leipzig for a month or longer, and should have played and sung the *Rhinegold* to the Härtels several times if I had had the slightest hope that our purpose would in that manner be advanced by a hair's breadth. What I laid particular stress on with Härtel, apart from the intrinsic importance of the whole quality and essence of your work, was the possibility and the all but absolute certainty of its performance, which of course is denied on all sides.

At last I told him : " This I will guarantee, by word

and deed, that between the completion of the *Nibelungen*, which may be expected by the end of the next year, and its performance, scarcely a year will elapse, and that the friends of Wagner, and I foremost amongst them, will do all that is possible to bring that performance about. In this firm conviction I think it desirable that the work should appear in print, so that the necessary standpoint for its judgment may be supplied," etc., etc., etc.

I am sorry to bore you with all this stuff, and only ask you *not to give way to irritation*, and not to say or to write a single rash word, because the matter is of decided importance, and a trustworthy publisher is not easily found. The publication of the *Nibelungen* in full score and pianoforte arrangement will require an outlay of at least ten thousand thalers, for which few firms will be prepared. For the present I should advise you to keep quite quiet, and to invite the Härtels simply, and if need be repeatedly, to visit you, leaving all further discussion as to the terms of publication till you have given them more accurate insight into the matter; that is, till your meeting at Zurich.

Your

FRANZ.

What is your present address?

Richard Pohl has asked me to inquire of you whether you will be at Zurich in July, and whether he may pay you a visit there?

244.

ZURICH, *June 28th*, 1857.

At last, dearest Franz, I am able to give you an answer by letter.

First of all, receive my heartiest congratulations on

the good state of your health.   Your letter has joyfully surprised me, and, to my greatest delight, has made me feel ashamed of my intrusive anxiety about you.   Your organisation is a perfect riddle to me, and I hope that you will always solve that riddle in as satisfactory a manner as this time, when I looked on with real anxiety.   Heaven grant that your profession of good health may not be that of a Spartan !

All the more sorry do I feel that you have not been able to dispel my anxiety as to the Princess also.   At our last meeting at Zurich my impression of your (to me) strange and very exciting mode of life frightened me so much that I am really less astonished at the Princess being on a sick bed than at your being up again.   My very eager anxiety about both of you is perhaps in bad taste ; for you are accustomed to taking care of yourselves, and acknowledge probably no special right on my part to trouble about you.   Heaven grant that patience and good advice may restore our magnanimous friend as soon as possible ; when she is once well again I shall be quite willing to plead guilty to the charge of impertinence.   You say nothing of the health of her daughter, who was also severely indisposed.   May your good star guide you ; in one important point I shall always remain a stranger to you all.

I shall have no further trouble with the Härtels, as I have determined finally to give up my headstrong design of completing the *Nibelungen*.   I have led my young Siegfried to a beautiful forest solitude, and there have left him under a linden tree, and taken leave of him with heartfelt tears.   He will be better off there than elsewhere.   If I were ever to resume the work some one would have to make it very easy for me, or else I should have to be in a position to present it to the world as a *gift*, in the full sense of the word. These long explanations with the Härtels—my first contact with that world which would have to make the realisation of my enterprise possible—were quite enough to bring me to my senses, and to make me recognize the chimeric nature of this undertaking. You were the only person of importance, besides myself, who believed in its possibility, but probably for the reason that you also had not sufficiently realised its difficulties. But the Härtels, who are to advance solid coin, have looked into the matter more closely, and are, no doubt, quite right in believing the performance of the work impossible, as the author did not even see his way to its completion without their help.

As regards myself, there was a time when I conceived, commenced, and half finished the work without the expectation of its being performed during my lifetime. Even last winter your confident tone, as you took leave of me, and your hope of releasing me soon from my mute and soundless exile, gave me the courage (which by that time had become a difficult matter) to continue. Such encouragement was indeed required, for, after having been without any stimulus, such as a good performance of one of my works might have given me, my position was, at last, becoming unbearable. Our trials at the piano further contributed towards my becoming thoroughly conscious of the misery of such musical makeshifts ; indeed, I felt that a good many things would be explained to myself only by a good performance. Since then my last hope has vanished

again, and a terrible bitterness has come over me, so
that I can no longer have any faith in mere chance.
You, my rarest friend, do everything in your power to
rouse me again in one way or other, and to sustain
my freshness and love of work, but I know that all you
say is only for this particular purpose. So I have at
last decided to help myself. I have determined to
finish at once *Tristan and Isolde* on a moderate scale,
which will make its performance easier, and to produce
it next year at Strassburg with Niemann and Madame
Meyer. There is a beautiful theatre there, and the
orchestra and the other not very important characters I
hope to get from a neighbouring German Court-theatre.
In that manner I must try (D.V.) to produce something
myself and in my own way which will once more restore
freshness and artistic conscientiousness to me. Apart
from this, such an undertaking offers me the only possible
chance of sustaining my position. It was only by a
somewhat frivolous proceeding—the sale of *Tannhäuser*
to the Josephstadt Theatre at Vienna—that I succeeded
in preserving my equilibrium, and this will soon again be
threatened, or, at least, is so absolutely insecure, that I
had to think of something which would free me from
care. For so much I may assume that a thoroughly
practicable work, such as *Tristan* is to be, will quickly
bring me a good income, and keep me afloat for a time.
In addition to this, I have a curious idea. I am thinking
of having a good Italian translation made of this work
in order to produce it as an Italian opera at the theatre
of Rio Janeiro, which will probably give my *Tannhäuser*
first. I mean to dedicate it to the Emperor of Brazil,
who will soon receive copies of my last three operas,

and all this will, I trust, realise enough to keep me out of harm's way for a time. Whether, after that, my *Nibelungen* will appeal to me again I cannot foresee ; it depends upon moods over which I have no control. For once I have used violence against myself. Just as I was in the most favourable mood I have torn Siegfried from my heart, and placed him under lock and key as one buried alive. There I shall keep him, and no one shall see anything of him, as I had to shut him out from myself. Well, perhaps this sleep will do him good ; as to his awaking I decide nothing. I had to fight a hard and painful battle before I got to this point. Well, it is settled so far.

Your three last Symphonic Poems have once more filled me with painful joy. While reading them I was forced again to think of my miserable condition, which makes such things mute to me, to me who knows so little how to help himself. God knows the greatest delight, such as your *Mountain Symphony*, is thus turned to sorrow for me. But I have made these complaints a thousand times, and there is no help for it.

Some unfortunate person has again sent me a whole heap of ridiculous nonsense about my *Nibelungen*, and probably expects an approving answer in return. With such puppets have I to deal when I look for human beings. These are the kind of people who continually trouble themselves about me with astounding faithfulness and constancy. Good Lord ! it is very well for you to talk.

I shall receive R. Pohl with all the respect due to the Weimar art historiographer. I shall stay in my "refuge," and shall be pleased to see him.

To speak at last of something hopeful, let me express my greatest joy at your giving me hope of a visit from you in September. Let me pray you earnestly not to treat this matter lightly, but to turn my hope into confidence. Try to imagine that you have undertaken to conduct a musical festival here, and then I am sure your passionate conscientiousness will not allow you to stay away. Really, dearest Franz, such a meeting is a necessity to me this time. I shall enjoy it like a true *gourmet*. Let me soon hear something definite, and greet Altenburg and all its precious contents from the bottom of my heart. *Remain* well, for you say that you are well, and once more, love me.

Your

R. W.

As regards my address, the very blind know my footsteps at Zurich. About *Tristan* ABSOLUTE *silence*.

245.

ZURICH, July 9th, 1857.

MY DEAR FRANZ,

I forgot to ask you something. At Zurich I told you that that poor devil Röckel was longing to see one of my new scores. Recently he has again reminded me of it, therefore I repeat my request to you to lend him your score of *Rhinegold* for six or eight weeks. His wife, who lives at Weimar, will, no doubt, gladly undertake to send him the score. He is a clever fellow, and I should like to count him amongst those who occupy themselves with my recent works. It will cheer him up considerably, and I see from his last letter that he is gradually becoming low-spirited. You would, no doubt, increase his delight if you were to add copies of all, or some of your symphonic poems. I have drawn his attention to them, and he is very curious to know something of them. You might let him have them just as a loan. Do not be angry with me for troubling you with this.

How are you, and have you any comforting news of the Princess for me?

The Grand Duke of Baden recently wrote me a surprisingly amiable and friendly letter, which is of real value to me, as the first sign of a breach in the timid or courtly etiquette hitherto observed towards me. The occasion was a little attention which I showed to the young Grand Duchess, and for which he thanks me in a moved and moving manner in her name and his own.

Eduard Dervient stayed with me for three days last week, and inaugurated my little guest-chamber. To him I also spoke of my *Tristan* scheme; he highly approved of it, but was against Strassburg, and undertook, although generally a careful and timid man, to arrange about its first performance at Carlsruhe under my direction. The Grand Duke also seems to have got wind of something of the kind, probably through Devrient, for in one passage of his letter he pointedly alludes to his confident hope of seeing me soon at Carlsruhe.

Well, as God wills. This much I see, that I must, once more, perform a little miracle to make people believe in me.

About my work I am, as you may imagine, in a state of great and continual excitement.

Let it be settled that I have you in September ; that is the chief thing.

A thousand cordial greetings to your dear home.

Ever thine,

RICHARD WAGNER.

246.

DEAREST RICHARD,

At your recommendation I am reading the Correspondence between Schiller and Goethe. Your last letter found me at this passage : " It is one of the greatest happinesses of my existence that I live to see the completion of these works, that they fall into the period of my activity, and that I am enabled to drink at this pure fountain. The beautiful relation existing between us constitutes a kind of religious duty on my part to make your cause my own, to develop every reality in my being to the purest mirror of the spirit which lives in this body, and to deserve by that means the name of your friend in a higher sense of the word " (p. 163, vol. i.).

I must weep when I think of the interruption of your *Nibelungen*. Cannot the great *Ring* free you of all the little chains which surround you ? You have certainly many reasons for being bitter, and if I generally observe silence on the point I feel it none the less sadly. In many quarters I am, for the present, unable to achieve anything more, but it would be foolish to abandon all hope. A more favourable hour will come, and must be waited for, and in the meantime I can only ask you not to be unjust to your friend, and to practise the virtue of the mule, as Byron calls patience.

Tristan appears to me a very happy idea. You will, no doubt, create a splendid work, and then go back refreshed to your *Nibelungen*. We shall all come to Strassburg and form a *garde d'honneur* for you. I hope to see you at the beginning of this autumn, although I am not yet able to settle on a definite plan. The Princess is still confined to her bed, and her recovery is, as yet, in a bad way.

I, for my part, shall be compelled after all, and in spite of obstinate resistance, to use the baths of Aix-la-Chapelle, which is very unpleasant to me. Next week I shall go to Berlin for a few days, and from there I proceed straight to Aix, where I intend to go through the cure from July 22nd till August 10th. On August 14th I shall be back in order to receive the commands of the Grand Duke with regard to the festivities in September. The excavations which have been made for the monument of Schiller and Goethe will, it is feared, cause a dangerous settlement of the soil near the theatre, and the two "fellows" may possibly not be able to find a secure position in Weymar. A telegram has been sent to Rietschel in order to decide in what manner the danger can be prevented. Perhaps they will order me to make no more "Music of the Future," so as not to ruin the city from the bottom. In that case I should have to fly to Zurich in order to produce the *Faust* symphony and my last symphonic poem, Schiller's *Ideals*, at your villa. The former has been increased by a final chorus of male voices singing the last eight lines of the second part, the *Eternal Feminine*.

It is still very doubtful whether the Princess will be fit for travelling this year, and the Child will, in any case, not leave her mother.   If both are able this autumn to perform the Swiss journey, which they missed last year, I shall of course stay with them at the Hôtel Baur. Your wife, in that case, must not refuse me the boon of getting me excellent coffee and a practicable coffee machine, for the abominable beverage which is served at the hotel as coffee is as disgusting to me as a *pièce de salon* by Kücken, etc., and embitters my morning hours.

By what manner of means have you got at H.M. the Emperor of Brazil ?   You must tell me this.   He ought by rights to send you the Rose Order set in brilliants, although you do not care about flowers or orders.

Rosa Milde is going to give a few performances at Dresden, and has asked for Elizabeth as her first part. If the voice of Frau Meyer does not improve I advise you to choose Frau Milde as Isolde.   I believe you will be satisfied with her, although our *friend* Hiller praised her so much.

Your faithful

F. L.

WEYMAR, *July* 10*th*, 1857.

247.

You have not come, after all, dearest Franz ; without a word of explanation, simply remaining silent, you have not come.   In two letters you had given me hope of your visit, and I wrote to M. that I had thought of a way of receiving you under my roof.   Has my message been given to you ?   Perhaps not.   M. was kind enough to write to me some time ago, but my last invitation was not mentioned with a single word.   You wrote to me a few lines, but not a word as to whether you were coming or not. My dearest Franz, whatever there may have been in my conduct to make you angry with me, you must, I pray you, forgive me for the sake of our friendship, while I, on my part, am quite willing to forgive the person who may have set you against me.

B. will bring you a copy of the poem of *Tristan*, which I wrote during his visit. While I was at work, and had a visitor, I found it impossible to make a copy and send it to M. Kindly excuse this.

Farewell, dearest Franz, and let me hear soon that you still think of me in a friendly way. The successful performance of your *Faust* has pleased me immensely. I wish I could have heard it.

Farewell.

Your

R. W.

248.

HÔTEL DE SAXE, No. 17, *November 3rd*, 1857.

DEAREST RICHARD,

How could I think of you otherwise than with constant love and sincerest devotion in this city, in this room where we first came near to each other, when your genius shone before me? *Rienzi* resounds to me from every wall, and when I enter the theatre I cannot help bowing to you before every one, as you stand at your desk. With Tichatschek, Fischer, Heine, and others of your friends in the orchestra here I talk of you every day. These gentlemen appear well inclined towards me, and take a warm interest in the rehearsals of the *Prometheus* and *Dante* symphonies, which are to be given next Saturday at a concert for the benefit of the Pension Fund of the chorus of the Court theatre.

The Princess and her daughter will arrive this evening. The Child is mad about your *Tristan*, but, by all the gods, how can you turn it into an opera for *Italian singers*, as, according to B., you intend to do? Well, the incredible and impossible are your elements, and perhaps you will manage to do even this. The subject is splendid, and your conception wonderful. I have some slight hesitation as to the part of Brangäne, which appears to me spun out a little, because I cannot bear confidantes at all in a drama. Pardon this absurd remark, and take no further notice of it. When the work is finished my objection will, no doubt, cease.

For February 16th, the birthday of the Grand Duchess, I have proposed *Rienzi*, and I hope Tichatschek will sing in our first two performances. The third act will necessarily have to be shortened very much. Fischer and some others even thought that we might omit it altogether. The Weymar theatre, like the Weymar state, is little adapted to military revolutions; let me know on occasion what I am to do. The rehearsals will begin in January.

My daughter Blandine has married at Florence, on October 22nd, Emile Ollivier, *avocat au barreau de Paris*, and democratic deputy for the city of Paris. I am longing to get back to my work soon, but unfortunately, the inevitable interruptions caused by my innumerable social relations and obligations, give me little hope for this winter. I wish I could live with you on the Lake of Zurich, and go on writing quietly.

God be with you.

Your

F. Liszt.

249.

My dear, dear Franz,

I want you to receive these lines just as you are going to the first performance of your *Dante*. Can I help feeling grieved to the very depth of my existence, when I am compelled to be far from you on such an evening, and cannot follow the impulse of my heart, which, were I but free, would take me to you in all circumstances, and from a distance of hundreds of miles in order to unite myself with you and your soul on such a wedding-day? I shall be with you, at least in the spirit, and if your work succeeds as it must succeed, do honour to my presence by taking notice of nothing that surrounds you, neither of the crowd, which must always remain strange to us, even if it takes us in for a moment, nor of the connoisseur, nor of the brother artist, for we have none. Only look in my eye just as if you would do if you were playing to me, and be assured that it will return your glance blissfully, brightly, and gladly, with that intimate understanding which is our only reward.

Take my hand and take my kiss. It is such a kiss as you gave me when you accompanied me home one evening last year—you remember, after I told you my sad tale. Many things may lose their impression upon me. The wonderful sympathy which was in your words during that homeward walk, the celestial essence of your nature, will follow me everywhere as my most beautiful remembrance. Only one thing I can place by the side of it, I mean that which you tell me in your works, and especially in your *Dante*. If you tell the same thing to others to-day, remember that you can do so in the sense alone in which we display our body, our face, our existence to the world. We wear ourselves out thereby, and do not expect to receive love and comprehension in return. Be mine to-day, wholly mine, and feel assured that by that means you will be all that you are and can be.

Good luck on your way through hell and purgatory! In the supernal glow with which you have surrounded me, and in which the world has disappeared from my eyes, we will clasp hands.

Good luck!

Your

RICHARD.

250.

January 1st, 1858.

I want to consecrate my pen for the new year, and cannot do so better than by a greeting to you, my dear Franz. Above all other wishes is my wish of seeing and enjoying you to my heart's content. The worst loss of the past year has been that of the visit you had promised me. If I were to try to imagine the greatest delight that could be vouchsafed to me, it would be to see you suddenly in my room. Are you inclined at all for such a stroke of genius? If I were only free you would experience such a surprise from me, but I must no longer hope for miracles; everything comes to me in a laborious and gradual way, and, after all, I have to share it with a host of Zurich professors. You perceive I am not very many-sided. My ideas move in a somewhat narrow circle, which, fortunately, through the objects it comprises, becomes as large as the world to me (I do not count the Zurich professors amongst those objects). If I have a grudge against your eternal and manifold obligations and engagements, you will understand my very special reason, viz., that they take you away from *me* so much. Candidly speaking, my being together with you is everything to me; it is my fountain, all the rest is but overflow. When I sit down to write to you I do not know what to say. Nothing occurs to me but what I cannot write. To speak to you of " business " is altogether an abomination to me, for when I deal with you my heart grows large, while business narrows it in the most deplorable manner. It is bad enough when, as formerly was too often the case, I am compelled to trouble you with my private sorrows. Especially to-day these must be far from me, for the first stroke of my pen in the new year is to convey nothing but a pure, sonorous greeting to you. I want to tell you, however, that yesterday, at last, I finished the first act of *Tristan.* I shall work at *Tristan* assiduously; at the beginning of the next winter season I want to produce it somewhere.

My reading is, at present, confined to Calderon, who will at last induce me to learn a little Spanish. Heaven forbid that in that case I should remind you of H. Nägeli. The necessary *cache-nez* I possess. My wife has given me one, together with a splendid carpet with swans on it, *à la Lohengrin.* I heard recently of your Dresden life with Gutzkow, Auerbach, etc., etc. Oh, you tremendous fellow! You can do anything. Perhaps you, too, will appear to me in a Spanish light, when I shall have a good laugh at you. I have struck up a friendship with the X.'s for the sole purpose of not being again left out of their invitation when the time comes. But I begin already to regret having done so, and any amount of enthusiasm cannot make me appreciate this abominable race of professors. But you will see by my having made the attempt that I wish to get rid of my roughness, in order to be quite amiable at your next visit. Did I recently write something stupid to the dear Child? I cannot remember exactly, but God must forgive me all my sins, just as I forgive Him many things in His world, and where God forgives, the Child should not be sulky. You ought to be angry least of all, for you must know that I love no one as I love you, and that it was you who taught me to love. If the Princess is angry with me I want her to give a good scolding one of these days to Professor M., or Professor V., etc., for it is in reality the fault of this type of men if I make any one angry.

I am delighted above everything at your being well again, although I find it difficult to believe that there are men who can go through what you go through. I am in fairly good health, and still have to thank Vaillant for it. I wish I could reward him.

Let me hear from you soon, and do not mind my nonsense. Greet the Altenburg with a will, and tell the dear ladies that they are to hold me in kind remembrance.

The blessings of a world on you, my Franz. Farewell.

Your
R. W.

251.

DEAREST FRANZ,

I intend to go to Paris in order to look after my interests there. If it is too far for you, or if you do not like to come to Paris, we might as well meet at Strassburg. I should like to consult you about my whole position, in order to have the consent of my only friend to my new undertakings. For the present you will see, at least, that I am not acting hastily. I wait for some money coming in. Everything leaves me in the lurch. I have had to send a power of attorney to Haslinger in Vienna, in order to compel the manager there to pay me some considerable sums which he owes me, but I cannot with any certainty reckon upon success within a month. At Berlin they have given *Tannhäuser* exactly once during last quarter, and for the first time I received very little money, while formerly I used to draw considerable sums from there during the winter. The Härtels, to whom I made some days ago the offer of *Tristan* on certain conditions, I cannot ask for an advance of money, even in the favourable case of their accepting my offer, because I should not be able to send them the manuscript before the end of February. The housekeeping money of my wife is in the last stage of consumption, and she longingly expects funds from me to meet the new year's bills. In such circumstances, and being absolutely without resources, I am in the painful position of having to delay my necessary journey, which I could not undertake, even if I had only the actual travelling money, because I must not leave my wife without means for ever so short a time. I shall therefore require at least one thousand francs in order to get away. By Easter at the latest, and perhaps sooner, I shall ask Härtel for a considerable sum on account of the first act, and promise faithfully to return the money then. Please consider from whom, and how, you can get the money for me. Send me the money, and let me know at the same time where you can meet me, at Strassburg or in Paris.

Farewell! *Au revoir very soon.*

Your

RICHARD.

252.

DEAREST RICHARD,

At Weymar I cannot raise ten thalers just at present, but I have written at once to Vienna, and in a week's time the sum of a thousand francs, named by you, will be handed to you by my son-in-law, M. Emile Ollivier (*avocat au barreau et député de la ville de Paris*). Call on him at the end of next week. He lives *rue St. Guillaume, No. 29, Faubourg St. Germain.*

If it is of use to you to have some conversation with me, I will come to Strassburg for one day, although I find it difficult to leave Weymar at the present moment.

The Princess has had an excellent idea, of which you will hear more before long. She will write to you as soon as she has had an answer with regard to it.

God be with you!

F. L.

FRIDAY, *January* 15th, 1858.

Your telegram arrived a day before your letter which I received last night. Let me have your address; *poste restante* is not safe.

253.

DEAREST FRANZ,

Tired to death and worn out, I write only to tell you that I have arrived at Paris, and that my address is *Grand Hôtel du Louvre* (No. 364).

In a modest room on the third floor, overlooking the inner courts, I found at last the quiet position which is necessary to me.

I expect help from you. My difficulty is great. In a few days I shall write more calmly.

Your
R. W.

254.

GRAND HÔTEL DU LOUVRE, No. 364, PARIS.

You dear, splendid man! How can I be unhappy, when I have attained the supreme happiness of possessing such a friend, of participating in such love? Oh, my Franz! could we but live always together! Or is the song to be right after all: "Es ist bestimmt in Gottes Rath, dass von dém liebsten was man hat, muss scheiden"?

Farewell; to-morrow I shall write about other things. A thousand greetings!

Your
R. W.

255.

Yet another friend, dearest Franz, has a kind fate vouchsafed to me. I was permitted to feel the delight of becoming acquainted with such a poet as Calderon in my mature stage of life. He has accompanied me here and I have just finished reading *Apollo and Klymene*, with its continuation *Phæton*. Has

Calderon ever been near to you? I can unfortunately approach him through a translation only on account of my great want of gift for languages (as for music). However, Schlegel, Gries, who has translated the more important pieces, Malsburg, and Martin (in the Brockhaus edition) have done much towards disclosing the spirit and even the indescribable subtlety of the poet to us. I am almost inclined to place Calderon on a solitary height. Through him I have discovered the significance of the Spanish character—an unheard-of incomparable blossom, developed with such rapidity, that it soon had to arrive at the destruction of matter, and the negation of the world. The fine and deeply passionate spirit of the nation finds expression in the term "honour," which contains all the noblest and at the same time most terrible elements of a second religion; the most frightful selfishness and the noblest sacrifice simultaneously find their embodiment in it. The essence of the "world" proper could never have been expressed more pointedly, more brilliantly, more powerfully and at the same time more destructively, more terribly. The most striking imaginings of the poet have the conflict between this "honour" and a profoundly human pity for their subject. This "honour" determines the actions which are acknowledged and praised by the world, while wounded pity takes refuge in a scarcely expressed, but all the more deeply moving, sublime melancholy, in which we recognise the essence of the world to be terror and nothingness. It is the Catholic religion which tries to bridge over this deep chasm, and nowhere else did it gain such profound significance as here, where the contrast between the world and pity was developed in a more pregnant, more precise, more plastic form than in any other nation. It is very significant for that reason that almost all the great Spanish poets took refuge in priesthood in the second half of their lives. It is a unique phenomenon that from this refuge, and after conquering life by ideal means, these poets were able to describe the same life with greater certainty, purity, warmth, and precision than they had been capable of while they still were in the midst of life. Yea, the most graceful, most humorous creations were given to the light from that ghostly refuge. By the side of this marvellously significant phenomenon, all other national literatures appear to me without importance. If nature produced such an individual as Shakespeare amongst the English, we can easily see that he was unique of his kind; and the fact that the splendid English nation is still in full blossom, carrying on the commerce of the world, while the Spanish nation has perished, moves me so deeply, because it enlightens me as to what is really important in this world.

And now, dear friend, I must tell you that I am very satisfied with myself. This curious and unexpected fact is particularly useful to me for my stay in Paris. Formerly Paris used to fill me with fears of boding evil ; in one sense it excited my desire, while on the other it repelled me terribly, so that I continually felt the sufferings of Tantalus. At present only the repulsive quality remains, while every charm has lost its power. The nature of that repulsiveness I now fully understand, and it appears to me as if my eyes had always possessed an unconscious faculty which has at last become conscious to me. On a journey, in carriages, etc., my gaze always tried involuntarily to read in the eyes of fellow-travellers whether they were capable of, or destined for salvation, that is, negation of the world. A closer acquaintance with them often deceived me as to this point ; my involuntary wish frequently transferred my divine ideal to the soul of another person, and the further course of our acquaintance generally led to an increase of painful disappointment, until, at last, I abandoned and violently cut short that acquaintance.

First sight is less fallible, and as long as my intercourse with the world is of a passing kind, my feeling with regard to it is free from any doubt, resembling, as it does, that perfect consciousness which comes to us on better acquaintance with people, after we have thrown off prolonged and laboriously sustained illusions. Even the passing sight of individuals, in whose features I see nothing but the most terrible error of life,—a restless, either active or passive, desire, —affects me painfully ; how much more then must I be terrified and repelled by a mass of people whose reason for existence appears to be the most shallow volition. These finely and very clearly cut physiognomies of the French, with their strong feeling for charming and sensuously attractive things, show me the qualities which I see in other nations in a washed-out, undeveloped state, with such precision as to make illusion even for a moment impossible. I feel more distinctly than elsewhere in the world that these things are quite strange to me, just because they are so precise, so charming, so refined, so infallible in form and expres-

sion. Let me confess to you that I have scarcely been
able to look at the marvellous new buildings erected
here ; all this is so strange to me that, although I may
gaze at it, it leaves no impression on the mind. As no
delusive hope, that might be excited here, has the
slightest attraction for me, I gain by my absolutely
unimpassioned position towards these surroundings a
calmness which—let me say it with a certain ironic
humour—will probably be of advantage to me in
gaining that for which I strove here in my early days,
and which now, as it has become indifferent to me,
I shall probably attain.

What this possible " attainment " may be I can only
briefly indicate to you. The object of my journey has
been the securing of the rights of property in my operas,
and beyond this I can look for nothing except what
is freely offered to me, and the only person who seems
inclined to make a definite offer is the manager of
the *Théâtre Lyrique.* I saw his theatre ; it pleased me
fairly well, and a new acquisition he had made, a tenor,
pleased me very much. In case he is prepared for
more than ordinary efforts, as to which of course I
must have every security, I might give him *Rienzi,*
provided that I succeeded (perhaps through intercession
of the Grand Duke of Baden with the Emperor of the
French) in obtaining the exceptional privilege of having
my opera performed at this theatre *without spoken
dialogue.*

Ollivier, whom I did not meet till yesterday, and with
whom I am going to dine *en garçon* to-day, received me
with such amiable kindness that I imagined I had arrived
at Altenburg. He made me an unlimited offer of his

services with the manager of the *Théâtre Lyrique*, a personal friend of his, amongst other people. Well, we must see what will come of it; in any case, I should surrender, without much scruple of conscience, *Rienzi*, to gain me an entry, but of course only on the supposition that considerable pecuniary advantages would accrue to me.

I had got so far when Berlioz called on me. After that I had to go out, and found soon that I was not well, the cause probably being a cold, which pulls me down more than usually, because as I remember only now, my food has lately been very bad, I being feeble and very thin in consequence. I had to make my excuses to Ollivier and stop at home in bed. In consequence of this prudent measure I feel a little better, and am expecting Ollivier, who will call for me at two to take me to the concert of the *Conservatoire*; so I will go on talking to you a little about practical things.

It was a real shame that I was once more compelled to take money from you, but this time it is quite certain to be a loan, which I shall repay to you in any circumstances. From the letter of the Princess, I see that you have to use all manner of stealth to get *Rienzi* accepted at the Weimar theatre. This grieves me very much, and I am afraid that a serious conflict between myself and the management will be the result. If this should be the case, the repayment of the thousand francs would become more difficult, but by no means impossible, and in any case I count upon returning the money to you by Easter. As to the employment of what you sent to me, and for which also I thank you cordially, you must please set the mind of the good Princess at rest. I am sorry that this also should trouble her.

Apart from you and Calderon, a glance at the first act of *Tristan*, which I have brought with me, has roused me wonderfully. It is a remarkable piece of music. I feel a strong desire to communicate some of it to some one, and I fear I shall be tempted to play some of it to Berlioz one of these days, although my beautiful performance will probably terrify and disgust him. Could I only be with you! That, you know, is the burden of my song.

Something more about business. The Härtels have replied to my offer of *Tristan*. It was quite amusing. Whatever I may do, the Philistine will think more or less impossible ; to that I am accustomed, and must comfort myself with the success achieved so far by my impossible creations. To sum up, the Härtels accept, in spite of their great doubts, the publication of the work, with a reduction, however, of my demands. Even so they think they are offering a great sacrifice to me, but they say that they are prepared to have the full score engraved at once, and I think that I cannot do better than accept their offer.

I am always loth to write to you about business, and have done so only when I expected you to help me, which unfortunately was the case often enough. This time, however, I want to give you a short synopsis or the state of my Paris expedition. At the beginning or the winter a M. Léopold Amat, *chef* or *directeur des fêtes musicales de Wiesbaden*, wrote to me from Paris, and set forth the results of his voluntary exertions for *Tannhäuser* (at Wiesbaden with Tichatschek and in the

French press). He asked me to authorise him to take the necessary steps for the performance of *Tannhäuser* at the *Grand Opéra*. I informed him that my only and indispensable *condition* would be that an exact translation of the opera, without omission or alteration, should be given. Soon afterwards a M. de Charnal, a young littérateur without reputation, applied to me, asking me for permission to publish a good translation in verse of the poem of *Tannhäuser*, in one of the first *Revues de Paris*. That permission I granted him, on condition that the publication in the review should not imply any further copyright. I am now expecting the pianoforte arrangements of my operas, in order to secure my rights, which will be of importance, whether I want my operas to be performed or whether I want to prevent their performance. The management of the *Grand Opéra* has made no move, but M. Carvalho, of the *Théâtre lyrique*, seems to be lying in wait for me. In case I should do anything with him, I am determined, as I said before, to leave *Rienzi* to his tender mercies, first because that work causes no anxiety to my heart, and may be transmogrified a little for all I care ; second, because the subject and the music are certainly less strange to the Paris public than are my other works. What do you think of it ? To me the whole thing would be purely an *affaire d'argent*, and as such it would no doubt turn out well.

Here you have plenty of business, but I must add one thing more. I have lately laid your poor Vienna cousin under contribution. As my manager at Vienna sent me no money, I asked Haslinger, on the strength of your friendship, to enforce my demands, and as he (being prevented by illness, as I afterwards heard) did not reply, I hunted up the address of your cousin (from 1856), and again invoking your sacred name, asked him to prod on Haslinger. That had the desired effect, and to both I owe it that my manager will probably discharge his debt before long. You see, it is always Franz Liszt, even if he knows nothing about it.

Here you have a very long letter from me. Next time the good Child shall have one equally long; I am deeply in her debt. The practical Princess also shall have a regular professor's letter from me. For to-day I send a thousand thanks and greetings to you all from the bottom of my heart. Be assured of my most faithful veneration.

Long live Altenburg!

Farewell, you dear unique one.

Your

R. W.

Hôtel du Louvre, No. 364.

256.

January 30th, 1858.

You have struck up a regular friendship with Calderon in Paris, dearest Richard; à la bonne heure, he is one of the right sort in whose society one may forget many blackguards and blackguardisms. Unfortunately I know him only very superficially, and have not yet succeeded in making him part of myself. Grillparzer used to tell me wonderful things about him, and if you remain much longer in this element I shall have to read some of his things after you. Let me know on occasion which are the pieces I ought to begin with. His two chief elements, Catholicism and Honour, are both dear to my heart. Do you think something musical might be made of this? I once read the translation by Cardinal Diepenbrock of a wonderful sacred drama, in which heaven, and air, and earth, with all their powers, are set in motion. I forget the title at this moment, but shall find out.

Perhaps you may tell me, some day, how to mould and handle this subject-matter for musical purposes.

I shall have to postpone *Rienzi* till May. We shall invite Tichatschek for it. All that *is possible* will be done, but I am annoyed that the result will again be very small. Fischer of Dresden writes me a very sad letter about the frustration of his hope of producing *Rienzi* there in the course of the winter. He and Tichatschek and many others are cordially devoted to you, and we shall certainly not fail to do our duty as far as in us lies.

Lohengrin will be given here very shortly; I have already had a few rehearsals, because Ortrud, the Herald, and the King will be in new hands. I cannot tell you how deeply the work moves me every time. The last time we performed it I felt proud of my century, because it possessed such a man as you show yourself to be in this work. With *Lohengrin*, the old opera world comes to a close; the spirit moves upon the face of the waters, and there is light.

As to your chances in Paris I have not much to say. It is true that *Rienzi* is amongst your works the most congenial to the Parisians. But whether they will take you up in earnest, and whether in that case you will be able to count upon the sympathy of the manager, the artists, and the press, appears very questionable to me.

Nevertheless you have done well to go to Paris yourself. Go on reading Calderon industriously; it will help you to bear the state of things there, which are in glaring contradiction with your genius and your nature.

Keep me *au courant* of your Paris adventures, and if I can be of any service to you, I need hardly say that you may freely dispose of

Your faithful

FRANCISCUS.

257.

DEAREST FRANZ,

People take care to give me plenty of diversion. From the enclosed letter, which please seal before you forward it to the person in question, you will see that in addition to other troubles I have been robbed. The thief is near you at Jena, where he has had to go for a short time on military duty. You will, I hope, find no difficulty in finding a person attached or semi-attached to the police, who could deal with E. W., late waiter at the hotel here, in the manner indicated by the letter. I think it will be best to frighten the fellow into restoring the money. If we were simply to put him in prison he would deny the charge in order to save himself, and it is always difficult to prove a money robbery in legal form.

Show me your practical wisdom as a police agent. But it must be done very quickly, as the fellow will stay at Jena or Weimar for a little time only. As I start the day after to-morrow, and shall therefore not be in Paris when he comes back, it would be difficult to lay hold of him here.

So much for to-day. I hope I shall find time to write you a rational letter from Paris.

A thousand thanks for your faithful love.

Your

R. W.

The money, if recovered, should be sent to Zurich.

258.

If it were given to me, dearest friend, to give you comfort and strength, I should joyfully make any sacrifice. From Dresden nothing much can be expected as yet, but I shall make another attempt soon. At Carlsruhe they are well inclined towards you, and the day before yesterday I had a long conversation about your sad position with the Grand Duchess of Baden, who, like the Grand Duke, seems to take a lively interest in you. Do not neglect your *Tristan*. For the first performance I should advise you to choose either Carlsruhe or Prague. Weymar would of course follow at once; for the moment, however, I think it more advisable that another stage should take the initiative, and have spoken in that sense to Thomé in Prague. In any case I shall not fail to attend the first performance, and you will oblige me by sending me the score as soon as you have finished it. I intend to lay the work before the Grand Duke, and to ask him earnestly that he may get you from Dresden the permission of conducting the opera here. May God grant that this step will, at last, lead to a favourable result.

Rienzi cannot be given here this season. Frau von Milde is expecting her confinement, and has not been singing these two months, besides which, we are at present unable to fill some other parts properly, and must wait till the end of the year, when several new engagements come into force. I had, as you know, proposed *Rienzi* as gala opera for February 16th ; but a light opera was preferred, and, as such, your tribune of the people would scarcely pass.

You are probably in direct correspondence with Eckert concerning the performance of *Lohengrin* at Vienna. He informed me that the work would be given this autumn. The principal parts will be splendidly cast : Ander (Lohengrin), Meyer (Elsa), and Csillagh (Ortrud), and if Eckert throws his heart into the thing, a great success is beyond all doubt.

Of my performances at Prague, Vienna, and Pesth, you have probably heard from others. Although I have no reason to complain, I am very glad that they are over, and that I may stop at home again; for I must candidly confess that the wear and tear connected with similar occasions is very unpleasant to me, and becomes almost unbearable if it lasts more than a few weeks.

Do not desert *Tristan* ; he is to lead you back soon, and *victoriously*, to Siegfried.

Your
FRANZ.

May 7th, 1858.

259.

I send you to-day a *wonderful fellow,* dearest Richard ; receive him kindly.

Tausig is to work your Erard thoroughly, and to play all manner of things to you.

Introduce him to our mutual friends at Zurich—Herwegh, Wille, Semper, Moleschott, Köchly—and take good care of him.

Your
F. Liszt.

Weymar, *May 18th*, 1858.

260.

Zurich, *July 2nd*, 1858.

At last, dearest Franz, I have once more got so far as to be able to carry out my long-delayed intention of writing to you.

I have to thank you very much for your last letter, to which I thought, upon the whole, silence was the best answer. I hope you understood me rightly. I am generally too talkative, and chat about many things which it would be better to keep to myself. This would be more advantageous to others also, for he who refuses to understand a silent friend will find a talking one troublesome.

Cordial thanks also to the good Princess for her letter.

Of *Tristan* I have sketched the second act; whether I have succeeded I shall see when I come to work it out. It was amusing to me to see you treat this peculiar affair as a matter of literary business in your letter. I explained to the Princess some time ago that the belief of the Prague manager, that I was writing this opera for a first performance at his theatre, was a pure misunderstanding. I could not help smiling at your believing in the assertion of this odd man sufficiently to speak to me seriously of the matter, and to offer me your amiable assistance. You must, of course, have been puzzled at my having the score engraved in this early stage of the proceedings. But there is a very simple reason for it. I had, as you know, no money, and, as *Rienzi* came to nothing, I saw no other way except " doing business " with the Härtels. For that purpose I chose *Tristan*, then scarcely begun, because I had nothing else. They offered to pay me half the honorarium of 200 louis d'or, *i.e.*, 100 louis d'or on receipt of the score of the first act, so I hurried to get it done head over heels. This was the reason of my business-like haste in finishing this poor work. Altogether, the fate of my works, including *Tristan*, has become a matter of great indifference to me ; as to how, where, and when, I care little, as long as I may be present.

The Grand Duke has probably given you my greetings, for which he asked me in a very amiable manner. I did not think it proper to charge him with such a message. H. R. H. wanted to know whether, in case I were permitted to return to Germany, I should go to Weimar, or whether I should prefer another " engagement," and I explained to him that the only advantage I expected from my amnesty was, to be able to visit Germany periodically, and that for that purpose I had chosen your house, because it was your house, as my *pied-à-terre*. That house, fortunately, being at Weimar, the only danger would be that you might refuse to receive me, and his wish of having me at Weimar would entirely depend upon your friendship, which, therefore, he should try to perpetuate. With that he was quite satisfied.

You have given me great pleasure with little Tausig.

When he came into my room, one fine morning, bringing your letter, I shook you cordially by the hand. He is a terrible youth. I am astonished, alternately, by his highly developed intellect and his wild ways. He will become something extraordinary, if he becomes anything at all. When I see him smoking frightfully strong cigars, and drinking no end of tea, while as yet there is not the slightest hope of a beard, I am frightened like the hen, when she sees the young ducklings, whom she has hatched by mistake, take to the water. What will become of him I cannot foresee, but whisky and rum he will not get from me. I should, without hesitation, have taken him into my house, if we had not mutually molested each other by pianoforte playing. So I have found him a room in a little hole close to me, where he is to sleep and work, doing his other daily business at my house. He does, however, no credit to my table, which, in spite of my grasswidowerhood, is fairly well provided. He sits down to table every day stating that he has no appetite at all, which pleases me all the less, because, the reason is, the cheese and the sweets he has eaten. In this manner he tortures me continually, and devours my biscuits, which my wife doles out grudgingly even to me. He hates walking, and yet declares that he would like to come with me when I propose to leave him at home. After the first half hour he lags behind, as if he had walked four hours. My childless marriage is thus suddenly blessed with an interesting phenomenon, and I take in, in rapid doses, the quintessence of paternal cares and troubles. All this has done me a great deal of good; it was a splendid diversion, for which, as I said before, I have to thank you. You knew what I wanted. Of course the youth pleases me immensely in other ways, and, although he acts like a naughty boy, he talks like an old man of pronounced character. Whatever subject I may broach with him, he is sure to follow me with clearness of mind and remarkable receptivity. At the same time it touches and moves me, when this boy shows such deep, tender feeling, such large sympathy, that he captivates me irresistibly. As a musician he is enormously gifted, and his furious pianoforte playing makes me tremble. I must always think of you and of the strange influence which you exercise over so many, and often considerably gifted, young men. I cannot but call you happy, and genuinely admire your harmonious being and existence.

My wife will return in a fortnight, after having finished her cure, which will have lasted three months. My anxiety about her was terrible, and for two months I had to expect the news of her death from day to day. Her health was ruined, especially by the immoderate use of opium, taken nominally as a remedy for sleeplessness. Latterly the cure she uses has proved highly beneficial; the great weakness and want of appetite have disappeared, and the recovery of the chief functions (she used to perspire continually), and a certain abatement of her incessant excitement, have become noticeable. The great enlargement of her heart will be bearable to her only if she keeps perfectly calm and avoids all excitement to her dying day. A thing of this kind can never be got rid of entirely. Thus I have to undertake new duties, over which I must try to forget my own sufferings.

Well, and how about you ? Will you come to my assistance again this year ? Your kind heart promises me to do so every year, but, during the nine years of my exile, I have succeeded only twice in tearing you away from your great dense world. Although you have promised me your visit for this year, you will find it natural if I am not too certain of seeing my wish fulfilled. I must add several marks of interrogation and of prayer.

Cordial thanks to the dear, heavenly Child for her last letter ; I hope my silence was eloquent.

A thousand greetings and cordial responses to you three dear ones ! I also wish to be remembered to F. Müller, who sent me a beautiful letter of congratulation on my birthday. I shall write to him soon, without fail.

Farewell, dear Franz. You can imagine how often I am with you, especially when Tausig is sitting at the piano. Between us, all is one. Farewell, and continue to love me.

Your

R. W.

261.

DEAREST RICHARD,

When I saw the Grand Duke last night for the first time after his return, he told me much about the visit you paid him at Lucerne. I do not know what impression your acquaintance with him has left on you, as we have had no news from you for such a long time, but from what I have heard, and what has already happened, I conclude with tolerable certainty that we shall see you here for the first performance of *Tristan*, *at the latest.* May God grant that it will be sooner; and I need not tell you that nothing I can do will be left undone.

Dingelstedt will shortly write to you about *Rienzi*, which is to be performed next season, in December or January. Last winter we were unable to get on with the work for reasons which, as they exist no longer, are not sufficiently important to be discussed.

Let me soon hear from you.

Your

F. L.

July 3rd, 1858.

I enclose a letter to Tausig, which you will be kind enough to hand to him.

How is he getting on at Zurich, and what do you think of him?

262.

ZURICH, *July 8th,* 1858.

This affair of T. and X., dearest Franz, has become very significant to me. It has shown me most clearly and definitely that even amongst the best of friends a certain mode of action may be perverted beyond recognition into its very opposite; and I look with horror upon the cares of this world, where everything is ruled by confusion and error to the verge of madness. It was absolutely terrible to me to read your charges against T. What I felt is difficult to describe; it was like a longing for death. About this young T. I recently wrote to you in a very unconventional manner. Two things make me overlook all his shortcomings, and attach me to him to such a degree that I feel inclined to place much confidence in him. One of them is his boundless love for you, the absolute abandonment of his impertinence as soon as you are mentioned, his most tender and deep reverence for you; the other, the beautiful warmth and genuine friendship which he shows at every moment for X. In the present case also he defended the latter in a really touching manner, and speaks of him always with enthusiastic praise of his heart and his intellect. Were it not for these two traits I should not know what to think of this young man, who speaks of God and the world in the most ruthless manner. Curiously enough, your reproach hit him in this particular point, and when he showed me your letter there was a peculiar desperate question in his glance. With such experiences the boy will become quickly, almost too quickly, mature.

My words will show you how deeply this matter has affected me; it is one of the thousand things which, when they occur to me, estrange me more and more from this world.

Farewell, and write to me again soon.

Always cordially your

R. W.

263.

I cannot understand in what manner I have caused *you* grief, but I feel the painful rebound of your wounded heart. My admonition to T. proceeded from a pure cause. X. himself knew nothing of it, and T.

would have done well if he had kept silence towards
you. "Insinuations" and "diplomacy" are surely out
of the question. I greatly dislike mixing myself up
with other people's affairs, and if I have done so
this time, it was certainly not because I was led to
it by others (I give you my word, that not a word
has been said or written about the whole matter), but
merely because it had been imposed upon me as a kind
of duty to act as guardian to T., and it appeared only
too probable that his conduct had not been very correct.
The young Titan sometimes gives way to an absence
of mind and a state of overexcitement, against which
those who wish him well should warn him. His
exceptional talent and his genial and prepossessing
manner generally incline me towards being overin-
dulgent with him, and I do not deny my genuine love
and partiality for this remarkable specimen of a "Liszt
of the future," as T. has been called at Vienna. But for
that very reason I expect him to be a good and steady
fellow in all respects.

Be thanked for the kindly friendship and care you
bestow upon him. I hope he will not only profit by
them, but honour them. The rare happiness of living
near you, and of being distinguished by you, should
form and mature him as an artist and as a man.

Ever thine,

F. L.

July 18th, 1858.

264.

DEAREST RICHARD,

Before the 18th inst. I cannot get away from

here ; the centenary celebration of Jena University will take place on the 15th, 16th, and 17th, and I have promised to take part in it. Apart from this, I expect in a few days a visit, which is of importance to me.

It was my intention to see you at the beginning of September, but I will gladly undertake the journey a few weeks sooner. You on your part must delay your journey by a fortnight, and write to me by return whether I shall find you at Zurich on the 20th instant. I should, of course, not make this journey unless I could be certain of being a few days with you. Trips of pleasure or recreation are not my affair any longer, and I could not consent to one. On the other hand, I shall be genuinely pleased to see you again.

Your

F. LISZT.

August 6th, 1858.

265.

GENEVA, *August 20th,* 1858.

DEAREST FRANZ,

Kindly make inquiries whether I might stay a short time at Venice which does not belong to the German confederacy without being claimed, extradited and otherwise molested. The *visé* of my passport I got from the Austrian minister without any difficulty. I daresay the Saxon minister would have given me his *visé* too (in order to get hold of me).

If there is any danger, kindly let the Grand Duke intercede for me, so that I may stay at Venice without being bothered.

I should be very thankful to him, for that quiet, interesting city tempts me greatly.

I shall delay my departure till I hear from you ; in any case I must wait till the heat is over.

Farewell, and be thanked for all your friendship.

Your

R. W.

MAISON FAZY, 3° ETAGE.

266.

GENEVA, August, 24th, 1858.

DEAREST FRANZ,

Best thanks for your reply. It somewhat startled me, and I made inquiries through a friend in Berne of the Austrian minister there. I enclose his answer, from which you will see that for the present I have nothing to fear at Venice. Whether they will allow me to stay there for any length of time is a different question which is of great importance to me. I feel the necessity of living in strict seclusion for some considerable period, in order to devote myself entirely to my work. The country will not, in the long run, do for this, and in an indifferent town I might, at last, be reduced to making acquaintance with commonplace people—the worst of all evils. One of the interesting, large cities of Italy is exactly what I want. In such surroundings one can most easily keep to oneself, for every walk presents objects of an important kind, and satisfies the want of men and things. But in large towns the noise of carriages is absolutely unbearable to me ; it drives me wild. Venice is notoriously the quietest, <i>i.e.</i>, most noiseless city in the world, which has decided me in its favour. Apart from this Dr. W. and K.R. have given me the most attractive accounts of life in Venice ; the latter will spend the winter there.

Finally, Venice is more convenient for my frequent communications with Germany than any other Italian town would be ; by way of Vienna my letters, etc., will reach the centre of Germany in no time. In short, I am obstinately fixed on Venice, and do not want to think of any other choice, because it is not travelling about, but settling down as soon as possible that I care for.

Listen, therefore. Kindly ask the Grand Duke in my name, for the special favour of securing for me, by his intercession in Vienna, an undisturbed sojourn in Venice. This is indispensable for my future, for such a permission would permanently open to me Venice and Austrian Italy generally. Let therefore the Grand Duke show himself my well-inclined protector, and do all in his power to comply with my wish.

It will further be necessary that your friend should graciously take the necessary steps as soon as possible. If, in the meantime, I should get into difficulties, I should at once claim his protection.

Therefore, please, please go to court at once ! Help me and do what I wish.

From Venice I shall write again ; till then continue to love me.

Your

R. W.

VENICE, *poste restante.—Dépêche télégraphique.*

BERNE, *Le 24 Août, Tuesday,* 1858.

To RICHARD WAGNER,
Geneva,
Maison Fazy.

Austrian minister thinks you have nothing to fear if your passport has the Austrian *visé.*

He can guarantee nothing, but is morally certain that you will not be molested. Telegraphic inquiry of the *Gouverneur* of Venice, he thinks imprudent because exciting attention and necessitating inquiry at Vienna. Answer would take too long. Dangerous refugees are notified to the embassy to prevent *visé* of their passports, which is not the case with you. Minister thinks your journey quite safe, but cannot personally give you any further information. *Bon voyage,* dear friend.

FRÖLICH.

267.

DEAREST RICHARD,

Bad news again! All the inquiries I have made agree on the point that your stay in Venice will by no means be secure. The Grand Duke, to whom I communicated the contents of your last letter, has commissioned me simply to advise you against the journey, and to recommend to you (as I have already done) Genoa or Sardinia. From Dresden I hear that there is at present no hope of your amnesty, and that the statements to that effect in several newspapers have not been confirmed. Nevertheless, I hope that some "measure" in your favour, I mean the permission of staying for a time at one place or another in Germany, will be taken, through means of the Grand Duke of Baden or the Grand Duke of Weymar. The performance of *Tristan,* at Carlsruhe or elsewhere, will offer the best opportunity, and as soon as you have finished ·the work, I beg of you to neglect nothing which may facilitate your return to Germany, although at first only for a few months for the special purpose of conducting *Tristan* in person. As far as I know your situation, or rather your connections and relations, I think you will have, in the first instance, to apply to the Grand Duke of Baden ; the young Prince is much in your favour, as is also the Grand Duchess. With our Prince I have, of course, discussed the matter frequently and at great length. I have, it is true, not been able to get a positive promise from him, but I think it very probable that when the time comes for *Tristan* he will not fail to give you a proof of the interest in you which he has frequently ·expressed, and, as you know, has shown by several letters and intercessions in your favour.

I wish, dearest Richard, I could give you pleasanter and more desirable news, but certain things cannot be changed or broken through all at once. From Austria you cannot expect much for the recovery of your personal liberty. It would be half a miracle if anything of the kind should happen. Even the performance of your operas at Vienna is an example of exceptional toleration, considering the customs of the country. To demand more would appear to me illusory. Your *political* expectations in Austria are as small as are your *artistic* expectations in Paris and Italy. Performances of your works in the French or Italian language must for the present be looked upon as *pia desideria*, or else as newspaper *canards*.

I am sometimes surprised (forgive my candour) that you fail to perceive that if a performance of *Tannhäuser* were given at Paris or Milan, it would take place in very unfavourable circumstances. (I do not speak of London, where a good *German* opera troupe might have a chance.) For several years to come the only true soil for your works is Germany; that soil they will occupy more and more firmly, and in advance of all other productions. Do not allow yourself to be led away by vague talking, and preserve your justifiable pride. . . . .

. . . .

I start to-night with the Princess and her daughter for the Tyrolese mountains. Address your next letter, *Hôtel de Bavière*, Munich, whence it will be forwarded to me. I cannot say, for the present, where we shall make a longer stay. About September 20th we shall once more pass through Munich, and shall be back here on October 1st at the latest.

When you can spare a quiet hour, let me know why you did not care to stay a few days longer at Zurich, where I intended to visit you on the 20th inst. at the latest. Several business matters (mostly in connection with the Grand Duke), and the University celebration at Jena, on August 15th (where I had undertaken to conduct some of my compositions), made it impossible for me to leave here sooner.

However that may be, I remain invariably your faithful and loving

F. Liszt.

Weymar, *August 26th*, 1858.

268.

Venice, *September 12th*, 1858.

Dear Franz,

I have just received your letter, dated 26th ult., which had lain at Geneva all that time. I see from it that you are very near me, and I hope I need only tell you that I am here in order to be able to expect your visit. Descend the Tyrolese mountains on this side, and you are with me. I should like much to reply by word of mouth to all you tell me, including your most curious ideas as to my designs on Italy.

Let me see you soon. A thousand greetings from

Your

R. W.

CANAL GRANDE, PALAZZO GIUSTINIANI,
CAMPIELLO SQUILLINI, No. 3228, VENICE.

269.

VENICE, *September 27th*, 1858.
PALAZZO GIUSTINIANI,
CAMPIELLO SQUILLINI, 3228.

DEAREST FRANZ,

Your letter of 23rd ult. was forwarded to me from Geneva very late, and I saw from it that you were near me,—" in the Tyrolese mountains," you said,—and this raised the hope in me that I should see you and speak to you soon. I must doubt, however, whether my letter to that effect, addressed to you *Hôtel de Bavière*, Munich, reached you in time, because I have neither seen nor heard anything of you. I feel that my desire of personal communication with you will not be realised, and I therefore write to you as to certain points, in connection with which I owe you an explanation.

Altogether this cannot amount to much ; you had to attend to University celebrations, etc., which, pardon me for saying so, appeared extremely trivial to me. I did not press you any more, but I must confess that when at last I received the news of your intended arrival on the 20th, it did not impress me very much.

Of my desire of selecting Venice for my place of abode, I gave you a full account in my last letter from Geneva, in which I also informed you of the satisfactory news I had had from the Austrian minister at Berne. I am in quest of repose and absolute retirement, such as only a larger town can offer to me. My attitude towards my surroundings must be an absolutely negative one; in that manner alone can I gain leisure and the proper mood for my work.

Your warnings and admonitions not to rely on the performance of my operas in Italy I pass over. Whatever can have given you the curious and mistaken notion that my journey to Italy had this ambitious, artistic purpose, I fail to see. I have selected an Italian town because I hate Paris, and because here in Venice I am certain to be removed from any possible contact with artistic publicity. This was not the case even at Zurich, which for that reason had long since become disagreeable to me. That newspaper writers explain my sojourn in Venice as a political manœuvre in order gradually to open Germany to me, is quite in accordance with the spirit and intellect of such people. I hope you will soon divest yourself of the idea that anything similar was in my mind. As an Austrian city, Venice exists for me only in so far as it does not belong to the German Confederacy, and as I may consequently live there in security. This has proved to be true. Unfortunately I could not prevent my landlord from trumpeting about my stay here, which in consequence was made public sooner than I desired. The police which, once more, asked for my passport, has, however, returned it to me with the remark that there is nothing against my undisturbed stay at Venice. Whether this was the result of the intercession of the Grand Duke, for which I had asked, I cannot tell.

You will be pleased to hear that Venice has not disappointed my expectations. The melancholy silence of the Grand Canal, on the banks of which I live in a stately palace with large rooms, is sympathetic to me. Amusement and an agreeable diversion of the mind is afforded by a daily walk in the square of St. Mark, a trip in a gondola to the islands, walks there, etc. It will be the turn of the art treasures later on. The entirely new and interesting character of the surroundings is very pleasant to me. I am waiting for my grand piano, and hope to resume my work without interruption next month. My only thought is of completing *Tristan*, nothing else.

Farewell; accept my corrections in the benevolent spirit of a true friend. Pardon the seriousness which pervades me, and all my opinions and judgments. Let me hear something kind from you, and, before all, answer this letter soon.

Always and ever thine

R. W.

270.

SALZBURG, *October 9th*, 1858.

The news about you, contained in the papers during last month, was so different and so contradictory that I did not know where to write to you. At last your arrival at Vienna was announced, and when this premature statement was contradicted, some one wrote to me that you had gone to Florence or Paris. By your last letter, which reached me on the day of my departure from Munich, I see that for the present you intend to remain in Venice, and that the Government does not object to your stay there. I wish with my whole heart that you may find rest at Venice, and be able to settle comfortably, and to resume and complete your works. *Fiat pax in virtute tua* is a prayer in the service of the Mass, which I repeat to you from the bottom of my heart. The information which I received as to the security of your stay at Venice was not of a kind to make me think your domicile there, even for a short time, an advisable thing. Even now I entertain some doubts, which, however, I hope will prove futile. It is a great pity that we cannot live together, and I long unspeakably for the day when this will be possible. Lately, again, I spoke to the Grand Duke about your situation, and conjured him to set everything in motion in order to open your return to Germany. He promised that he would do so. The remarks in my last letter in reference to the performances of your works in the French or Italian language you seem to have misunderstood. By several things which you had previously written to me, and by your last journey to Paris, this possibility was suggested to me for discussion, and my only intention was, of course, to explain my view of the matter to you, without in the least wishing to prejudice you. The Queen of England had told you that an Italian performance of

your works would be desirable; of Roger's *Tannhäuser*
we had spoken several times, and you had also come to
an understanding with Ollivier as to the *a, oits d'auteur.*
My expectations of all this are small, and I cannot agree
with others of your friends as to the opportuneness and
desirability of performances in a foreign language;
indeed I should think it more advisable not to attach
any importance to them for the present, and to make
no attempt in that direction. But you must not charge
me with having evolved the whole matter from my
imagination. In the worst case, my view would simply
be an erroneous one, but you should not misunderstand
or disapprove of my intention of saving you unnecessary
trouble. You have struck your roots entirely in German
soil; you are, and remain, the glory and splendour of
German art. While theatrical affairs abroad are in
their present condition, while Meyerbeer and Verdi
reign supreme, while theatrical managers, singers, con-
ductors, newspapers, and the public are under their
immediate influence, there is no need for you to mix
yourself up with this muddle.

Another point in your letter, dearest Richard, has
almost hurt me, although I can well understand that
you think the official impediments which prevented
my journey to Zurich trivial, and that you fail to give
due importance to the University Jubilee of Jena, and
to the many considerations which I have to observe,
were it only in order to be occasionally useful to you
in small matters. In a calmer mood you will easily
understand that I cannot and dare not leave Weymar
at every moment, and you will surely feel that the
delay of my journey to Zurich was caused by no kind

of *triviality*. When I wrote to you that I should be with you on August 20th, I made no doubt that even in case of your earlier departure from Zurich you would appoint another place, Lucerne or Geneva, for a meeting. As you failed to do so, I came to a conclusion which I am only too happy to abandon on your word.

Enough of this, dearest Richard: we shall remain what we are—inseparable, true friends, and such.another pair will not be found soon.

During the first half of September I roamed about the Tyrolese mountains with the Princess and her daughter, and we stayed a few days quite alone in the Ötz-valley. Driven away by bad weather, we returned to Munich, quietly witnessed the festivities, and saw our friend Kaulbach every day. Lachner told me that he had had some correspondence with you about an early performance of *Rienzi*. *Tannhäuser* I heard again at Munich, but *Lohengrin* had to be postponed owing to the sudden indisposition of Herr Lindemann. Since I heard some passages of it from you, I know more of it than all the performances can teach me.

In order to carry out our original plan, and assert our rights even against the bad weather, we have come to Salzburg, and shall be back at Weymar in about a week. Probably I shall find there the proofs of my *Dante* symphony, which I shall send to you at once, as the true child of my sufferings.

When shall I have the joy of reading *Tristan*? The Härtels informed me that the pianoforte score was in print. Have you quite settled as to where the first performance is to take place? According to all accounts the Carlsruhe people reckon upon it for certain. May God grant that *Tristan* will put an end to your exile. This is my hope.

Rienzi with Tichatschek is to be given at Weymar in the course of the winter. Previous to that I shall go to Dresden, where I have promised Rietschel to pay my *old* debt to Weber, and to make *one* exception by playing several of Weber's pianoforte compositions at a concert for the benefit of the Weber monument, the model of which Rietschel has executed with incomparable mastery. On that occasion I shall ask for a performance of *Rienzi* at the theatre, in accordance with which I shall arrange that of Weymar, so far as our means will allow us. If I had a little more money I should have preferred to pay the balance which is still due on the subscription for the Weber monument in hard cash, instead of playing to the people a few hackneyed pieces. Weber must forgive a poor devil like me that I can do nothing better for him. You wrote to me about this matter many years ago, and now that the model of the monument is ready, it is a point of honour to make an end of the matter and commence casting it in metal. Write to me at Weymar how you like the city of the Lagunes. I presume that C. R. is with you. Remember me to him kindly, and tell him that I sincerely approve of his sonatas published by Härtel.

With invariable friendship, I remain cordially and sincerely

Your
F. LISZT.

271.

Be thanked, dear friendly friend; your beautiful friendship is the only thing that still impresses me; you give it me purely, fully.

As regards my fate, I look forward with patience to calm, clear, quietly active years. My work has become dearer to me than ever. I have resumed it lately; it flows from my spirit like a gentle stream.

In all my relations to the suffering world one thing guides and determines me—pity. When I give myself up to it unconditionally, all my personal suffering ceases.

I have at last got my Erard. It stands in the large echoing hall which serves me as a study. There *Tristan* is to be finished this winter. The first act, dearest friend, is quite complete; ask the Härtels to give you the proof-sheets of the full score, which is already engraved. In the completion of the second act, which I have only slightly sketched, I am continually interrupted by visits. I have just begun working at it again; it will be very beautiful, and is to be finished and printed by the end of this year at the latest. By March the last act will follow, and if all goes well I shall witness the first performance about Easter. You are aware that, through Eduard Devrient's intercession, the Grand Duke of Baden has acquired a right in this work. If he can arrange to get me permission to go to Carlsruhe for the performance, it will take place there. But of this hope also I do not make a vital question; I can wait.

Venice continues to be most sympathetic to me; my

choice was guided by instinct, and has turned out well. This kind of retirement is most pleasant to me. I see just enough to occupy my fancy agreeably ; nothing disturbs me. That, looking upon this peaceful scene, I also was allowed to look upon you, and that you appeared to me in so beautiful and blissful a light as you did in your last letter, has crowned my happiness.

Be thanked my dear, noble, unique friend ! Shall I say more ? You know all that these words imply.

Greet the Princess and the good Child ; they are to be annoyed by nothing in the world, and they are to love me as much as they can.

I hope that these lines will affect you as sympathetically as yours have made me happy.

Farewell, and be always assured of my responsive love.

Your
RICHARD W.

It would be a good omen if this letter were to reach you on your birthday.

272.

VENICE, October 23rd, 1858.

After I had settled with R. on the 21st that we were to congratulate you jointly on your birthday, he came to me on the 22nd and told me that he had just sent you a telegram. By way of revenge I ordered a dinner with oysters and champagne in the Square of St. Mark, to which a military band played the overture of *Rienzi* most excellently. We drank your health and clinked our glasses, and had a most pleasant evening.

Of this I send you documentary evidence by this letter.

Your
R. W.

273.

VENICE, October 26th, 1858.

DEAREST FRANZ,

I have just had a letter from Munich telling me that they have given up *Rienzi* owing to religious scruples. I want money, much money, in order to get honestly through my difficult position, and am looking out everywhere for a little business. I have just offered my *Lohengrin* to the Cassel management. If you can help me there, do so.

I should not like myself to write to Coburg, where I have been neglected in a surprising manner. Do you know of a channel through means of which you could bring it about that they should buy *Lohengrin* and the *Dutchman* as well? Think of this and help me in the old way.

A thousand greetings from your

R. W.

274.

DEAREST RICHARD,

R.'s telegram of October 21st was received with joyful acclamation, and your letter, which arrived on the same evening, was the most welcome birthday present on account of the calm, conciliatory mood which I felt in it. May you soon resume your work joyfully! I hope you are getting on with *Tristan*, of which as yet I do not know a single note. In accordance with your last letter, I have asked the Härtels to lend me the score for a few days when the engraver does not want it any longer.

Your hints as to the performances of *Lohengrin*, *The Flying Dutchman*, and *Rienzi* in Cassel, Gotha, and other cities will not be neglected, and I need not assure you again that I shall do all in my power. First of all you will receive a letter concerning *Rienzi* from my chief and friend Dingelstedt. The opera is to be given here in January. Be kind enough to reply to Dingelstedt's letter with some *politeness*, and do not be annoyed at my making this remark. I wish very much to incline Dingelstedt a little more favourably towards the performance of your works and to co-operate with him in perfect sympathy. That co-operation is of importance to me not only as regards *Tristan*, which will meet with no difficulty, and, as I hope and longingly wish, will open your return to Germany, but chiefly with a view to the performance of the *Nibelungen*, which is our ultimate goal. The honorarium of 25 louis d'or which our theatrical exchequer can offer you is very small, but I advise you to accept it, and take it upon myself to get you a small *douceur* from the Grand Duke's privy purse later on.

I should like to have Tichatschek for the first two performances of *Rienzi*, although that would increase the expense considerably. But I have a great liking for him, and wish to get him some distinction from the Grand Duke on that occasion.

Last Sunday we gave *Komala* by Sobolewski. I do

not know whether you have seen a small pamphlet
" Opera, not Drama," which he published last year as
an introduction to his opera. The following beautiful
comparison occurs in it: " The words are the hard,
transparent pieces of incense, the melody is the beautiful scent which emerges from the thick clouds of smoke,
when the incense has been lit." In many other things
I cannot agree with him, especially not as regards the
marks of punctuation, by means of which he tries to
distinguish himself from you, when at the end of the
pamphlet he exclaims : " Wagner says, *Opera not,*—
Drama; I say *Opera, not Drama.*" His *Komala* is
better than his comma, and his practice much better
than his theory. There is much in it that would please
you, and has undoubtedly been originated by *Lohengrin*.
Sobolewski wrote *Komala* at first in three acts, and had
it done in that form at Bremen. Afterwards, in honour
of operatic theory, and probably persuaded by the
critics who thirst for contrasts and operatic tunes, he
added two acts more, in which he introduced vocal
pièces de salon, reminding one of the Queen in the
Huguenots, and the inevitable drinking chorus. By
his desire I preserved the five acts at the first performance, but at the second I omitted the two additional
ones without any consideration, or rather, for very good
considerations, and shall even take the liberty of altering
his *finale*, which has been fashioned after your *finale*
of the second act of *Tannhäuser* ("*nach Rom*"), and
after the last act of *Iphigenia in Aulis*. In that manner
the work will appear in its only true form, and may
keep its place as a fine musical cloud-and-mist picture
in perfect accord with Ossian's poem.

For your private benefit I send you a few motives from *Komala,* which I copied for you.

About the middle of November we shall perform here a comic opera, *The Barber of Bagdad,* founded on a tale from the " Arabian Nights," words and music by Cornelius. The music is full of wit and humour, and moves with remarkable self-possession in the aristrocratic region of art. I expect a very good result. *Rienzi* will be taken in hand immediately afterwards.

Excuse me for having delayed writing to you so long. I am up to the ears in all manner of business and correspondence, and have not had a free hour since my return. Please do not retaliate, and let me have good news of you soon.

Your

F. Liszt.

November 5th, 1858.

Kindly give the enclosed few lines to Ritter. The additions to the *Dante* symphony and to the Gran Mass will be ready before Christmas, and I shall send you both together.

275.

Venice, *November* 21*st,* 1858.

My dear Franz,

Many thanks for your kind letter ; I had nothing particular to tell you, or would have replied to you sooner. In addition to this I was ill during the whole first half of November, which was more than I had bargained for, especially as it interrupted my work in the most unpleasant manner. Now I am well again and all will be right. I am looking forward to

the Mass and *Dante* which you promise to send to me.
Mind you keep your word. I have asked the Härtels
to send you proof sheets of the first act of *Tristan.*
Perhaps you have received them by this time. The
Härtels treat me with much forbearance. At first
when I thought that the score would be finished this
autumn, I prodded them on terribly. Since then I
have left them miserably in the lurch. Before the end
of December I cannot think of sending them the second
act. I cannot help this, because I must wait for the
most favourable mood to go on with the work. The
Nibelungen question has also been mooted again by us.
I shall have these things engraved now, and shall leave
the discussion of the honorarium till after the performance. In this matter a very droll intermezzo has been
played, or rather it has not been played out yet,
because its conclusion will probably take place in a few
days. I shall relate this adventure to you when it is
finished.

My affairs are in a somewhat miserable condition.
Rienzi is not getting on in spite of the continued
success of the Dresden revival. The first disappointment came from Munich where I had expected to get
an honorarium of fifty louis d'or. They wrote to me
that the reading committee objected to the subject on
religious grounds. I pity that dear religion! It is
partly your fault that it is put to such uses now ; why
do you write beautiful Masses for the parsons ? From
Hanover also I expected an immediate remittance, and
could not understand the delay, when I heard that
Niemann, after having heard Tichatschek in *Rienzi*, did
not feel competent to sustain the part with equal voice-

power. Therefore it was given up. Breslau alone is sufficiently bold, and will venture upon it. I wish I could find some one who would do justice to the real character of the part, in which case he need not be afraid of singing it even before Tichatschek. I have hinted so much to Niemann. I am thus, once more, reduced to my old capital, *Tannhäuser* and *Lohengrin*, and they are no longer sufficient for my present difficult position.

D. wrote to me five and a half lines, inquiring as to my terms. You probably know my reply. I wish the inhuman creature had sent me the money at once. Good Lord, what Jacks-in-office you all are! None of you can put himself in the place of a poor devil like me who looks upon every source of income as a lucky draw in a lottery. Please, tread gently upon his toe.

K. R. left me to-day, probably for a few weeks, in order to congratulate his mother on her birthday at Dresden. If he finds it possible he will pay you a visit at Weimar.

W. remains with me in his place ; he arrived from Vienna with a Russian family a month ago, in order to spend the winter here. Fortunately, he keeps quiet and does not molest me, for being by myself is the boon which I enjoy, and watch over with painful care. In the Square I am literally run after by foreign princes ; one of them, D., who boasts of knowing you personally, I was unable to avoid. He lives where I have my dinner and, occasionally, waylays me. He is an odd and apparently good-natured person. To-day he dropped down upon me with much enthusiasm between the soup and the cutlets, in order to tell me that he had heard one of your symphonic poems beautifully played on the piano, and by whom? By a Venetian music-teacher, who has been made an enthusiast for German music by you and me. This amused me very much. D. also has been gained for your cause. What more can you desire? And all this happened in the Square of St. Mark at dinner, the weather being infamously cold.

Be of good cheer then, and may God bless you. Continue to love me. Write to me soon, and greet Altenburg a thousand times for

Your
R. W.

276.

VENICE, November 26th, 1858.

I enclose you a beautiful autograph.

I cannot tell you how comic it appears to me that I have to transact Weimar business with F. D. I have a good mind to tell *him* that he had better leave my opera alone. Weimar has lost all its charm for me since I have to meet so formal a person before I can get at you and the Grand Duke. You are a very tedious set of people.

You told me two years ago that you were in possession of a score of *Rienzi* which I had left there on my flight. If that is so, I should be glad if you would not attach much importance to its possession. My original score is always at your disposal in case, as I scarcely believe, you should care much about this opus. I have only a very few copies left. At the time I had no more than twenty-five copies made, more than half of which I have squandered away. If it *must* be, get a copy from Fischer in Dresden, and submit it reverentially in my name to the great Dingelstedt. Have you had your score altered by Fischer? In the third act there is a long cut and a change necessitated by it which I made for Hamburg.

Good Lord! it is miserable that one has to take all this trouble for a little money. I am once more confined to my room, and cannot even get up from my chair; a neglected abscess in my leg causes me terrible pain; sometimes in the middle of my music I call out loudly, which has a very fine effect.

Have the Härtels sent you the first act of *Tristan*? You will have copies of the poem before long.

Farewell for to-day. I have to indulge in a few shrieks, which in a letter would not sound well.

A thousand greetings—oh!

From your
R. W.
(oh!!)

Have I really to wait for the wretched twenty-five louis d'or—oh!!—till after the *performance*? Lord only knows when that will take place—oh!!

277.

VENICE, *December 5th*, 1858.

I made haste, dearest friend, to write to D. in accordance with your summons sent to me through our Princess.

I wrote to him that doubts had arisen in me whether I still desired the performance of *Rienzi* at Weimar, and I ask you to agree with me and give up the plan.

If anything could have induced me to push my *Rienzi*
at this time of day it would, as you will understand,
have been the desire of deriving a good income from it,
such as would have been welcome in my poor and uncertain condition.   In itself I look upon this revival as
an anachronism which, moreover, would be quite premature.   After the recent great success of the opera at
Dresden I was in hopes that the rapid sale of this opus
would supply me with sufficient means for my present
wants.   That hope, however, has been deceived in the
most important points, especially with regard to Munich
and Hanover, as I recently informed you.   By offering
this opera broadcast I had to humiliate my pride very
much, and I have now become very sensitive as to this
matter.   At Weimar, too, the opera is, properly considered, an intruder, and is evidently being looked
upon as such.   You enlightened me upon this point
last winter, when you explained to me the reason for
its delay.   But I do not desire that you should force
this juvenile production upon any one in Weimar.   The
reasons for keeping on good terms on such an occasion
with this person or that person do not exist for me, and
my sincere wish is, that they should not exist for you
either.   In this matter we two should agree.   Whether or
not I perform my *Nibelungen* at some future time is at
bottom a matter of indifference to me.   I shall complete
it in any case, for my enthusiasm and strength for such
works I do not derive from any hopes, for the realisation of which I should require certain people.   All that
the world and my "admirers" and "worshippers" of
whom I have to hear so much can do for me, is to look
upon my whole situation in a serious and sympathetic

light, and to do all in their power to ease my heavy
cares and to preserve to me the pleasure and leisure
which I require for my work. Beyond this I want nothing.
But to attain it, very different efforts are necessary
from those which have hitherto come to my knowledge.

Enough of this. I can do without the Weimar
honorarium and *douceur* for *Rienzi*, which, in any case,
would come too late to be of service to me. By next
Easter, till which time I should have to wait, I shall be
able to help myself in other ways; in the meantime it
will be a hard struggle, but I shall manage somehow.

Even the Weimar receipts would, unfortunately, not
have enabled me to repay your 1,000 francs.

To sum up : you will, undoubtedly, save yourself much
trouble and unpleasantness by giving up *Rienzi*. If
you have Tichatschek in the spring let him sing Lohengrin ; that will give you much more pleasure.

Imagine that for a week and a half I have not been
able to move from my chair. This illness was just what
was required to finish me up. I had just resumed my
work a little, after a gastric and nervous indisposition,
when I was obliged to give in again. However, I am
getting better, and hope to be able to walk and work
again next week.

Farewell, and be pressed to my heart a thousand
times.

Your
R. W.

278.

Dearest Richard,

Härtel has sent me a divine Christmas present.
All the children in the world cannot be so delighted

with their trees and the golden apples and splendid gifts suspended thereon as I, in my own person, am with your unique *Tristan.* Away with all the cares and tribulations of every-day existence ! Here one can weep and glow again. What blissful charm, what undivined wealth of beauty in this fiery love-potion ! What must you have felt while you created and formed this wondrous work ? What can I tell you about it beyond saying that I feel with you in my heart of hearts !

However, in my capacity of practical friend, I must speak to you of commonplace things. Your negative answer to D., much as it grieved me in many respects, came at the *right moment.* I proposed, as you know, *Rienzi* for performance eighteen months ago, and your small opinion of my small influence on our affairs is, unfortunately, too correct. Without troubling you with the details of local matters, I only tell you that I quite approve of your conduct, reserving to myself, however, the right of asking for your *Rienzi* if a favourable moment for the performance of this opera, long desired by me, should arrive. In the first instance, the *Prophet* and Auber's *Bal Masqué* are to be given, and I, for my part, have declared that I shall not enter the orchestra for some time to come. By next spring I hope your personal affairs will have taken a more favourable turn, to which I may, perhaps, be able to contribute something. When *Tristan* is completed, and you have sent the dedication copy to the Grand Duchess of Baden, you must write to me at length as to what remains to be done.

With K. R., who delighted me with a visit of several days, I discussed a good many things which he will shortly communicate to you. I flatter myself that he has taken a good impression away with him, and that some old friendly associations will be even more firmly established in years to come. His musical gift appears very considerable to me, and I have advised him to concentrate himself on an operatic subject, which he had better arrange for himself. You should encourage him in this ; by your advice and influence he will no doubt achieve something excellent, and a musico-dramatic work will help him to proper recognition in the quickest and best way.

I wanted to send you the *Dante* symphony for the new year, but the corrections have taken me longer than I expected, and the publication will not take place before January. I shall send you a respectable parcel, for the Gran Mass will also be included in it. I wish I could bring you these things personally, stay with you, accompany you in *Tristan.* Let us hope that the new year will put an end to our separation, and chain us to each other in the body, as we are already in spirit and heart.

Your

F. L

December 26th, 1858.

You may expect a dedication from the composer of the opera *D. v. S.* ; accept it in a friendly spirit, although you will find yourself in the strange company of Meyerbeer. The composer is well inclined towards you, of which I recently had a very convincing proof. Do not mention this until the dedication actually reaches you. Later on you will probably have to write a few lines in reply.

279.

Cordial thanks for your New Year's greeting, dearest Richard. I expect to see the explanation of the last words of your telegram in your next letter, for I have no knowledge of the event which you describe as "wonderfully miserable." In certain quarters, however, the *miserable* appears no longer *wonderful* to me. I hope the new year will bring some things to a better issue, and have many good things in store for you. Enclosed I send you this week's *répertoire* of the Weymar theatre, in which you will see the announcement of *Lohengrin* for next Sunday. For the first time I shall not conduct this work to which I am attached with my whole soul. *Tannhäuser* also I have left to my colleague, and when I come to explain to you the circumstances which determine me to this negative attitude, I feel sure that you will see in it no neglect of my artistic conviction, much less of my duty as a friend to you.

If your operas have elsewhere been given for the purpose of getting money, the responsibility lies with those concerned; but here, where these works have been guarded and watched with so much love, I cannot make myself an accomplice of the brutal mercantile spirit in which they are now regarded, especially not after we two have been treated with such total want or consideration in this *Rienzi* affair, which has been allowed to drag on for more than eighteen months.

As I said in my last letter, I fully approve of your resolution not to sell *Rienzi* to the management here. If you should be applied to by letter *I advise you to make no concession.* If the time for relenting should come I shall send you word; you know how deeply your interests concern me.

In the first instance, the *Prophet, Bal Masqué, Don Pasquale,* and *Antigone,* have to be studied and performed, which will leave no time or goodwill for *Rienzi.* As regards goodwill, C. R. can relate to you the circumstances of the first performance of Cornelius's opera, when my passive attitude during this season will be explained to you. Really I often require the patience beseeming a *confrater* of the Franciscan order to bear so many intolerable things.

Your

F. L.

January 1st, 1859.

280.

VENICE, *January 2nd,* 1859.

My DEAR FRANZ,

The time has come when I must once more speak with calmness and in a decisive manner of the subject which has been so rich a source of my life's troubles, and which last New Year's Eve caused the storm I let loose upon you, no doubt to your sorrow. Such storms must not occur again, that I feel deeply. Even this last attack was caused only by a moment of the most violent excitement. I must, in fact, undergo an absolute change in order to gain a position more worthy of myself. It is for this reason that I apply to you, for the last time, and perhaps it would be better if I did not trouble you in the matter, even for this last time. But if I omitted to do so at the moment when I am about to take a decisive step, I might perhaps have to reproach myself with having neglected my nearest, most helpful, and most influential friend in an unaccountable manner.

Let me come to the point.

After living in exile for ten years, my amnesty has become of less importance to me than the guarantee of an existence free from care and secure from discomfort for the rest of my life. Do not be surprised. The return to Germany is of relative value to me. The only positive gain would be my seeing you often and living together with you. The possible performances of my operas under my direction, would certainly bring me less enjoyment than exertion, care, trouble, and annoyance. I never had much pleasure in the performance of one of my operas, and shall have much less in future. My ideal demands have increased, compared with former times, and my sensitiveness has become much more acute during the last ten years while I lived in absolute separation from artistic public life. I fear that even you do not quite understand me in this respect, and you should believe my word all the more implicitly. Your nature and position in life and in the world are so entirely different from mine that you can scarcely realise my sensitiveness in this respect from your own consciousness.

Believe me implicitly when I tell you that the only reason for my continuing to live is the irresistible impulse of creating a number of works of art which have their vital force in me. I recognise beyond all doubt that this act of creating and completing alone satisfies me and fills me with a desire of life, which otherwise I should not understand. I can, on the other hand, do quite well without any chance of a performance.

I see clearly that before the completion of *Tristan* my amnesty would absolutely place me in an awkward position ; no expectation, not even that of producing *Lohengrin*, could induce me to leave my present place of abode before I had finished my work. From this you may guess at other things. Any offer of a secured and comfortable existence would be of no value to me if it were coupled with the condition of my accepting the amnesty, and of doing certain services made possible thereby. I cannot and shall not accept an appointment or anything resembling it. What I demand, on the other hand, is the settlement upon me of an honourable and large pension, solely for the purpose of creating my works of art undisturbed and without regard for external success.

Being without property or subvention of any kind, I have to rely for my income upon my operas. He who has real knowledge of the nature of my works, and who feels and esteems their peculiar and differentiating qualities, must see that I, in my position towards such an institution as our theatre, ought to be entirely relieved from the necessity of making commercial articles of my works. Any just-minded man must perceive that it would be quite unworthy of me to relinquish my freedom by giving my operas to managers without stipulating for their artistic interest, without choice, without preference for any particular theatre, or even by being compelled to offer them to such managers. This necessity has already filled me with much painful bitterness, and the worst of it is that even if I suppress my sense of honour to that extent, the receipts accruing to me are of such a nature that they place me, pecuniarily speaking, in a painful and alarming position. At times those receipts come in plentifully and unexpectedly, and in consequence bring with them all of a sudden perfect security and a certain tempting plenty. At other times they fall off for a long period and again quite unexpectedly; and this falling off, just because it could not be foreseen, is followed by want, care, and tribulation. If this is to be mended I must be relieved from the necessity of counting upon these receipts, and be placed in a position which will enable me to look upon them as an accidental increase of resources, which I can employ in adding certain comforts to my existence, and which I am able to dispense with without interfering with my sufficient and settled income, as soon as I find it desirable to withhold my operas from those theatres, the strength or the direction of which does not enable me to credit them with honest zeal for my work. In this manner, and by the position towards our abominable theatrical institutions thus attained, I should be protected by my contemporaries, and enabled to continue my creations in accordance with my earnest desire and with the peculiarity of my artistic nature. An ample and fully secured pension can alone do this for me, and only a combination of several German princes whom I have inspired with sympathy can accomplish the desired object.

On such a combination I should have to insist, for the reason, more especially, that this pension, if it is to fulfil its object and to satisfy my somewhat refined and not altogether ordinary wants, must amount to at least 2,000 or 3,000 thalers. I do not blush in naming such a sum. My experience of what I want in accordance with my nature, and, perhaps I should add, the nature of my works, teaches me that I cannot well do with less ; and on the other hand, it is well known that artists like Mendelssohn (although he was rich), have received equally large honorary salaries from one single quarter.

I ask you therefore, definitely and finally, whether you will take the initiative in this matter ? At the same time I would draw your attention to the fact that, after mature consideration, I must abide by the character of my demand. An appointment at Weimar, although it might leave me at perfect liberty and even be equal to yours, I could not accept, because the salary would not be sufficient for my purpose. It would not help me radically, and would therefore imply all the dangers of a palliative measure. Once more, I require an absolute settlement of my external circumstances, which will provide for and exercise a decided influence on my future artistic creativeness. I shall be forty-six next birthday, and therefore speak of about ten years at the utmost.

If you have reasons for not entering into my request, or for declining to concern yourself with it personally, let me know plainly and definitely. I could explain those reasons from your peculiar position, and they would not in the least interfere with our friendship. Let me know in that case whether you advise me to apply *myself* to the Grand Duke of Weimar, in order to induce him to place himself at the head of the aforesaid combination of princes.

If you do not think this advisable, I am determined to ask D. whether he will intercede for me with another prince. If he also refuses, my last resource will be to apply to that prince myself. On the success of this step will depend my further relations to Germany, as to which in such circumstances I have quite made up my mind.

My request, whether it be addressed to you, or D., or one of the princes, will be accompanied by a clear and convincing exposition of my circumstances, my position towards the artistic world, and my individual qualities, and wants. At the same time I shall state precisely what I promise to do in return for such a pension. In the first instance, and whether my return to Germany will be granted or not, I shall undertake to continue the creation of new works. All my works, present and future, will be given to the various court theatres gratis. Finally, as soon as I am allowed to return to Germany I will, by special desire, undertake to superintend in person the study and production of my operas, and, if it should be wished, of other works, the representation of which would be for the benefit and honour of art.

This letter, dear Franz, is the first I have written in this fateful new year 1859. It is addressed to you, and deals with a subject which will be of decisive influence on my future life. May Heaven and our friendship reward it with success!

Answer me soon definitely and decisively, for I repeat that I do not want my request to be in any way connected with the amnesty.

A thousand cordial greetings to the ladies, to whom
I shall soon write a pleasant letter.

Your
R. W.

281.

DEAREST FRANZ,

Have you *nothing at all* to say to me ?
What is to become of me, if *every one* ignores me ?

Your
R.

VENICE.

282.

MY DEAR FRANZ,

On reading my letter again, you will probably
have discovered what was the meaning of my jocular
complaint—" You answer me much too pathetically and
seriously." You must have seen by the exact terms
of my letter, somewhat loosely worded though it was,
that by your answer I meant the manner in which you
speak of my conduct towards D. with regard to *Rienzi*.
As this part of my letter has remained obscure to you,
I add the following words of explanation. My letter
about the withdrawal of *Rienzi* was written with a
view to being shown, because I had referred D. to
you. I thought, however, you would see that I was
annoyed by the difficulties he made about the honorarium, and by the remote date for which payment was
promised. I was in hopes that my letter discussing
the withdrawal of the opera would help me quickly to
the honorarium, and perhaps increase the amount a
little. I had unfortunately reckoned upon this income

before the new year, and relied upon it all the more
because I had on a former occasion explained my difficult position to your sympathetic heart.   When I
forwarded D.'s last letter to you my intention was to
complain of his pedantic statement : " The honorarium
will be paid to you after the first performance,"—a statement to which I am no longer accustomed at any other
theatre.   I further hoped to induce you—as indeed I
clearly indicated—to effect at least the immediate payment of the honorarium.   As my letter about the
withdrawal of *Rienzi* was written with a view to being
shown, it may very likely have puzzled you ; but I know
that it was intended only to frighten D., and to supply
you with a weapon for forcing him into a decent and
business-like attitude.   In consequence, I hoped that
the success of this little manœuvre would secure me
the receipt of the wretched twenty-five louis d'or before
the new year.   Upon this sum I looked as my only
certainty, because you were there to get it for me,
while the moneys which I expected from other quarters
represented only so many hopes which might be
delusive.   At last New Year's Eve came.   My money
was all gone ; my watch, the snuff-box of the Grand
Duke, and the *bonbonnière* of the Princess, the only
valuables I possess, had been pawned ; and of the
money I had got for them only one and a half napo-
leons remained.   When, on New Year's Eve, on entering
my lonely room, I found your letter, I confess I was
weak enough to hope that it would announce to me the
imminent arrival of the twenty-five louis d'or, in consequence of the successful demonstration against D.
which I thought I had made.   Instead of this, I found.

in reference to this matter, a serious explanation of your relations with D., which, as I see from this letter, have already become matter of bitter and troublesome experience to you. I had foreseen this, and made you silent reproaches when D. was called to Weimar through your means. I quite understood that, owing to prolonged irritation, you were, on receipt of my last letter, in a mood which misled you as to the character of my threat to withdraw *Rienzi*. You recognized in me also the sympathetic annoyance at all the unworthy things we meet with, and you overlooked the fact that a poor devil like me cannot afford to be serious. Therefore you entered seriously and bitterly into my withdrawal of *Rienzi*, which, after the insults you had received, was welcome to you, and I, for my part, had to witness on that wretched New Year's Eve the destruction of my last secret, but none the less certain, hope of receiving money. The great disappointment of that moment would, at any other time, have probably made me reticent and silent, but the long-expected and ardently-longed-for boon of your sympathy for *Tristan* evoked in me a kind of convulsive excitement. Once more, your joy at my first act had brought you so near to my innermost heart that I thought I might, at such a moment, make the most outrageous demand on you. That feeling I expressed, if I remember rightly, in the words, " For my paroxysm of joyous excitement your delight at *Tristan* is responsible." Dearest friend, at that moment I could not even think of the possibility of a misunderstanding. Everything being so certain and infallible between us, I went to the opposite extreme of reproach-

ing you because you had left me in the lurch with
regard to money matters, and because you had taken
my diplomatic demonstration against D. in a much too
earnest and pathetic sense, my only interest in him
being comprised in a little money. I further indicated
that the various considerations, which to you, being
on the spot, and holding an official position, might
appear serious and of great moment, did not exist for
me at all, the only connection between myself and the
theatres, and their public art, being solely that of
money.

THAT OF MONEY! Yes, so it is ; and with that you
reproach me. You should rather pity me. Do you not
think that I should prefer *your* position in regard to the
performance of your own works because money is no
object to you ? My first letter of this year will have
shown you that I also am capable of considering the
matter in a serious and literally pathetic, *i.e.*, *suffering*
mood.

Enough of this. Your letter, received to-day, has
affected me deeply, as you will easily understand. Yet
I am calm and full of hope. Your curious misunderstanding in applying my reproach, that you answer me
in " too earnest and pathetic a style," to your delight
at *Tristan*, must by this time have become clear to
yourself. I feel quite confident that any unprejudiced
friend, to whom you may show our last letters, will
persuade you, in spite of your prejudice, that my
humorous and playfully extravagant reproach referred
only to your idea of my intended withdrawal of *Rienzi*,
and, generally speaking, to the expectation I had of D.
and the whole slough of our German operatic theatres.

You now know the position which excited me to this kind of desperate humour, and I hope it will be a long time before I again have to change my last napoleon at the telegraph office.

It is you, dear friend, who are suffering and needing comfort ; for the extraordinary letter which you found it possible to send me can only have sprung from a terrible mental irritation. I hope in the meantime that this lengthy explanation and disclosure of the mis-understanding into which you had succeeded in falling will be some comfort to you.   I have none other to offer.   If your irritation concerned me alone, this letter should dispel it altogether.   Let me further assure you that you have hurt me in no way, for your arrows did not hit me ; their barbs stuck in your own heart.   This letter, I hope, will free you of them.

One more thing let me ask you to-day.   Do not answer my letter of January 2nd.   Look upon it as if it had not been written, or, at least, not received.   I am fully aware that you are not able to put yourself in my place with such goodwill and understanding as would enable you to do justice to my letter.   Please forget it altogether ; in that case, I will on my part pardon your reproaches, you curious, dear, dear friend.

Farewell for to-day.

I am sure I have not lost you.

Your

RICHARD WAGNER.

VENICE, *January 7th,* 1859.

In order to set your mind at rest, I inform you that, by a curious and lucky accident, some money,

which I had long expected and already despaired of,
arrived here from Vienna in the first week of the new
year.   My three valuables (let a kind world forgive me
this luxury!) are out of pawn.   For the present I am
provided for, and do not apprehend any new stoppage
of my resources just yet.

May the friendly remembrance of me be revived in
you.

Your
RICHARD W.

283.

Your greeting, dearest Richard, has brought
me the enchanting forgetfulness of all that should
ever be far from us.   Receive my thanks, and let us
continue to suffer patiently together.

Before you had written to ask me not to mention
your proposal, I had communicated it at some length
in the proper quarter.   As I might have expected, after
numerous similar conversations (which I never mention
to you) there were several reasons for not accepting it.
Perhaps I shall be able to broach the subject again later
on, and obtain a more favourable result; to the extent,
I mean, that a small sum will be sent to you.   Anything
more cannot be hoped for.

I must ask you to believe that I am extremely grieved
always to have to tell you things of this kind.

In your letter to Princess M. you speak of a change
of abode, and of your desire to settle in a large town.
In case, against my sincere hope, the permission to
return to Germany should be permanently refused
to you, and you prefer to live in a large town, I still

think that Paris would be the most comfortable, the most convenient, and even the cheapest place for you. I know your dislike of this city *pleine de boue et de fumée;* but I think that if you were to live there for any length of time you would feel more at home, apart from which we should be tolerably near each other, so that I might visit you frequently.

Have you had any further news from Carlsruhe? The newspapers continue to announce a performance of *Tristan* in September, and I do not relinquish the hope that at that time a favourable turn in your affairs will take place. Anyhow, this summer must not pass without our seeing each other.

Once more, thanks for your greeting; the song is indescribably beautiful.

Most cordially your

F. L.

WEYMAR, *February* 17th, 1859.

From Vienna you will soon receive through my cousin a small collection of *notes.*

All that is kind to C. R.

284.

VENICE, *February 22nd,* 1859.

I have just received your letter; as I am expecting R. and W., who may come in at any moment, I must defer answering you at length until to-morrow. But I will not go to bed to-day without thanking you most sincerely for the great benefit you have conferred upon me by your letter. I am often in a state of convulsive excitement, and must then look very ugly. But that state has now disappeared entirely ; you took it away to-day.

I shall say more about this to-morrow, and you will find me in a willing frame of mind for confessing my sins.

One word more. If I have understood your short hint rightly, let me ask you, for Heaven's sake, not to send me any money now. I could not bear it. Send me your *Ideals*, and, when it is ready, your *Dante* those I am looking for longingly.

The boys have just come in ; the well-brought-up K. thanks you a thousand times for your remembrance of him.

More to-morrow, God willing.

My blessings on you !

Your
R. W.

285.

VENICE, *February 23rd*, 1859.

DEAR FRANZ,

To my hurried lines of yesterday I add a more comprehensive letter to-day. I have many things to tell you.

Lately I felt the urgent desire of sending you a word of comfort and sympathy. I thought that you were in need of such. For I had heard, to my horror, how great your annoyance must be, and B.'s account confirmed my impression that you were deeply annoyed and grieved by ingratitude, faithlessness, and even treachery.

Suddenly, however, I felt quite stupid, and all I intended to say to you appeared to me trivial and superfluous. I could think of nothing better than to copy out for you a few fragments of my last work. They are not the really important things, for those can be understood only in their larger context, and I am all the more obliged to you for your kind reception of my good intentions, which count for little in art, but for a great deal in friendship.

I must almost thank you for the alarming New Year's greeting which you sent to me. I believe it has been beneficial to me ; I am aware that I have too little control over myself, and rely upon the patience of others to an undue extent. An occasional lesson, therefore, does me good. Although I remain firmly convinced that you have misunderstood me in one essential point (as, indeed, well you might), I feel, nevertheless, that I must have cut a very ugly figure. That was proved to me by the effect I had upon you, for we know little of our appearance until we see ourselves in a looking-glass, and in your irritation I recognized my ugliness. These attacks of my violence ought surely to have calmed down by this time ; indeed, I long for that unruffled calm which I esteem so highly and recognize to be the finest quality in man. It appears to me that I have arrived at the turning point of my life, and I deeply long for a state of quiescence. I am aware that that quiescence must, at last, come from the inner man, and our position towards the outer world must become one of apathy, if nothing from there contributes to the contentment of our mind. Let us see then.

I am intent at present upon gaining a clear and

definite view of my fate. My mental disposition you
know from my letter to M. As regards external matters,
after mature consideration, I am taking every step
to place my future relations with Germany on the
necessary definite basis. I heard from Dresden that
the king would on no account swerve from his decision
to reserve the amnesty for those who had submitted
to the investigation and judgment of the law-courts.
I was advised to submit to that condition, but after
mature consideration, and after weighing all the
chances, I am firmly resolved never to fulfil that condition. In order to do all that was possible, I lately
wrote to the Minister of Justice, asking him to discuss
the matter with the King once more. This measure
was suggested to me by my latest experience in this
place. I ought to tell you and the Grand Duke for your
satisfaction that, by desire of the Saxon Government,
I was to be banished from here. I was advised to submit unconditionally, but to send a medical certificate to
the Governor-General, praying that I might be allowed
to stay for a few months longer for urgent reasons of
health. For the moment this has answered, and I am
allowed to stay. If I refuse to be examined or perhaps
to be locked up a few months in Saxony, I base that
refusal towards the Government entirely upon my state
of health, which I need only exaggerate a little in
order to show good and sufficient cause for my refusal.
In other respects I submit most humbly to the decree
pronounced against me, recognize my guilt and the
justice of the proceedings without reserve—and only
ask H.M. to remit the conditions of my amnesty by an
exceptional act of grace on account of my health, which

has become so weak that the doctor has strongly advised me not to undergo that strain. In that manner I think I have taken the only step which may lead me straight to the goal of certain knowledge as to my fate. If the King refuses to grant me this request it is clear that I shall have to give up all hope from that quarter for ever. But even in that case I am resolved to make one more last trial. I shall apply direct to the Grand Duke of Baden, placing the case before him, and asking him for his permission to approach the Emperor of Austria, the Prince of Prussia, the Grand Duke of Weimar, the Duke of Coburg, and perhaps one other friendly Prince with the prayer to grant me an exceptional privilege of residence in their respective states, either by agreement amongst themselves, or by a decree of the National Diet. Avoiding anything of the nature of a complaint against the King of Saxony, I shall base this request solely upon the same circumstance, viz., the very serious state of my health and my nervous irritation, which do not permit me to undergo the risk of a criminal investigation at Dresden, although I fully recognize the justice of that investigation, and do not expect the King to alter his decree in my favour. I shall further ask the Princes in question to suspend the treaty of extradition in my favour after due consultation with the Saxon Government, the object being to secure my personal efforts for the advancement of German art. It will depend upon the consent of the Grand Duke of Baden whether I take further steps in that direction. I do not venture to say that I expect a successful issue, but one thing I shall gain in any case, and that the most necessary of

all, viz., certainty as to my position.   I must no longer
delay gaining that certainty, because my whole future
life depends upon it.   Before telling you what further
steps I have in view in order to gain certainty in
another direction also, I must answer your question as
to Carlsruhe.

Devrient wrote to me that in case *Tristan* were
finished by that time, September 6th, being the birthday
of the Grand Duke, would be the best day for the
performance ; and he added that the Grand Duke
counted with certainty upon my personal attendance.   As
to this last point, which of course I had made the chief
condition from the first, I have recently received further
information.   The Grand Duke intends to invite me for
the time in question to Carlsruhe on his own responsibility.   Nothing is to be known beforehand, and my
presence is to be simply an accomplished fact, for
which the Grand Duke takes the personal responsibility.
This seems a princely way of doing things, and the
young sovereign inspires me with confidence.   But I
must assist him by denying any intention of a journey
to Carlsruhe altogether.   You will therefore oblige me,
dearest Franz, by ostensibly assisting me in this matter.
You might cause some paragraphs to be inserted in the
newspapers, contradicting that rumour which, unfortunately, has been spread about a good deal, and
stating that nothing was settled, and that my personal
attendance at Carlsruhe was quite out of the question,
as, as yet, there was not the slightest chance of my
amnesty.

Concerning your own recent steps in my favour, I
must charge you in all friendliness with having acted

too delicately towards me by not letting me know the motives of the refusal you have met with.   Even now you do not state those motives plainly, for the reason apparently that you fear to wound me unnecessarily by their communication.   On the other hand, I ask you to consider that it would be better if I saw quite clearly in this matter.   This would finally and for ever free me from all the illusions into which my strong desire tempts me while things are in this uncertain state, and an unpleasant feature of our mutual relations would disappear altogether.

All my transactions with the Härtels as to the edition of the scores, etc., of the *Nibelungen* to be prepared at once, have again been abandoned recently. The only thing they were willing to grant was the immediate commencement of the engraving (provided always that a performance was guaranteed), without payment of an honorarium, and with the undertaking only on their part to share the profits of the edition with me.   How loath I am to agree to this latter proposal I need not explain.   The profits to be derived from such a work increase as the years go on, and will probably become lucrative only after my death.   In any case, those profits would accrue to me at a time of life to provide for which at present would be folly, considering how urgently I require immediate assistance and freedom from care.   Heirs I have none.

Your advice to settle in Paris in case Germany remains closed to me quite coincides with my own plans.   The dear Child has communicated to you what my immediate views of life are.   I cannot bear this state of inactivity any longer ; my health is ruined for

want of life and action.   Paris is the place, appointed
to me by fate.   I quite agree with you in thinking that
I shall get accustomed to living there as time goes on.
Apart from any plans, I shall there have at least the
occasional use of a fine orchestra which I have missed
for so long.   Without considering for the present any
possible performances at French theatres, I should
there also have the best chance of witnessing a performance of my own works.   A well-managed scheme
of German opera would be all that would be required.
But it is impossible for me and my wife to lead, once
more, a half-starving life in Paris.   Some comfort and
freedom of action must be secured to me, otherwise I
cannot think of it.   I shall probably leave my furniture,
etc., at Zurich.   The pretty little house will be kept for
me, and I hope to inhabit it again later on in the
summer, which would be an agreeable change.

The hope you give me of receiving frequent visits
from you in Paris is the real bright point in the picture
of the future.

Believe me, dear Franz, when I consider the advantages which my desired amnesty would offer to me, there
is only one which appears to me worth a real sacrifice,
I mean that of being together with you more frequently
and for longer periods.   What else is there that could
very strongly and decisively attract me?   Performances
of my operas I should, in most instances, carefully avoid,
although I might in rare and particular cases take part
in first performances of my works, which would of
course be very desirable.   The question, whether in
that case encouragement and new strength, or grief,
annoyance, and overexcitement would be the lasting

effect upon me, I fear I must decide in favour of the
latter alternative, and no external success, no applause,
could make up for this.   If I was sensitive before, I am
so now to the verge of excessive irritation, and I dread
every contact with theatrical matters, singers, con-
ductors, etc., to such a degree that I feel almost inclined
to bless the fate which keeps me apart from them.
But we, we two, want to cultivate our friendship by
personal intercourse; we are to each other the only
enjoyment which the world can offer us.   Only think
how painfully we have always been kept separated,
during how few weeks of the long and beautiful years
of our friendship we have looked into each other's eyes.
This fountain of generation of inner strength and fire
is fully appreciated by me, and I feel it to be the direst
deprivation that I can approach it so rarely.   If you
promise me this boon for Paris, you may look upon my
determination to go there as certain and immutable.

Let me have a full account of yourself, dear friend ;
of all your troubles I hear from others, sometimes even
through the newspapers.   That is not right ; neither
should you be too brief in your statements ; it looks like
want of confidence.   I want to gain a closer view so as to
know how to stretch out my hand, which would comfort
you with a friendly touch.   It is natural that you are
too great, too noble, too beautiful, for our dear, gossipy
Germany, and that you appear to the people like a god,
whose splendour they are not accustomed and not
inclined to bear.   It was left to you to illustrate this
phenomenon, for so bright, so warm a being as yourself
had never before appeared in Germany.   But I should
like to know to what degree this miserable conduct

touches your heart, annoys you, embitters you. I have grown so indifferent to similar impressions, that I often find it very difficult to discover the exact point where the impression is made.

If, on the other hand, I consider what happiness is in your possession, what crowns of life and of eternity are on your forehead, if I think of your sympathetic and nobly refined home, free as it is from the serious cares of common life, if I finally observe how your personality and your ever-ready art enchant and delight all around you, I find it difficult to understand what your sufferings really are. And yet you suffer, and suffer deeply ; that I feel. Sink your pride for once, and write to me as plainly and as comprehensively as I too frequently do to you, much to your annoyance. I must conclude, in order not to begin the fourth sheet, and will only tell you in the margin that I thank you cordially for your love, and shall always remain faithfully and lovingly

Your friend,

RICHARD W.

286.

MILAN, *March 25th*, 1859.

MY FRANZ,

I am once more on my travels without having told you anything about them ; tired out as I am by the Brera, the *Cena*, the Cathedral, etc., I do not want to go to bed before sending you two words of news.

In order not to interrupt the composition of my third act, I came to the conclusion that I ought to begin it in a place where I might finish it. I have selected Lucerne for the purpose ; you know how dearly I love the Lake of Lucerne ; the Righi, Pilatus, etc., are indispensable remedies to me and my blood. I shall live there in solitude, and at this time of the year shall easily find a most desirable lodging. There I mean to work splendidly. My Erard has already preceded me.

My health gives me still much trouble, otherwise I am fairly well off, but with your friendly cousin in Vienna, who thinks so little of your advantage, I have still a bone to pick. About that next time. I should, no doubt, have had news from you if, in my last letter, I had not again given you such a dose of gravy. I should have been only too happy to receive a sign of life from you, even if that matter had not been mentioned with a word. I hoped for it from day to day, and in that idle hope neglected advising you of my intended change of abode.

As soon as I am settled again I shall write better and more, without waiting for you to ask me. For to-day these preliminary lines must suffice. A thousand cordial greetings.

Your
R. W.

Lucerne, *poste restante.*

287.

Be heartily welcomed on the Lake of Lucerne, my dear, great friend. *Tristan* will once again enjoy and derive strength from Alpine air before he leaves you for ever to shine on others. At Carlsruhe they are afraid that he will not arrive punctually at the appointed time. Devrient, whom I saw here and at Jena, told me so lately. The first performance is wavering between September and December—the birthday of the Grand Duke or that of the Grand Duchess, and I have already announced myself as the *inevitable* guest.

Your dose of gravy, as you put it, was not particularly palatable. At our next meeting I shall have to say much about it, unfortunately of the negative kind. Nevertheless, I hope to be able at the same time to propose to you a different arrangement (if that is the name) with which, no doubt, you will agree. First of all, however, *Tristan* must be finished, engraved, and performed, and after that we will, without delay, take the *Nibelungen* affair seriously in hand, and set it right to your satisfaction.

The Princess and her daughter are going to Munich next week (Kaulbach is painting the portrait of Princess M.). I stay here till Easter, and then go on a visit to Prince Hohenzollern at Löwenberg, Silesia. From the middle of May to the beginning of June I shall pitch my tent at Leipzig, where all manner of things will happen. Later on, for Whitsuntide, grand Schiller festivities are announced here. Whether they will take place is very questionable, but in any case I shall have to get the music for the festival-play by Holm (*Vor hundert Jahren*) ready, which will be something of an effort.

My health, fortunately, gives me no trouble, and I have no lack of patience. The rest may come and will come.

Farewell and persevere. Such is the wish of

Your

F. L.

WEYMAR, *April 6th*, 1850.

288.

Tell me, dearest Franz, how would you feel if you were in my position? I have repeatedly asked you to send me your new works as they appear. The *Ideals* has appeared, but you are silent on the subject. Now I read the publisher's announcement of the appearance of *Dante*. How would you feel if this happened to you? Do you still harbour your strange illusions about me? That surely is impossible.

The weather is bad; I am absolutely alone, and seldom in the right mood for work. So I drag on amidst mists and thoughts.

Let me hear, let me see.

Your

R. W.

289.

DEDICATION OF THE "DANTE" SYMPHONY.

As Virgil guided Dante, so have you guided me through the mysterious regions of life-tone imbued worlds. From the bottom of his heart calls to you:—

"*Tu se' lo mio maestro, e'l mio autore!*"

and dedicates this work to you with invariably faithful love

Your

F. LISZT.

WEYMAR, *Easter* 1859.

290.

I should prefer not to write to you to-day, dearest Franz, because I am not in the proper mood

for it, but as I must not think of working, I make at
least this attempt at some sort of activity, without
knowing exactly what the result will be.   If you
suddenly were to enter my solitude,—that would
be a chance of the possibility of a possibility.   But
you seem to have disposed of your summer,—Löwenberg and Leipzig, while the third L. (Lucerne) has
been totally forgotten.   Well, I stick to Lucerne, and,
carefully considered, it is the only place in the world
which is at present possible to me.   You know, or
might imagine, that I do not live a life in the proper
sense of the word ; the only thing that could help me—
art, art to the verge of drowning and world-forgetful-
ness, of that I have still less than of life, and this state
of things has lasted for a period which I soon shall
count by decades.   Excepting the servants, I see and
speak to no one ; just imagine how I must feel.   My
good people, I fear you leave me too much alone, and
the meaning of "too late" will one day be brought
home to you in connection with me.   It is very well
to say : "Get *Tristan* ready, and then we shall see."
But how if I did not get *Tristan* ready because I could
not get it ready?   I feel as if I should break down
pantingly in sight of the goal.   Once at least every day
I look at my book with a right good will, but my head
is waste, my heart empty, and I stare at the mists and
the rain-clouds, which, ever since I have been here,
have debarred me even from the chance of shaking up
my stagnant blood by pleasant excursions.   People
say : "Go to work, then all will be right."   Very well
in its way, but I, poor devil, lack routine, and if ideas
do not come to me of themselves, I cannot make them

A pleasant state of things this! and what is worse, there is no chance of helping myself in any other way. All is shut and locked against me. Work alone is to help me, but who is to help me to the possibility of work? I have evidently too little of what you have too much.

I am full of enthusiasm for the German Confederacy of the Teutonic nations. For heaven's sake do not let the villain L. Napoleon touch my dear German Confederacy! I should be too deeply grieved if any change were made. I am curious, however, what will become of my intended migration to Paris. It is surely most unpatriotic to look for a comfortable existence at the head-quarters of the enemy of the Teutonic nation. The good Teutons should really do something to save the most Teutonic of all Teutonic opera-composers this terrible trial. Moreover, in Paris I shall be pretty well cut off from all my German resources, and yet I shall be obliged to apply in a very high quarter in order to get permission for permanent settlement in Paris, for my Swiss settlement is coming to a close. Germany is evidently intent upon driving me forcibly to the enemy. Very well! There is a possibility of my going in the autumn for six months to America, where offers have been made to me which, considering the friendly sympathy of the German Confederacy, I cannot very well neglect. This will be decided before long. What makes me hesitate is that the *Tristan* scheme at Carlsruhe would be crossed thereby in such a manner that I should have to give it up for the present, and should probably not resume it at any future time. The last act of this child of sorrow is now on the verge of the "to be or not to be;" a slight pressure of some spring of the

vulgar fate, at whose mercy I am, might kill this child
at the very moment of its birth.   Everything with me
depends now upon the turning of a hand ; there may
be a way and there may be a complete stoppage, for
I, my Franz, am in a bad way.

I have heard nothing for a long time of any of my
friends ; they probably think that I am very happy in my
dear Switzerland, in this splendid solitude, in the joy of
composing, forgetful of all the world.   I am not angry
with them because they make themselves such illusions.
If they only knew that I had to threaten violence in
order to get out of you the *Dante* symphony dedicated
to me, they might draw further conclusions from this
fact.   What do you say to that ?   I have, after all,
arrived at *Dante*, of which I did not wish to speak
to-day, because I love it too much to involve it in my
present mood.   Let me tell you, however, that we had
better keep the dedication, written in my copy, to
ourselves.   I at least shall not mention it to a soul.
Your words have positively made me blush, you may
believe me.   I cannot tell you too often how miserably
weak I feel as a musician.   I know, in the depth of my
heart, that I am an absolute blunderer.   You ought to
watch me when I am at it ; now thinking " it must do after
all," then going to the piano to puzzle out some wretched
rubbish, and giving it up again in a state of idiocy.
Oh, how I feel then ! how thoroughly persuaded of
my musical wretchedness !   And then come you, whose
pores are running over as with streams, fountains,
cataracts, and tell me such words as those which you
have said to me.   I find it difficult to think that this is
not the purest irony, and I must recall your friendship

in order to believe that you have not been cutting a joke at my expense after all. This is a peculiar story, dearest friend; believe me, I am not up to much. I really begin to think that Reissiger must have helped me with *Tannhäuser* and *Lohengrin*. With my new works you have most certainly helped me, and now that you leave me in the lurch, I can do nothing more.

About *Dante* only so much to-day that I was specially pleased to see how perfectly well I remembered it from your playing it to me. As I come to study it more closely I perceive that no feature of any importance had escaped me, even the smallest and finest details were perfectly familiar to me from that time. This at least is good evidence of my receptive faculties; but I believe that the credit is really due to the peculiar grandeur and quality of your work.

Generally speaking, if you wish to know, I am again in exactly the same condition as when I wrote the letter about you to M. Concerning that letter I recently had a brand-new experience. K. R. had not read it, when I found it accidentally amongst my papers at Venice, and gave it to him. After that he came to me, and told me that people who were near to you had told him in connection with this letter that I expressed myself in it in an evasive manner, and was evidently intent upon saying nothing definite about you. He himself had been made anxious by this, and now, having read it, was truly delighted at perceiving the *enormous* significance I had attributed to you. Astonished at the possibility of an ill-natured misunderstanding, I read the letter once more, and was compelled to chime in with K. R.'s impetuous declamations at the incredible dulness, superficiality, and triviality of people who could have misunderstood the meaning of this letter. I have taken a solemn oath not to publish *another word*. What we are to each other we know and tell one another at intervals for the sake of encouragement and comfort. But what we are to the world I will be d——d if I——!

It is *too* incredible.

Good Lord! I cannot get out of my trivial mood in this letter, and therefore must not discuss anything noble, least of all the *Ideals*. If you want to be sure of hearing something rational from me, come to me and play all your things to me, especially the Crusaders' chorus (splendid!!); then at least *you* will know once more accurately what is in me.

For the present I spend all the good humour I can dispose of on my wife. I flatter her and take care of her as if she were a bride in her honeymoon. My reward is that I see her thrive; her bad illness is visibly getting better. She is recovering, and will, I hope, become a little rational in her old age. Just after I had received your *Dante*, I wrote to her that we had now got out of Hell; I hope Purgatory will agree with her, in which case we may perhaps, after all, enjoy a little Paradise. The whole thing is splendid. Remember me to the Prince of Löwenberg, or whatever his name may be, and tell him that if the German Confederacy does not recall me soon I shall go to Paris and betray the length and breadth of Germany.

God be with you. I hope you will pardon this absurd letter.   Ever thine,

R. W.

291.

What a terrible storm is your letter, dearest Richard ! How desperately it lashes and knocks down everything. What can be heard in the midst of this roaring thunder ? Where shall I find, and what is the good of, words, words, words ?

And yet my confidence in you is unshaken. Hamlet's dilemma does not apply to you, for *you are* and cannot help being. Even your mad injustice towards yourself in calling yourself a "miserable musician and blunderer" (! !) is a sign of your greatness. In the same sense Pascal says, "*La vraie éloquence se moque de l'éloquence.*" It is true that your greatness brings you little comfort and happiness, but where is happiness, in the narrow monotonous sense which is absurdly given to the word ? Resignation and patience alone sustain us in this world. Let us bear our cross together in Christ—" the God whom one approaches without pride, before whom one bends the knee without despair." But I must not be betrayed into needless Franciscan sermons.

Candidly speaking, I do not think much of your American project, and fear that New York would appear even more uncanny to you than London. Nevertheless, write to me some particulars about the offer which has been made to you, without the slightest fear of alarming the German Confederacy. As I frequently said, Carlsruhe is, for the present, your best chance, and I am persuaded that the Grand Duke of Baden, who is very well inclined towards you, will not fail to give you practical proof of his kindness. Devrient does not expect to give *Tristan* before December, on the birthday of the Grand Duchess.

You need, therefore, be in no particular hurry to finish the work. In any case, I shall visit you before that at Lucerne, or wherever you like, and will play to you a lot of my stuff if, as you tell me, it amuses you. The noblest reward of my work would be if it were to bring home to you the truth that you are and remain an *immense musician*, and if by that means you were incited to renewed industry.

In spite of all the war troubles the meeting of musicians will take place at the beginning of June, as announced, and I have to take up my quarters at Leipzig for that purpose as early as next week. Do not laugh at me too much because I continue to take an interest in similar things ; they are not without influence on your *tantièmes*, and from that point of view I may ask for your toleration. I hope the weather will soon be finer on the lake, and a milder spirit will illumine your soul.

Cordially your
F. LISZT.

WEYMAR, *May 14th*, 1859.

I told you at the time how deeply your letter to M. about the Symphonic Poems had rejoiced me. The twaddle which dulness, triviality, and spite have talked about it is not worth notice.

292.

LUCERNE, *May 15th*, 1859.

DEAREST FRANZ,

Thiele, of Berne, the, trombone player, has just called on me, and told me that he recently visited you at Weimar, not knowing at that time that the place of trombone player would be vacant there. He asked me to recommend him to you, because, as a native of Weimar, he would like much to be employed there. I am cordially pleased to recommend him to you most warmly, not only for the sake of Thiele, but for that of your orchestra. He took part in 1853 in my famous May concerts at Zurich, and on that occasion gained, I may say, my whole heart by his enthusiasm. He had two very weak players with him, but managed to carry them along with him by his energy to such an extent, that in the passage

one might have thought that one was listening to a whole host of trombones. Thiele, in short, is excellent, and known all through Switzerland as a trombone genius. I congratulate you on his acquisition. Do not let him escape you.

Farewell for to-day, dearest friend. What state I am in you may unfortunately see from the fact that a few days ago I felt bound in conscience and duty to ask Devrient not to rely on *Tristan* or me any longer. This was bound to happen, and there is an end for the present.

Much luck to the Leipzig festival.

Farewell, and accept the best wishes of

Your
RICHARD W.

293.

May 21st, 1859.

DEAREST FRIEND,

Send Tausig to me; I hear he is disengaged. My wife has even written to me that he wished to come to me.

Otherwise I have nothing rational to tell you to-day.
I feel miserable; you will soon hear more. A thousand
cordial thanks for your letter.

Your

R. W.

LUCERNE.

294.

DEAREST RICHARD,
My excellent friend, Felix Dräseke, is on his way
to you. Receive him kindly as one of "ours," and
reveal to him your *Nibelungen* treasure, on which he is
worthy of gazing with heart and soul.

I hope to be with you at the end of August; let me
know where I shall find you then.

Your

F. L.

WEYMAR, *July* 19*th*, 1859.

295.
Telegram.

WEYMAR, *August* 9*th.*

TO RICHARD WAGNER,
LUCERNE,
HÔTEL SCHWEIZERHOF.

On the completion of *Tristan* the most cordial
congratulations of your invariably faithful

FRANCISCUS.

296.

LUCERNE, *August* 19*th*, 1859.

DEAREST FRANZ,
I should like to thank Princess M. for the news
contained in her last letter, and to congratulate her

cordially on her impending marriage, but I am ill, and a feverish cold has suppressed all rational thoughts in me. But as I wanted to give you some news of me without delay, I ask you, for the present, to be the very eloquent interpreter of my sincere feelings to our amiable Child. The effort thus made, in spite of my indisposition, enables me to add that, although the disappointed hope of your visit, which would have been most welcome just now, fills me with grief, I fully understand that the sacrifice in my favour would have been too great. On the other hand, I lay the sacrifice made by me at the feet of the happy Child with joyful pride.

As to my fate I can tell you nothing, not knowing myself whither I shall direct my steps. I should like to live in Paris in absolute retirement, but the French Minister refuses to give me his *visé* for my passport. In answer to my remonstrances, he wrote to Paris a fortnight ago, but has had no answer. I am probably taken for an obstinate conspirator, an opinion which the treatment I receive at the hands of Germany seems to countenance. I wait for my fate in my little room here, neither longing for Paris nor attracted by any other place that is open to me. Dräseke is still with me, and I enjoy his visit. Soon he will go too.

Excuse me from writing any more. Even the effort of these few lines has put me in a perspiration.

Continue to love me, and greet Altenburg a thousand times from   Your

R. W.

Tristan has received your welcome with pride and joy.

297.

DEAREST FRIEND,

Your letter, received to-day, has increased my grief at not being able to be with you. Although I am not much worth as a sick nurse, I should nurse you well, and assist you in passing the time with more ease. Alas! we are miserable creatures, and the few who have penetrated the deepest secrets of life are the most miserable of all. That snarling old cur, Schopenhauer, is quite right in saying that we are ridiculous in addressing each other as *Monsieur* or citizen. *Compagnon de misère et de souffrance*, or fellow-sufferers, and worse we are, *tutti quanti*, and nothing we can do can make any essential change in this. The worst is that we know it quite well, and yet never like to believe it.

What is this about the *visé* of your passport? Probably the impediment has been removed by this time ; otherwise make inquiries as to the quarter from which it arises, whether from the Saxon embassy in Paris, or from the French police. Steps must be taken accordingly. It is understood that I am quite at your service in this matter, but I should not like to make a *faux pas*, and it is necessary, therefore, that I should be more accurately informed by you, in order to apply at once to the right people.

In my opinion Paris is the most comfortable, most appropriate and cheapest place for you while things in Germany remain in their wretched state. Although you may not agree with the artistic doings there, you wil find many diverting and stimulating things, which will do you more good than your walks in Switzerland, beautiful though the Alpine landscape may be.

I am surprised, it is true, at your speaking of a permanent settlement in Paris at this moment. I thought that your relations to Carlsruhe had reached such a point as to secure to you an asylum in the Grand Duchy of Baden (perhaps at Heidelberg, unless the *Professors* should frighten you there). How about the first performance of *Tristan* at Carlsruhe? Devrient informed me, with tolerable certainty, that the intention was to give the work on the birthday of the Grand Duchess in December, and that you would be invited to conduct it. I hope no change has taken place in this. Let me have particulars. Perhaps I shall be able to assist you in simplifying the matter.

Do you know what I did a few days ago? Looking at your portrait, which you had signed *Santo Spirito Cavaliere*, it occurred to me to write a *Rienzi fantasia* for pianoforte. If it should amuse you for a moment my time will have been well employed. I should tell you that your little bust adorns my writing desk. You are of course without the company of any other celebrities—no Mozart, no Beethoven, no Goethe, or whatever their names may be. To this room, which is the heart of the house, none of them is admitted. What a beautiful day it will be when I see you here.

M. will leave us soon, probably in October; until then I cannot get away from here. If you should happen to remain in Switzerland till after that, I shall visit you in the late autumn. Otherwise I shall see you at Carlsruhe or Paris.

Remember me cordially to Dräseke. I am very glad you have taken a liking to him. He is a splendid fellow. In our small circle of most intimate friends he is called the "hero." Has he shown you his ballad, "König Helge"? It is a glorious thing.

Be good enough to tell him that *I invite him specially* to stay with me on his return journey, and that I should think it very shabby of him if he played me the trick of flying past me under my very nose.

Try to get well again as soon as possible, dearest friend, and continue to love

Your

FRANZ.

WEYMAR, *August 22nd*, 1859.

298.

PARIS, *October 20th*, 1859.

I hope, dear Franz, these lines will reach you exactly on the 22nd.

Accept my cordial wishes for your birthday. It is of great significance to me that just at present, while I am seriously and deeply considering our mutual relations, I should come upon this day which Nature herself, no doubt, counts amongst her most fortunate days. For what she succeeded in creating on this day has borne such rich fruit that, without this gift of your existence, there would be a chasm in the essence of things, of the depth of which he only can judge who loves you as I love you, and who might suddenly imagine that you existed no longer. Gazing down this terrible chasm, such as my imagination pictured it, I turned my eyes to you as one awaking from a terrible dream, and was so sincerely delighted, so deeply moved by your real existence, that you appeared to me as one newborn. In this spirit I greet you on this, to me, highly important birthday. Your friendship is an absolute necessity to me; I cling to it with my last vital strength.

When shall I see you at last?

Have you an idea of the position in which I am, of the miracles of faith and love which I require in order to gain new courage and patience? Think this out for yourself, without my telling you. You *must* know me sufficiently to understand this, although we have not lived much together.

I ask you, once more, when shall we meet again? Carlsruhe is more than uncertain. *Tristan,* altogether, has become a shadowy and half impossible thing. Do not wait for an external occasion which may bring me to you. In the most favourable case the *Tristan* period, with its desperate and terrible exertions, would not be fit for our meeting again for the first time. Be guided to me by your innermost heart, and may it impel you to come to me soon. By the middle of November I expect my wife. Could I not have you *before*? It is bad enough for me that I have to call you, and that you do not come of your own accord. I heard of the marriage of Princess M. through B. yesterday; he does not inform me where she is going to live. Kindly tell me where I am to write in order to convey my wishes to her.

Farewell; I am just on the point of moving into my new lodgings. So I am " settled " once more, without faith, love, or hope.

Farewell, and accept my wishes kindly; in congratulating you I congratulate myself.

Your

R. W.

16, Rue Newton, Champs Elysées.

299.

Paris, *November 23rd*, 1859,
16, Rue Newton.

Believe me, dear Franz, I find it very difficult to give you news of myself. We live too little together, and must necessarily become strangers in one important aspect of friendship. You wrote to me to Venice and Lucerne that you liked my migration to Paris for the reason that you would be able to visit me more frequently. I have often assured you that I desired an amnesty particularly because I should be able to pay you more frequent and longer visits, and I informed you again that your promise induced me to look upon my Paris settlement in a more favourable light. In spite of this, my first request for your visit addressed to you from here has met with a refusal. You say you cannot come to Paris, and propose a two days' meeting at Strassburg instead. What will be the use of these Strassburg days to us ; what to me ? I have nothing to tell you in a hurry, no plans that we need discuss. I want to enjoy you, to live with you for some time, as we have hitherto seen so little of each other. Why do you all of a sudden object to Paris, where, if you do not wish it, no one need know of your presence ? I can get you rooms near me in a very remote quarter. We shall spend the days at my lodging, where you can see whom you like. Why need you always be a public man apart from the private friend ? I cannot understand this. My poor deserted life has made me incapable of comprehending an existence which casts a side glance at the whole world at every step. You must pardon me for declining the Strassburg meeting, greatly as I appreciate the sacrifice which you offer me.   It is just this sacrifice which appears to me too great at the price of a few hurried days in a Strassburg hotel.

I am extremely sorry that the Princess was unable to find me; her very valuable letter I fail to understand.   By the spontaneous joy and cordiality with which I should have received her, she would have recognized what she is to me.   She has often experienced this, and surely does not suspect me of affectation.   I do not know what to say to all this, and remain silent.

My silence extends to everything else that otherwise I might have told you about myself.   If one has to tell such things at all, it is better to be silent about them. As to the Carlsruhe plan you are probably sufficiently enlightened.   Devrient has thought it desirable to make an excuse for the bungling and neglectful way in which he has taken up the idea of a first performance of *Tristan* at his theatre, by saying that it is impossible to execute the work.   To that *also* I do not reply. Why should I speak?   *I* know my fate and my position, and remain silent.   It is more serious to think of the consequences which the wiping out of my new work from the list of living things will have for my means of subsistence.   However, why should I point out those consequences?   He who is endowed with five senses must know what my position is.   I can complain no longer, for that would mean to accuse, and I do not even want to accuse friend Devrient.   I have not said a word to him.   You know enough now, and more than will please you.

My wife has arrived here.   She is a little better, and

I hope things will go on tolerably well. She told me, without complaining, that you had been at Dresden without paying her a visit. I tried to comfort her as well as I could.

Farewell, my dear Franz. Do not misunderstand me; I wanted to write to you, and for a long time did not know how to set about it. Heaven only knows whether I have done it in the proper way. Be always assured that you are dear to me above all else, even if I fail to comprehend many things which determine your action.

Farewell. Greet the Princess, and tell her that her letter pleased me, although I failed to understand it. Greet also Princess H——. May you all think of me in a friendly spirit.

Farewell.

Your
R. W.

300.

BRUSSELS, March 29th, 1860.

DEAREST FRANZ,

Once more I give you a sign of life. That one lives at all is perhaps the most wonderful case in point, and when one arrives at the end of things, one need not care any longer. Death, which at this moment mows down men so recklessly, leaves us standing in a bare field by a mere whim. One is astonished and a little thoughtful for awhile.

My fate is very odd. While the real thing for which alone I care remains enveloped in the most German mist of impossibility. H.'s diplomatic skill has arranged for me all manner of Paris glories, which float before me mockingly like a *Fata Morgana*. Heaven only knows what will come of this *Tannhäuser* scheme. In my heart I do not yet believe in it, and for good reasons. It is of more importance to me to perform *Tristan* in Germany, and I am determined to set that old Dresden matter right if any decent concessions are made to me. If I succeed in this, I shall look to Vienna as the theatre which has the best singers, and presents the unique phenomenon of being conducted by a competent musician, with whom one can come to an understanding. This, as you know, cannot be found in the rest of Germany.

Of you, dearest friend, I have heard nothing for a long time, for even H. was unable to tell me anything. The comfort of your visits in Paris, which at one time you promised me so confidently, will not, it appears, be vouchsafed to me. Be not offended, therefore, if to-day I send you a visitor in order to give you some news of myself on the same occasion. I have been brought here by the absurd illusion of being able, by repeating my Paris concerts at Brussels, to recover some of the money which those Paris excesses had cost me. But of course the only results of this excursion were new expenses and a little propaganda. Amongst the most valuable conquests I have made here is first Herr A. Samuel, who is starting for Germany, and would like to be introduced to you. He has been very amiable towards me, both in deed and word. You will like him, too, and in that belief I recommend him to your welcome.

You also introduced some one to me here. Frau

Agnes Street-Klindworth brought me a letter from
you which 'you had given to her five years ago for
London.   I have to thank you for the most pleasant
acquaintance which you procure to me so unexpectedly
and after all that time.   I was soon at home with her
and Papa Klindworth, and owe the most pleasant
memories to these two people.   The old man amused
me greatly by his incredible wealth of diplomatic
anecdote.

I return to Paris to-day in order to have a closer view
of my brilliant misery.   M. Royer wants a large ballet
for the second act of *Tannhäuser*; you may imagine
how I relish the idea.   My only refuge in the face or
such demands is Princess Metternich, who is highly
esteemed by Fould, etc.   I must see whether I can get
rid of this ballet, otherwise I shall of course withdraw
Tannhäuser.

Well, you have now a good insight into the joy of
my existence.   Do not delay communicating to me a
fragment of your life.   The only thing that makes our
position towards this misery of world and life tolerable
is the growing contempt for world and life; and if one
can arrive at that in a good humour, things are all right
for a little while.   But when one perceives how few
things hold water, when one observes the terrible superficiality, the incredible thoughtlessness, the selfish
desire for pleasure, which inspire every one, one's own
earnestness appears often in a very comic light.   This
consideration is to me, at least, the only one which
sometimes puts me in a tolerable mood.

A thousand cordial greetings to you, my dearest
Franz ; with Mamma I get on very well.   The old lady

quite touches me by her love and sympathetic insight.
Farewell, and remember lovingly,

Your
R. W.

301.

Dépêche Télégraphique.

WEYMAR, *le* 22 *Mai.*

Déposée sous le no. 93 *a* 12 *heures* 31 *minutes s.*
Expédiee à domicile le 22 *à* 2 *heures* 15 *minutes soir.*

RICHARD WAGNER,

RUE NEWTON, 16, CHAMPS ELYSÉES,
CHEMIN DE VERSAILLES, PARIS.

Cordial wishes for your birthday from your

FRANZ LISZT.

302.

Your letter, dearest, unique friend, is to me more
beautiful than the most beautiful balmy May day.
May you rejoice in the joy which it has given to me.
I wish I could telegraph myself to Paris. Where
could I be more happy than with you, in the magic
circle of *Rhinegold*, the *Valkyrie, Siegfried, Tristan and*
Isolde—all of them the objects of my longing? But I
must not think of this for the present, although I shall
certainly come as soon as I can.

Your photograph has been announced to me by an
amiable hand, but has not made its appearance so
far. I told you before that your little bust stands on
my writing-desk as *unicum.* The photograph will find
its place in the same room, which otherwise contains
nothing *artistic.*

Beethoven, Weber, Schubert, and others of that stamp keep company to your portrait (that with the motto, " Du weisst wie das wird ") in the ante-room. *Here* I want to have you alone together with my St. Francis, whom Steinly has designed for me splendidly. He stands on heaving ocean-waves, his outspread cloak on, firmly, unmovedly. In his left hand he calmly holds burning coals ; the right is extended in the act of blessing ; his gaze is turned upwards, where the word " *charitas* " glows, surrounded by an aureole.

The great life-question of the Princess has been finally and favourably settled. All the villainous and subtle intrigues which were spun for a number of years have been dispelled.

After the return of the Princess from Rome (where she arrived last Sunday, and will probably stay till the end of July) all will be arranged. I wish I could soon have the pleasure of seeing you *chez nous*.

Through Fräulein Hundt (whom, together with her friend Ingeborg Stark, you received so amiably) I heard a good many things about your way of life in Paris. *Tannhäuser*, with ballet, and a contest of trans- lators as well as of minstrels, are immediately before you. It will be a tough piece of work for you, and I advise as many walks and cooling baths as possible. Fips should teach you a little philosophic patience during the rehearsals. Frau Bürde-Ney told me lately when she was " starring " here, that she intended to go to Paris for a few days, in order to study Isolde with you. She has the necessary stuff (" Wupptich " they say at Dresden) for it.

A thousand thanks for the score which Härtel has

sent me. You know best how all this is sung from my very soul. Let me know when convenient what you consider most desirable in regard to the performance of *Tristan*. At Carlsruhe it seems impossible, and Devrient was inclined to bet that *Tristan* could not be performed anywhere else either, unless you consented to considerable alterations. This is by no means my opinion, and as often as Devrient said *No*, I replied *Yes*. His stage experience is, no doubt, older than mine, but nevertheless I have perfect confidence in my opinion of such things. You know for what reasons I did not, at the time, beg *Tristan* for Weymar, and you will approve of my passive attitude. If, as I should not like to think, no favourable chances for the speedy performance of this marvellous work turn up, and if, for the present, you will be satisfied with a performance here, I firmly believe that I can arrange it for next season (1861). Let me know your views when you write again. Meanwhile I remain, with all my heart,

Your own

F. LISZT.

WEYMAR, *May* 31*st*, 1860.

I shall remain here till the return of the Princess. Whether Berlioz will reply to your letter, couched in the barbarous French of Genius, in *our* sense, appears somewhat doubtful. The more's the pity.

303.

PARIS, *June* 15*th*, 1860.

Can you induce Herr D. to send me a prompt reply to my last letter ?

The question at stake is whether or not I shall
be able to do something for the health of my wife
this summer in accordance with the doctor's pre-
scription. I *must* know this. At the same time I
must declare that I shall not accept less than 1,000
francs.

I do not want to encroach upon you, but what you
can do without injuring yourself, do please, as soon
as possible.

If they think me worth that sum at Weimar I shall
expect the bill of exchange by return of post.

Adieu.

Your

RICH. WAGNER.

16, RUE NEWTON, CHAMPS ELYSÉES.

304.

DEAREST FRANZ,

According to a letter just received, D. thinks it
necessary to refuse me the thousand francs I had
asked for, and offers me thirty louis d'or instead.

This puts me in an awkward position. On the
one hand I am, as usual, greatly in want of money,
and shall decidedly not be able to send my wife to
Soden for a cure, unless I receive the subvention I
had hoped for. On the other hand, I must despair
of ever prospering if, compelled by necessity, I have
to yield on every occasion. I have explained my
view of the question of honorarium to D. quite openly
and without any brusqueness, and have finally insisted
upon my first demand.

I should like to let my wife start as soon as possible.

The worst turn which this affair could take at Weimar would be, if my demand were simply refused, and if I had nothing at all to give to my wife.

You now know my position exactly. If your diplomatic genius could find a middle course (in case my demand cannot be carried) you would oblige me greatly. I suppose that you are on sufficiently good terms with D., and hope that, at the worst, you will discover such a middle course. Therefore kindly look after this trumpery matter. I am unfortunately surrounded by nothing but trumpery things.

Let me hear from you soon.

Adieu.

Your
R. W.

305.

Concerning the *Rienzi* honorarium, I could effect nothing beyond what D. had offered to you. Pardon me, dearest friend, for not having written to you at once, but I am very tired this week and as unwell as the normal state of my health will allow me to be. It is not of any consequence, and a few days' rest will set me right again. In the meanwhile I must unfortunately advise you to accept D.'s proposal. The G. D. is not here, and no other course is open until the performance actually takes place. After that I hope to get you a few hundred francs more. D. tells me that *Rienzi* is to take the place of the *Prophet* next season. Five (say 5) new decorations have been ordered, and are in preparation. Meffert will sing the title part, and the other characters will be decently represented, while the chorus will be increased by soldiers. Let it therefore take its course until we can do something better. Patience, says Byron, is the virtue of mules, but he who does not possess it remains a miserable ass.

I shall write to you in a few days about several things not connected with business. Most cordially

Your

F. L.

June 24th (birthday of the Grand Duke, who is not expected back here before eight or ten days. From Baden he has gone to Switzerland with his wife).

Your photograph has arrived at last, and lights up my room.

306.

MOST UNIQUE OF MEN,

Madame Kalergi's intervention in your concert affair gives me great joy. Beautiful and noble traits of that kind are, unfortunately, seldom met with. Will you kindly forward the enclosed lines to my gracious lady protectress? I do not know her present address. You are once more in the old *Tannhäuser* birth throes. Much luck! You will have to suffer much at the rehearsals, and have perhaps never undergone so hard a trial of patience as the re-writing and rehearsing of this work, which to you is partly "ein überwundener Standpunkt," as friend Brendel says. Through means of the *Presse Théâtrale*, which is kindly sent to me, I remain *au courant* of your exertions. Be not too much annoyed at being an immortal poet and composer; there is nothing worse in this world to

which one should apply the following modified version
of Leibnitz's well-known axiom : *Tout est pour le mieux,
dans un des plus mauvais mondes possible !*
Alas ! I lately again had a great misfortune. One
of my few friends, the bravest and most self-sacrificing
of all, is dead. Her name was Clara Riese, and she
lived as pianoforte teacher at Leipzig, where, on
Tuesday, I accompanied her to her last place of rest
in the old Johannes cemetery.

Up to the last day I was in hopes that her incredible
strength of character would keep her alive ; but in
vain.

Excuse this mournful message, but I am still so full
of her death that I cannot help thinking of it.

Nothing is happening here. D. showed me your
letter about *Rienzi,* and I am thankful to you for having
behaved in so accommodating and generous a manner.
The opera will be taken in hand at the commencement
of the season (September), and after the first performance I intend to have some conversation with His
Serene Highness.   Before that it would be useless.

Have you heard anything from Seebach ?   Madame
Kalergi will be the best and most useful intercessor
you could employ in this matter.

May everything succeed to your heart's desire.

Your
F. Liszt.

From the Princess I continue to have very good
news ; she will probably remain in Rome for some
time to come.

In October Härtel will publish the last two of my

twelve Symphonic Poems, *Hamlet*, and *The Battle of the Huns*.   As soon as I have an opportunity I shall send you my medley of songs to Paris.

307.

MY DEAR RICHARD,

It will be quite right and proper for you to pay a call of thanks to the Princess Regent at Baden-Baden. Considering the well-known favour in which you stand with the Princess, and the sterling quality of her sympathy, she will not fail to have a favourable influence on the course your circumstances will take in the immediate future.   Your presenting yourself personally to her is most likely to increase, if possible, her interest in your works.   All this is right, and as it should be ; on the other hand, it is a pity that I shall not be able to come to Baden.   Excuse me from mentioning my reasons ; you would perhaps think them miserable, but they determine me categorically.   Although I do not think that you will return to Paris as early as Saturday, the hurried character of our meeting, especially in the landscape surroundings of Baden, would be painful.   I had made arrangements to start to-night, and the resolution of resigning the pleasure of seeing you again costs me much.   Nevertheless, I think it preferable to wait for an opportunity more favourable to both of us, which, I hope, will occur soon.

B. was with me when your letter ot August 10th arrived.   He came from Wiesbaden, where they were expecting you for a performance of *Lohengrin* (with Niemann).   By-the-bye, there will be no lack of

Tannhäuser and *Lohengrin* performances in these regions. Be a little lenient and longsuffering with regard to their defects. Do not misinterpret my stopping at home for the present ; there is not an atom of laziness or egoism in it—*mais tout bien considéré je dois faire ainsi, parceque cela vaut mieux pour vous*—and I feel convinced that, later on, you will agree with me.

Your

F. L.

WEYMAR, *August 14th*, 1860.

My gracious master, the Grand Duke, spoke of you lately with the most lively interest, and expressed his wish to see you here, to which I replied, that for that a *special* occasion would be necessary. You should not forget, however, that he has more than once interceded for you with the King of Saxony by word and by letter.

308.

PARIS, *September* 13th, 1860.

At last I find time and the proper mood for writing to you in a more collected manner than is usually the case. My late brief letters left a debt to you unpaid.

The letter I received from you at Baden quite satisfied me, and I felt quite ashamed at having proposed so hurried, and to you so inconvenient, a meeting. The matter simply came to this :—

A longer excursion to Germany was on my part quite out of the question, and I had to abandon all hope of the long-desired proper visit to you for this year. A brief interruption of my anything but pleasant stay in Paris was, on the other hand, very desirable to me. I had promised my wife to fetch her, if possible, from Soden. The Rhine I had never seen. I was told at the Prussian Embassy that the Princess of Prussia would shortly arrive on the Rhine, and the Saxon ambassador told me that he would be very pleased, and that it would be agreeable to the King of Saxony also, if I were to thank the Princess for the interest she had taken in the decision finally made in my favour. These various motives I developed into the plan of a very short tour to the Rhine, such as suited my limited finances. One or two days more would have caused the most painful embarrassment to me. I could of course not have thought of staying a day in Frankfort without thinking of the possibility of embracing you, but as you were unable to come, I was unable to wait at Frankfort; you understand why. Therefore, I ventured to ask you to follow me to Baden, where my narrow financial circumstances compelled me to go. I fully understand the reasons which prevented you from coming there. Pardon me for having attempted to smuggle, so to speak, our meeting into another plan. The temptation to such an attempt was too great.

You are quite mistaken, however, in thinking that a " special occasion" would be necessary for inducing me to pay a visit to Weimar. Believe me that I abide by what I told the Grand Duke at Lucerne years ago, when he asked me whether I should be inclined, in case of an amnesty, to stay at Weimar now and then. I told him that the chief reason which would attract me to Weimar would be your society, and that, therefore, I should pay frequent visits to Weimar as long as you

were there. You will understand that in my relations
to Weimar no change whatever has, fortunately, taken
place ; on the contrary, I may hope that I shall no
longer be obliged to pay for the boon of your society by
my participation in insufficient artistic doings (I am
speaking of the opera). Be assured that I am joyfully
looking forward to the day when I may set sail for
Altenburg.

My position in Germany is still far from satisfactory.
As you know, I am neither amnestied nor has my
sentence been remitted. All I have obtained is the
promise that the claim to extradition will be abandoned
whenever, for the purpose of performing my works,
I wish to enter a German territory, the government
of which has given its consent, and asked permission
of the Saxon Government. Even my six days' journey
to the Rhine I could not have extended to Weimar
without previously complying with those conditions,
for otherwise I should have offended the Saxon Government at the very outset. Our German potentates
cannot enter into direct communication with me, for
I am still a political outlaw, neither must I hope for
important or sufficient measures in my favour at any
court, and the plans for the performances of my last
works have not been advanced much. This is all the
more evident, as the condition of our largest operatic
theatres is most disappointing. Of Berlin I could not
think at all without first contemplating the possibility
of a complete revolution of affairs, both as regards the
theatre and the management. I was not bold enough
to approach the Princess of Prussia with any hope of
producing a profound impression in that sense. I was

quite satisfied with meeting in her the *spirituelle*, intellectual, lively woman I had pictured to myself, and I limited myself to acknowledging and thanking her for the uninterrupted sympathy she had shown for my works without being in the least tempted to communicate to her any plan or wish of mine.

It remains therefore a perfect mystery where my *Tristan* is to see the light of the world. The birth would probably be most easy if I were to trust the King of Hanover with the delivery. Niemann declares that the King would engage any singer, male or female, whom I should require for the model performance of my work as long as that performance took place at Hanover. This might lead to something ; that King appears liberal and magnificent in his passion for art, and nothing else will suit me. Let us hope that my political situation will be no obstacle.

For the present my Paris enterprise occupies me altogether, and mercifully obscures my view of future German misery. I do not know what rumours are current with you as to the difficulties placed in my way. They may be well intended, but they are false. *Never yet has the material of an excellent performance been placed at my disposal so fully and unconditionally* as has been done at Paris for the performance of *Tannhäuser* at the Grand Opera, and I can only wish that some German prince would do the same for my new works. This is the first triumph of my art which I personally witness. I owe it to the success of my works in Germany, which has gained me such warm admirers, that the Emperor, on the strength of their word, has issued a truly imperial *command*, which makes me master of the whole material, and protects me from all intrigues. A translation, as excellent as could have possibly been expected, is another earnest of general success. I have secured the best singers that are to be had, and the preparations in every department are made with a zeal and a care to which Germany has little accustomed me. All the leading people go with pleasure to a task which offers them a more interesting occupation than is usual. I also take the matter seriously. I am removing such weak points as I have discovered in the score. I take great delight in the re-writing of the great Venus scene, and hope to improve the effect thereby. The ballet scene also will be executed on the larger scale designed by me.

Unfortunately I have not yet been able to begin this necessary work in the proper way. Before my journey to the Rhine the translation occupied me exclusively, and on my return here I had, first of all, to complete a little piece of literary work which has only just been finished. M. Frédéric Villot, about whom H. has probably spoken to you, asked me to publish an edition of my operatic poems in a prose-translation, and to add a preface explaining my ideas. This I have done, and I hope that the opus will appear about the beginning of October at the latest. The rehearsals are in full swing, but unfortunately I had to object to the baritone at the last moment. Fould had at once to give orders for the engagement of a new singer, but we have not yet found the right man, and this has caused a slight delay. There has, however, been no trace of ill-will on the part of any one. M., who is working here in his underhand way, will not, after all, be able to do anything against the Emperor and the cause; he is trying, however, to secure the good engagements which have been made for me for his own benefit later on. Well, I do not grudge him this ; the man has no real initiative.

You have now, dearest friend, an approximate view of my life and work. That I should be happy you can scarcely expect, but I feel the calm of the fatalist who surrenders himself to his fate, astonished perhaps a little at the often curious manner in which it disposes of me and leads me into unexpected paths, and saying to myself: " So it was to be."

With real horror I think of Germany and of my future enterprises in that country. God forgive me, but I discover nothing but mean and miserable things, conceit and a pretence of solid work without any real foundation ; half-heartedness in everything. After all I prefer to see *Le Pardon de Ploërmel* in Paris than under the shadow of the famous, glorious German oak tree. I must also confess to you that my treading once more German soil did not produce the slightest impression upon me, except in so far as I was astonished at the insipidity and impertinence of the language I had to listen to. Believe me, we have no Fatherland, and if I am "German" it is because I carry my Germany along with me. This is fortunate, because the Mayence garrison has certainly not inspired me with enthusiasm.

X. seems to be angry with me ; I at last got annoyed with him because his optimism irritated me.

I cannot understand a good many things, and allowance ought to be made for me on account of my curious life. X., it seems to me, fritters himself away; he undertakes too much, and by that means loses the compact, concentric quality which a true man needs. I cannot look on without being painfully affected. On the other hand, I am, no doubt, very wrong in not accepting so true a friend as he is; and I have much reason to acknowledge X.'s friendship. He must not be angry with me and do as he likes; but he should be sometimes a little more punctual with his letters.

Believe me, that in spite of my Paris surroundings I feel awfully lonely, while of you I can never think except as of some one who is surrounded by people, even at Weimar. Perhaps I have a good many erroneous notions in that respect; at least Madame Street gave me to understand as much when she described her visit to you. She said that you had been very sad, although in very good health. Well, I certainly cannot see why you should be particularly joyous; at the same time this news has struck me very much, and Madame W., to whom I spoke about it, was quite frightened. There is something about you which causes you to appear surrounded by splendour and light, and makes it difficult for us to understand what could make you sad. Least of all am I inclined to discover the cause of your irritation in the stupid reception which your works have met with now and then, for it seems to me that no one ought to know better than you that this animosity is caused not by your works, but by the false light in which you appear to the multitude. That light which reveals you as so exceptional a phenomenon, that a misconception of it is only too easily accounted for, is now and then too powerful, especially for German eyes. I think, therefore, you are right in withdrawing yourself from that illumination as much as possible, and in letting your works take their own course for a time without the least anxiety about them. One thing you will gain, the avoidance ot personal contact. In that, everything is misery, and believe me that while we try to " do violence to the kingdom of heaven," we only stir up the nether mud. No, the kingdom of heaven comes to us in our sleep. But enough of this vague talk! Let us soon meet, when we shall see how we can ward off all sadness. I shall soon make a long stay with you.

God bless you, my Franz! Pardon this long talk to my desire of being near you once more.

A thousand greetings from

Your

R. W.

309.

WEYMAR, September 21st, 1860.

Your glorious letter, dearest Richard, made me breathe the pure atmosphere of high mountains once more. You know what I require, and offer it to me in abundance. I was almost afraid that you might have misunderstood my non-appearance at Soden or Baden, and I am cordially delighted at being set right by you as to this. As I wrote to you before, it was *impossible* for me to get away from here before Thursday, August 16th. Well, all is over now, and you have pardoned me. Let us talk of something else. How proud I should be of your visit here, and how beneficial and strengthening prolonged intercourse with you would be to me, I need not tell you. I think it more probable, however, that I shall pay you a visit in Paris first. The exact date I shall not be able to determine until the continued uncertainty and wavering of all my circumstances here have ceased, which must happen shortly. As regards your visit here, I repeat what I have said to you and others. Weymar owes you a special distinction, and it is necessary that an appropriate and adequate opportunity of presenting yourself here should be offered to you. It is extremely amiable of you to mean principally me when you pronounce the name of Weymar. I wish that this *synonym* (in an artistic sense) were a little more pronounced; that my advice were followed, and my reasonable wishes complied with a little more readily. But this can scarcely be expected, and I must in this, as in other matters, show myself resigned, determined, and consistent. I quite agree with what you say of the "*insufficient* artistic doings" here ; however, many things *could* and *should* be done, especially for you and your works. You will understand that I cannot abandon this view, and that I shall do all in my power to realise it. The impending performance of *Rienzi* may do something towards it.

I consider Hanover a well-chosen ground for the first performance of *Tristan*. The King works magnificently for his theatre, and if the matter is placed before him in the proper way, it may be expected that he will carry out your wishes and intentions. Unfortunately I cannot be of service to you, for to the particular influence of some of my "*friends*" I owe a distinctly pronounced dislike on the part of His Majesty. All I can do in the face of this is to wait quietly and resignedly, until the King condescends to adopt a more

correct view. Fortunately Niemann is devoted to you,
body and soul, chest-voice and head-voice. He will, no
doubt, do all in his power to bring about the scenic
embodiment.

Berlin and Vienna will probably hold back a little in
existing circumstances, and the rest of Germany, which
is united at least in the spirit of *negation*, will probably
wait prudently until the camel comes walking along,
after which it will consult no end of folios in order
to describe and appreciate it properly. Oh! lazy
abomination, your name is—artistic conditions.

At Wiesbaden, Frankfort, and I know not where
else, they were waiting for Wagner, and wanted to see
him conduct, or at least listen to, *Tannhäuser*, *Lohengrin*,
etc., and there would certainly have been no lack of
enthusiastic demonstrations; but from a work like
Tristan, at the very first sight of the score of which
every one must exclaim: " This is something unheard
of, marvellous, sublime," they run away, and hide themselves like fools.

I have taken the liberty of making use of the passage
of your letter referring to the ready assistance you
receive from the artists, and the management of the
Grand Opera in Paris by Imperial command; and in
the next number of Brendel's paper you will read
something corresponding to your letter in the form of
an original correspondence. We had, of course, to
adapt some things too true in themselves to our
laudable habits here. As I have named Brendel I
should like to mention a request, viz., that you should
publish the preface to the French translation of your
dramas in Germany, simultaneously with the Paris

edition, and that you should for that purpose send the *original*, probably written in German, either to Brendel or some publisher. A translation of that preface will, no doubt, appear, unless you forestall it by the original itself, and thus prevent the travesty of your ideas, or at least of your style. If no German sketch should be in existence, my request of course falls to the ground, for it would be asking you too much to do the work twice over.

Then you are satisfied with the translation of *Tannhäuser*? I am extremely pleased, for I confess that I think it no easy task to Frenchify your works in your sense. I am very curious to see the new version of the Venus scene and the ballet. When you have finished it quite, and a copy has been made, you might perhaps lend me the sketch of the new version for a few days, but I hope that this will be made unnecessary by my visit to you.

Truly, dear Richard, we belong together and must come together at last. Cordial thanks for your kind letter, which in these dreary days has been a great and noble joy to me. Amongst other things you have taken a fine and strikingly correct view of the totally passive attitude with regard to the reception and promulgation of my works which I shall observe for the future. Other people have somewhat misunderstood my conduct. What a blessing it is to be able to dispense with the explanation and discussion of certain things !

God bless you, dearest Richard; keep fresh and brave and upright.   Your

F. Liszt.

I shall write to X. to-day, and give him news of you.

310.

ᴾARIS, *November 24th*, 1860,
3, RUE D'AUMALE.

DEAREST FRANZ,

Forgive me for writing but a few lines. I have been severely ill these four weeks, and my recovery is scarcely noticeable. I am still extremely weak.

I have an urgent request to make. Fancy! I do not possess *a single* copy of my poem of *The Ring of the Nibelung*. I want to publish it, and do not know where to get a copy for the printer. I remember that at the time I sent a great number of copies to Weimar, and there was such abundance there that (as I think Dräseke told me) the book was to be had second-hand. Be kind enough to get me one copy in consideration of my urgent need, and send it me as quickly as possible. If there should not be a single possessor who could make up his mind to part with his copy in spite of the author's great difficulty, I promise to restore to him the identical copy after the completion of the reprint. I may therefore fairly ask even the most ardent admirer of my poem to make this sacrifice on my behalf.

Alas! I begin to perspire, and can write no more. Come to Paris as you promised, and make me happy!

Your

R. W.

311.

DEAREST RICHARD,

I have managed to get a copy of your *Nibelungen*. Counsellor Müller was kind enough to give me his for you; it was taken yesterday to Paris by the courier of the French Embassy here, together with the volume "Wagner und das Musik-Drama," by Franz Müller, which has just been published. You will receive the little parcel from *Monsieur Lérée, chef de bureau des départs au ministère des affaires étrangères.* It is not customary for the ministry to transmit private messages, and you therefore must either call on M. Lérée personally, or send him a few lines.

I was in bed a whole week at the same 'time as you. There are moods and conditions in which we bear physical illness better than the uninterrupted sequence of every-day cares and tribulations.

When will the French edition of your three operatic poems appear, and what publisher undertakes the edition of the *Nibelungen* ? Have you arranged with Schott about the publication of the full scores of *Rhinegold* and the *Valkyrie* ? Send me word as to these three things.

The first performance of *Rienzi* is announced for Boxing-day. I have conducted several rehearsals, and have undertaken the others as well, but I have declined most positively to conduct the performance. That performance will be a brilliant one according to the circumstances here, and will probably realise D.'s expectations as to pecuniary success. Capellmeister Stör, who has conducted your three other operas ever since I left the theatre definitely, will undertake the direction of *Rienzi*. Our artists are full of enthusiasm.

As a trifle I may mention to you that Müller of Dresden (Messrs. Meser) will shortly publish two transcriptions by me,—the "Spinning Song" (*Dutchman*), and "Santo Spirito Cavaliere" (*Rienzi*).

I shall not talk to you about my coming to Paris until I am able to tell you the exact date ; it will be before long.

Your

F. L.

WEYMAR, *December 2nd,* 1860

312.

PARIS, *December 15th,* 1860.

DEAREST FRANZ,

I am very slowly regaining my strength.   What impedes my recovery, and indeed makes it impossible for the present, are the extraordinary exertions and excitements to which I have to expose my health, which is gradually coming back to me.   My daily occupation is this, that by the utmost care and by abstaining from any other kind of activity, however slight, I manage to attend the rehearsals at the opera.   The proofs of *Rhinegold,* which Messrs. Schott would have liked so much to have published at Christmas, have been lying on my table for seven weeks without my being able to make any progress with them.   Guess at my condition from this fact, and forgive me anything that I may have done to shock you.

Pardon, for example, my not having thanked you before for sending me Müller's copy of my *Nibelungen.* Good Lord ! I wanted so much to hasten the publication, and hurried you in consequence.   Now I possess the copy, and have not been able even to look at it.   I also found it impossible to send you the book before this ; I have a horror of undertaking anything, and apart from this, the Paris publishers treat one with abominable

negligence. The German original of my letter to Villot
you have probably seen. I have not been able yet to
address a single line to my Leipzig publisher in connection with this matter.

For *Tannhäuser* I have still to score the grand new
scene for Venus, and to compose the whole of the
Venusberg dance music. How this is to get done in
time without a miracle I fail to perceive.

I wish YOU would at last come to Paris.

But no more of this. I cannot speak of anything at
greater length, firstly, because I know too little, and
secondly, because I must absolutely conclude these lines.

Farewell, and a thousand greetings.

Your

R. W.

3, RUE D'AUMALE.

313

MY GREAT FRIEND,

How it is that we live for weeks and months *by
the side of each other* while I know all the time that we
are cordially united and, so to speak, welded together
in spirit, I will not explain to you to-day. You have
probably heard of the painful circumstances which prevented me from visiting you in Paris at the end of
February. God be thanked, my anxiety is now slightly
diminished, and I intend to arrive at Paris between May
7th and 9th. But I do not want to have it talked about
because the many impediments which have so far
frustrated my travelling schemes have made me a little
superstitious.

With your permission I should like to advocate the
offer made to you by Brendel, concerning the perform-

ance of the second act of *Tristan*, at the meeting of musicians (August 7th). Schnorr and his wife have undertaken to sing, and the other parts will be decently filled here. Of course, this fragmentary performance ought not in the least to disturb or interfere with your original and further plans concerning this work. I hope that you will credit me with sufficient knowledge of the circumstance to understand your hesitation at sanctioning this proceeding. Be good enough to tell me simply what you think about it. If you do not send us packing, and look favourably on our request, the proper steps will be taken.

Write to me, if possible, by return of post, because I leave here on the 29th inst.

Your

F. LISZT.

WEYMAR, *April 18th*, 1861.

314.

A thousand thanks, dearest Richard, for your kind letter. May the treacherous fate which has hitherto kept us apart soon be vanquished for ever. No one can understand better than I that a fragmentary performance of *Tristan* must appear quite absurd to you. I thank you for the gentle manner in which you reply to my proposal, and take into account the narrow circumstances and resources which impede my activity. You cannot believe how painful it is to me not to be able to do anything *proper* for your honour, benefit, and use. For several years all my steps and efforts in that direction have been in vain ; otherwise, not only *Tristan* but *The Ring of the Nibelung* would be in existence and do wonders.

I was told several times, and positively assured, that everything would be done here to further your efforts, and especially to effect the performance of *The Nibelungen* and of *Tristan*. I, for my part, have clearly demonstrated, by word of mouth and by letter, what they would have to do, viz., to invite you here for the purpose of mounting and conducting those works in accordance with your instructions and wishes. But the whole plan was always wrecked on the score of expenses.

I will not trouble you with the details of this affair, the failure of which, between ourselves, was my chief reason for giving up my connection with our theatre altogether.

The Carlsruhe performance of *Tristan* in September will be a great joy to me. The Grand Duke of Baden be praised and thanked for it. You will reward his kindness and grace in a glorious manner.

What will become of me in the course of this year is quite uncertain. First of all I shall see you in Paris.

Your

F. LISZT.

WEYMAR, *April 26th*, 1861.

An answer would be too late to find me here.

315.

PARIS, *June* 15*th*, 1861.

DEAREST FRANZ,

A few days ago I received a telegram from Leipzig for Tausig, in which he was requested to send his address. To-day followed a letter for him, accompanied by one to me, in which I am asked for information as to Tausig and his whereabouts. I think it unnecessary to give that information, because I assume that Tausig has either seen the person in question at Leipzig or given news of himself. I therefore ask you to transmit to our young friend these facts, and also the enclosed letter intended for him, as I do not know what to do with the latter.

Beyond this I have nothing to tell you, dearest Franz —no event, no plan, no hope—for not the slightest change has taken place in my position.

Farewell, and, if possible, make me happy soon by news of your well-being.

Cordially your
R. W.

3, Rue d'Aumale.

316.

Dearest Richard,

A letter from my daughter, Mdme. Ollivier, informs me that your wife will go to Soden by the middle of this week, and that you intend to come to Weymar by the end of the month.

Your presence here, coming as it does at the end of my too much prolonged stay, will be a beautiful spiritual ray of sunlight; let me urgently pray you not to refuse me this joy. On August 15th I intend to leave Weymar for a longer period, and have made the necessary preparations for my removal.

You will, of course, stay with me at Altenburg, where H. and T. also have quarters. To the Grand Duke I have announced your visit, and I expect that your personal relations to him will be of a most pleasant and satisfactory kind.

How about your settling at Carlsruhe? Have your pecuniary affairs been arranged in Paris, and how? Let me know something about this.

As to myself I know nothing definite, except that I am going away from Weymar. Many objections have of course been raised, which, however, have not been able to alter my resolution. Between this and the beginning of August I shall fix on my next place of abode, which will, in any case, not for the present be a large town, because I want retirement and work above all. Briefly speaking, my situation is indicated by this dilemma: Either my marriage takes place, and that soon—or not. In the former case, Germany later on, and especially Weymar, may still be possible for me. Otherwise no!

For the moment I am plagued with all kinds of business matters. Excuse me, dearest Richard, for writing you so little, and vouchsafe soon the great joy of your presence to

Your sincerely devoted

WEIMAR, *July 7th*, 1861.   F. LISZT.

P.S.—My daughter writes to say that she will arrive here with Ollivier on August 3rd. The performance of the *Prometheus* and *Faust* symphonies will be on August 6th.

INDEX.

A. (? Avenarius), ii. 41, 2.
B. A. (tenor), ii. 180, 4, 8, 94.
C. A., i. 302.
Abt, i. 79, 82.
Actor, Wagner's wish to have been, i. 75.
Actors and Singers, operatic, i. 77,9, 90, 2, 4, 8, 102, 55-6, 208 ;
   ii. 290.
   Personal instruction of, ii. 117.
Admirers, i. 137 ; ii. 41, 3, 8, 112, 207, 314, 25 ; "duty of his," ii.
   119, 61, 265.
Alberich, ii. 50.
Aldridge, the "black Roscius," i. 314.
Alexander's Indian expedition, ii. 99.
Alps, The, i. 86, 161, 210, 8, 87, 9, 313 ; ii. 28, 150.
Amat, Léopold, ii. 227.
Ambition, i. 23, 76, 234.
America, Wagner's idea of going to, ii. 9, 11 ; an offer for, ii. 112,
   114, 6, 9, 296, 300.
Amnesty and exile, i. 60, 74, 180, 96, 8, 234, 54, 61, 5-8, 71, 4, 80,
   285 ; ii. 10, 23-7, 42, 58, 141-7, 53, 5, 73, 6-7, 80, 94, 205, 32,
   235, 45, 51, 71-2, 85-7.
   partial, granted, ii. 321-2.
Ander, as Lohengrin, ii. 233.
Anderson, treasurer of " Old Philharmonic," ii. 57.
Animals, Wagner's love of, i. 135, 334 ; ii. 150.
Anschütz-Capitain, Frau (singer), i. 302.
Anxiety as to postal transit of MS. scores, ii. 120, 61.
Applause, ii. 144, 290.
Apt, Herr, i. 290.
Art v. Animalism, i. 236.
Art, Working hard at, i. 38, 40, 8, 56, 82, 143 ; ii. 18, 50.
Art-inspiration, i. 36, 49, 170 ; ii. 161, 295.
Art-mood ii. 5, 207.
Art-reform, i. 25, 32, 75, 97, 130, 51.
Art-review projected, i. 315-9.
Artistic creation, i. 123, 221 ; ii. 16, 92.

341

354   INDEX.

Original theatre, an, i. 151, 3, 6.
Ortrud, i. 186-7, 92-3.
Ossian, ii. 259.
Over-work, i. 213, 8 ; ii. 181.

P., Count (Hanover), ii. 115.
P., Manager, i. 4.
Paris, i. 1, 2, 26, 40, 8, 56-9, 62, 225, 308, 34 ; ii. 219, 21, 3, 7, 46,
    249, 304, 7-40.
    Liszt recommends, i. 33, 60 ; ii. 282, 8, 96, 305-6, 9.
    Publishers, ii. 335.
    Théâtre Lyrique, ii. 225.
    Wagner's concerts at, ii. 312.
Passport difficulties, i. 20, 321-2, 5, 7, 9-31 ; ii. 64, 244-5, 50, 96,
    304-5.
Patience, i. 248, 54 ; ii. 38, 81, 2, 147, 77-9, 210, 70, 93, 300, 8, 19.
Patronat-verein, First idea of, ii. 134.
Pawning his treasures, Wagner, ii. 277, 81.
Peimann, Baron von (Police Director, Prague), ii. 142.
Pension for Wagner, ii. 173-4, 9, 272-5, 81.
" Pension-Fund of Musicians," Liszt's concert for : Dresden, ii.
    213 ; Hamburg, i. 53, 9.
Peps (Wagner's dog), i. 334 ; cf. 298 ; ii. 150.
Philharmonic Society, New, want Wagner to conduct, ii. 102.
    Old, offer to Wagner, ii. 55-8, 60, 2 ; Concerts, ii. 71, 9 ;
    Wagner's opinion of orchestra ; ii. 71, 4, 85, 101.
Philipront (Brussels), i. 164-5.
Philistines, i. 108, 12, 35, 45, 208, 72, 86, 8, 305, 18, 52 ; ii. 4, 6,
    11, 27, 60-1, 82, 90, 4, 227.
Philosophical thoughts, etc., i. 55, 81, 151-3, 221, 54, 277-8 ; ii. 26,
    39, 53, 86, 93-9, 222-3, 84, 305, 11, 20.
Pianoforte-playing of neighbours, ii. 159, 83, 201.
Pictures of Madonna and S. Francesca, ii. 167.
Pitch in chorus-singing, i. 205.
Planers, the (Wagner's parents-in-law), i. 39.
Playful epithets, i. 231, 98, 313, 21, 48 ; ii. 154, 97, 200.
Poems for musical setting, ii. 15.
Poet, Wagner's first recognition as, i. 253.
Pohl, R., i. 329, 45, 9 ; ii. 19, 24, 203, 7.
Polemics, i. 34 ; ii. 145.
Police, i. 236, 71, 97 ; ii. 100, 250, 305.
Politics, i. 48, 271, 98, 328 ; ii. 143-4.
Portraits of Liszt, i. 182, 5, 94, 313, 48, 52 ; ii. 51.
    Wagner, i. 294 ; ii. 8, 23, 33, 86, 172, 306, 14, 9.
Postman, The, i. 270, 338 ; ii. 68.
Präger, Ferdinand, ii. 68, 86.

NOTABILIA, APHORISMS AND CHAR-
ACTERISTIC EXPRESSIONS.

Accent of sorrow in the voice, i. 208.
Art, Aristocratic region of, ii. 260.
    I only play with art to pass the time, ii. 54.
    Only as an artist can I live, i. 234 ; ii 144, 271, 95.
Azymen, ii. 186.

Beginning and end of the world (*Nibelungen*), i. 257.
Bell-simile, i. 46-7.
Berlin, Over-witty, ii. 135.
Black flag (*Tristan*), ii. 54, 161.

Cocoon, i. 347.
Confederation of friendly Princes, i. 31, 49, 50, 2 ; ii. 179, 273-4.
Core of art, We met at the, i. 123.
Creator of my actual position, You are the, i. 176 ; ii. 7.

Desire (or Will) of Life, ii. 224.
    Negation of, ii. 53, 86, 93, 95-9.
Dirt,—This dirt cannot touch you, ii. 90.
Dog's life, ii. 181, 295.
Drama *à la verre d'eau*, i. 25.

Early works left far behind him, i. 219, 22.
Error,—Through Error to Truth, i. 150.

Future of the human race, i. 278.

Germany, You are her glory, i. 133, 230 ; ii. 252, 96.
God's word revealed in Genius, i. 239.
Greatness,—Your greatness is your misery, i. 273.
Greek, I am so much of a, i. 43.

Half-heartedness, ii. 10, 327.
Happy.—To be entirely happy just for once, i. 324 ; ii. 11. *See*
    ii. 136.